A PLACE
TO STAND

A PLACE TO STAND

A REFORMED STUDY OF CREEDS AND CONFESSIONS

by Cornelius Plantinga, Jr.

Illustrations by Paul Stoub

Bible Way

©1979 by the Board of Publications of the Christian Reformed Church
2850 Kalamazoo SE
Grand Rapids, MI 49560

Printed in the United States of America

Library of Congress Cataloging in Publication Data

Plantinga, Cornelius, 1946-
    A Reformed study of creeds and confessions.

    Bibliography: p.
    l. Creeds. I. Title.
BT990.P67   238'.4'2   79-371
ISBN 0-933140-01-0

*"If the foundations are destroyed,
what can the righteous do?"*
Psalm 11:3

*My foot stands on level ground;
in the great congregation I will
bless the Lord.*
Psalm 26:12

CONTENTS

PREFACE

A Place to Stand is, in several ways, a "first" for the Christian Reformed Church's Education Department.

It's the first comprehensive adult study of ecumenical creeds and Reformed confessions in our history. The project is at least a decade overdue. In recent years, millions of books have told Christians how to read their Bibles, raise their children, grow their churches, cure their sorrows, and lose their fat. Radio and TV preachers have been plowing those same fields. Meanwhile, a good many Reformed people—across a spectrum of Reformed, Presbyterian, and other congregations—have begun to wonder who they are, where they came from, what they ought to believe, and why. *A Place to Stand* was planned, written, illustrated, and edited with those people and their questions in mind. We believe this is at least a substantial first response, though we have no illusion that our first response will also be the last word.

A Place to Stand is not only the title of a book, but also the name of a course, the first course in a complete, new, adult curriculum. Eventually, other courses will fill out this curriculum in such areas as biblical studies, church history, moral and ethical decisions, family living, and the church. If you read this book in connection with classroom discussions, the last section *(POSTSCRIPT)* should make sense to you. If you are not engaged in such a course, spare yourself sublime confusion by ignoring the *POSTSCRIPT.* And if you would like more information about this course, or the entire adult curriculum, you are invited to write the Education Department.

The *creeds* studied here (the Apostles', Nicene, and Athanasian) are among the oldest answers the church has given to the question, What do we believe? They are basic truths of basic Christianity, defended with equal zeal by Franciscan friars and Protestant preachers. They are universal, not parochial, and for centuries they've been at the core of the Christian religion.

Where the Reformed faith has been, there have also been the *confessions.* They are tracts which fueled the fires of the Protestant Reformation, though many began as gentle primers for children gathered near the hearth. Some were drafted by massive synods called to define heresy. Others were scribbled hastily, the last will and testament of a Reformer scheduled to die. Between the early sixteenth and mid-seventeenth centuries, confessions were issued by the score. Many were clearly Lutheran; many were clearly Calvinistic; some were neither, or both. To the extent that "Reformed theology" is Calvinistic rather than Lutheran, the "Reformed confessions" are also Calvinistic.

It isn't possible to be ignorant of the confessions and know the Reformed faith. While the Bible is the ultimate court of appeal in all Reformed churches, the confessions are (and have been since their adoption) the first line of defense. They are not a closed canon; new confessions may well be necessary. And the confessions we have are open to correction. But the historic statements are our first lessons in the school of Reformed faith, the foundation for everything that follows. They have shaped our teaching, defined our preaching, and tempered our character for better than four hundred years.

Three Reformed confessions are studied in *A Place to Stand. The Heidelberg Catechism* has been, since its introduction in 1563, the most widely loved and often cited of all the Reformed catechisms. Warm, lyrical, experiential, ecumenical, it was written with the soul of the psalmist David and the mind of the apostle Paul by a fledgling preacher and a rookie professor, neither of whom were yet thirty. The *Belgic Confession,* which consumes nearly half this study, is a classic statement of the Reformed faith; it is sturdy, carefully reasoned, and concisely biblical. The author of this Confession and those who joined him promised to "offer their backs to stripes, their tongues to knives, their mouths to gags, and their whole bodies to the fire." More than a few made good on that promise. The *Canons of Dort* show a church responding to theological challenge. Here is a response marked by consistently clear thought, firm biblical commitments, and a warmth which surprises some first-time readers. At the same time, the Canons are brutally frank and pointed, a feature which may account for the benign neglect to which this confession has been treated in recent years. The Canons are an affront to anyone who believes the church should be, above all else, nice.

The author of the textbook *A Place to Stand* is Cornelius Plantinga, Jr., a minister in the Christian Reformed Church. Rev. Plantinga is an alumnus of Calvin College, Calvin Theological Seminary, and Princeton Theological Seminary. In 1978 he was appointed to the department of

Neal Plantinga
8-22-

PAUL STOUB
1-10-79

Systematic Theology at Calvin Seminary. Rev. Plantinga has taken a look at his own theological heritage in *A Place to Stand*. When he surveys the great ecumenical creeds, he shows his grasp of both broad historical movements and narrow theological arguments. When he goes to work on the Reformation documents, it's clear he is not only a student of the confessions, but also one of their sons. In a consistently bright, sometimes even gripping narrative, the writer examines the confessions which are his own.

And the author's script has been punctuated with illustrations by Mr. Paul Stoub, Artist (and Art Editor) for the Education Department. As Plantinga's words tell about the confessions, Stoub's sketches show the confessors: Reformed people of various ages and callings. Most of the artist's sketches are of Reformed people who, like Stoub himself, come from Dutch Calvinist stock transplanted in America. But no attempt has been made either to limit or to represent "Reformed people"; rather, the illustrations simply remind us that confessions made in books and stored on shelves neither give wisdom in life nor comfort in death. Until confessions come to expression in the life of a confessor, they are merely relics.

For the past few months, the editors and I have been debating the title of this course, *A Place to Stand*. The publishing deadline stopped the debate, but we still wonder if the title is misleading. When we describe the creeds and confessions as "a place to stand," we don't mean them as a place to stand *still*. The theology of these confessions is not a static, unmoving, quiet place of refuge away from the world. The title is meant, rather, to reflect the well-shaped, solid platform on which Reformed people campaign vigorously for the kingdom of God—the place we take our stand because, God help us, we cannot do otherwise.

On behalf of the planners, editors, author, and artist, I offer you *A Place to Stand* in the Reformed tradition. We believe a keen look at our heritage will both strengthen our identity and confirm our calling. And that's important. Ultimately we'll be judged not on the grounds of which confessions we *held*; the Lord will, I think, make more of the confessions we *lived*.

May this course make better confessors of us all.

A. James Heynen
Director of Education

MEETING
INWOOD CRC
11·16·78

CHAPTER 1
The Nature and Shape of
the Ecumenical Creeds

Introduction—Beliefs and Creeds

People believe in all sorts of things. You will often hear people say things like this: "I believe in doing a job right the first time." Or, "I believe in having kids take a year of piano before they start the violin." Or, "I'm a firm believer in compulsory jail sentences for heroin dealers." Some beliefs even get set to music. The chorus to one 1970 popular tune, for example, repeatedly insists, "I believe in music. I believe in love."

So people believe in certain policies (doing a job right), certain sentiments (love), certain arts (music), and various propositions ("All women are human."). They also believe in certain *persons*. They will say, for instance, that they believed in Richard Nixon, but he let them down. They believed in Winston Churchill, and he never let them down. They believe in, that is, they *trust* a respected teacher, a beloved father, an honest political leader, a convincing salesman. Some people, reserving their trust for those whom they love deeply, believe only in themselves.

Roughly speaking, any statement of belief is a creed. The word *creed*, after all, comes from the Latin *credo* which simply means "I believe." But usually the term *creed* is saved for statements of belief which are formally, not just casually, expressed. And usually a creed includes not merely one, but a whole set of connected beliefs. Finally, we ordinarily use the term *creed* to refer to the formal beliefs of a large group of people instead of the personal beliefs of an isolated individual. So a creed, we may say, is *the formal statement of a group's set of beliefs.*

One might think all creeds are Christian. They are not. Social and fraternal groups of various kinds sometimes adopt creeds. Many non- or semi-Christian groups express their beliefs creedally. Followers of Islam, for example, have creeds. So do Mormons. Secular humanists have set forth creedal statements. Robert Ingersoll, one of the most notorious secular humanists of the modern age, once said his creed was this:

Happiness is the only good.
The place to be happy is here.
The time to be happy is now.
The way to be happy is to make others so.

The Variety of Christian Creeds

But even the most secular of creeds is indebted, no doubt, to the long Christian tradition of creed-making. From biblical times to the present, Christians have tirelessly fought heresy, defied persecution, taught beginners, and publicly worshiped by means of creeds. These have come in various shapes and sizes. Some, like the Second Helvetic Confession of 1566 (which offers thirty chapters of belief), are long. Others, like Paul's confession in I Corinthians 8:6, are short. A number of creeds—the Athanasian Creed, for example—seem highly technical and remote to the average Christian. Others, such as the Apostles' Creed, look simpler at first. Many creeds are sweet-tempered and peace-loving. But just as often creedal statements come smoking out of the heart of doctrinal debate.

Christian creeds are found in the Bible and in the early church. Many new creeds were distilled out of the ferment of the Reformation. There are modern American creeds, creeds of the emerging churches in Africa, and creedal statements from the World Council of Churches. Creeds are Eastern and Western; they are Catholic, Lutheran, Reformed, and Anabaptist; they are

Methodist and non-denominational.

Careful readers will be quick to say, however, that many such formal statements of Christian beliefs are not called creeds at all. Sometimes they are called confessions. Think, for instance, of the Belgic Confession, or the Westminster Confession, or the Presbyterian Confession of 1967. They may be called declarations (the Barmen Declaration), or canons (the Canons of Dort), or affirmations, or calls to unity, or formulas, or the like. This should not confuse us. There are no standard rules for the use of terms here. One simply notes what a particular statement has historically been called.

The Three Main Creeds

These first chapters consider three main ecumenical creeds of the early church: the Apostles' Creed, the Nicene Creed, and the Athanasian Creed. What are these creeds like?

First we note what is obvious: They are creeds; that is, they are *formal statements of a group's set of beliefs*. What do we believe? We believe *propositions* and we believe *persons*. We believe *that* propositions are true (I believe that God exists.), but we believe *in* persons (I believe in God the Father.). We *assent* to propositions and we *trust* in persons. The Apostles' Creed—and the Nicene Creed as well—includes both aspects of belief. "I believe *in* God the Father"—that is trust. I also believe that this Father in whom I trust is "Almighty, Maker of heaven and earth"—that is assent. The creeds do not separate the two, and we shouldn't either. Both trust and assent are essential ingredients of the Christian faith.

Another thing to note is how important the doctrine of the *Trinity* is in the three creeds. The Apostles' Creed frames its confession in a trinitarian way by means of articles I, II, and VIII. So does the Nicene Creed with paragraphs 1, 3, and 4. And over half the content of the Athanasian

DICK MULDER
11·16·78

Creed has to do with the Trinity.

These creeds are, moreover, *biblical* creeds. Crucial to all of them is a recital of the main events of Christ's profound work. All of them take data, however they shape it, not merely from human experience, but from what the Bible says.

Finally, these three creeds are *ecumenical.* This simply means they are broadly accepted by the churches. They express a core of belief which unites the Christian churches of the West. (The Greek East accepts only one of the three, the Nicene Creed.)

Origin and Purpose of Creeds

Why were creeds ever drawn up in the first place? What are they for?

Mainly creeds serve as a norm or a rule of faith. A norm was originally a carpenter's square; rules are still used to keep pencils and people in line. Because the followers of Christ were called to faith (as well as to hope, love, and many other virtues), it became necessary from the very start to know what and in whom to believe. So Peter says, "You are the Christ" (Mark 8:29), and Paul makes standard the confession that Jesus is Lord and that God raised Him from the dead (Rom. 10:9). The earliest creeds, then, were centered on Jesus. They were rules of faith for identifying who He was and what He did. They did so by summarizing the biblical teaching about Him.

These short rules of faith became useful in the first few centuries of the church in several ways. First, they *identified* not only who Jesus was, but also who His followers were. In oral form these tiny creeds served as passwords among the faithful. By using one of these secret signs, a devout Christian could be recognized by other believers, or condemned by persecutors. One of the most famous of such symbols, as they were called, was "I believe in Jesus Christ, the Son of God, our Savior." This was an acrostic; that is, it was a formula in which the first letters of the crucial terms combined to form in Greek the word

FISH. Soon just the outline of a fish was enough to get the message across. You still see such fish on people's doors and around their necks. They are giving the secret sign.

Early creeds were also used *to educate people for baptism.* Here again, because of the fear of making common the mysteries of the faith, the creed was kept out of public view and was not written down. A person who wanted to be baptized might be secretly told the main points of Christian belief. Then, as he was baptized, he would give them back for memory.

Again, short creeds were surely used *to unify and build up believers at public worship.* Philippians 2:6-11 was no doubt used this way even before it was written into Paul's epistle. Believers knew these creeds by heart. Many still do today.

It was not until creeds were called upon to defeat heresy that they were carefully written out. This is a final use of creeds we may mention here. They had a *polemical* (controversial) use. When somebody said strange and suspicious things about Christ or the Trinity, the church's experts would go to work, trying to spell out exactly what must be believed from the Bible on the matter in question. Creeds were ways of saying, "This is how the church reads the Bible." Sometimes, as you can tell by looking at the Athanasian Creed, the church read the Bible in a most technical way. But lives and careers were at stake, and the church's best minds tried mightily to confess the faith as exactly as possible.

CHAPTER 2
The Apostles' Creed

Introduction—The Apostles' Creed as Martyr

Many of us have known the Apostles' Creed for years. We recite it weekly at public worship. But, after repeating it hundreds of times, we no longer find it exciting. We say it mindlessly. Many people might not even be startled to hear the Creed begin, "Our Father who art in heaven. . . ." The Creed has become a well-worn shoe for us. It fits, but it does not pinch, and we scarcely know it is there. One standard commentator suggests that by "vain and thoughtless repetition" the Creed can even become a *martyr*. It can die for the faith.

Oddly enough, it is not because we understand the Creed so thoroughly that we are bored by it. Most of us would be hard put to say, for example, how it came into existence. We might also be unable to outline its structure. (For that, a person often needs to see the Creed written out in front of him.) And we might wonder, but not know, why some people think only the pastor should say these famous words.

These are the sorts of things we will discuss in this chapter. We will try to understand—and hence appreciate—this noble confession of faith. Nothing less is appropriate to a work praised as "the Creed of creeds."

Origin and Development

Until at least the fifteenth century, many people believed the apostles had written the Apostles' Creed. In fact, they assumed that each of the twelve apostles had contributed a small share of the Creed, and that this explained why it so readily fell into twelve articles! According to legend, after Jesus' ascension the apostles wanted to agree on one *basic* statement of the faith which each could carry with him. So, on or around Pentecost, being filled with the promised Holy Spirit, the apostles pieced together the

Creed which bears their name. Peter began: "I believe in God the Father, Almighty. . . ." Andrew added: "And in Jesus Christ, His only begotten Son, our Lord." James continued: "Who was conceived by the Holy Spirit. . . ." On it went, until Matthew finished by saying: "And the life everlasting. Amen."

No doubt this is only a pleasant tale and not an account of facts. (Several devout souls have even tried to attribute the composing of the Creed to our Lord Himself.) Still, the heart of the Creed *is* very old. In fact, in confessing three divine persons, the events of Christ's career, and the life of the redeemed community, the Creed plainly derives its material from the New Testament. Thus, even though the apostles did not write it, the Creed may legitimately be called apostolic because its teaching is apostolic.

But then how *did* the Creed come into being? The earliest formulas of faith, as we say in chapter 1, were simple and oral. They were seemingly too simple and too short to serve as suitable rules of faith for the growing Christian religion. But the group of Christian writings accepted by, say, A.D. 150 was too long and complex to serve this purpose. What the situation called for was something between a short saying like "Jesus is Lord," on the one hand, and the whole New Testament, on the other. What was needed was an intermediate *summary* of the New Testament's teaching.

So believers had to undertake the difficult task of lifting essential truths out of the New Testament writings and leaving the rest alone. Some beliefs—for example, the resurrection—obviously had to be selected. Others—for example, that Melchizedek was king of Salem—could be left unmentioned. Some—such as the assertion that Jesus "descended into hell"—would be borderline cases. Meanwhile, to strengthen the product of these decisions with apostolic authority, someone spread the story that the apostles themselves had done the deciding.

Why was such a summary rule of faith necessary? One of its first uses was to prepare converts for baptism. Taking the Great Commission (Matt. 28:19) as a model, the church in Rome (or Antioch, or Corinth) instructed the prospective convert about the Father, the Son, and the Holy Spirit. Then, as he was baptized, the convert was asked: "Do you believe in God the Father?" He answered: "I believe." "Do you believe in Jesus Christ, His only Son?" "I believe." "Do you believe in the Holy Spirit?" "I believe."

Soon the process moved on to a second stage in which, at a point late in the instruction, the local bishop secretly "handed over" to his pupil a trinitarian confession in which the questions and answers were sewn together. Then, at baptism, the convert "gave it back" by reciting it. Gradually, in various local churches, the originally lean confession, based on the Great Commission, was fleshed-out with solid meat from other parts of the New Testament. Soon the confession may have read something like this:

I believe in God the Father Almighty,
And in Jesus Christ, His only Son, our Lord,
And in the Holy Spirit, the holy church,
 the resurrection of the flesh.

> (from Paul T. Fuhrmann, *An Introduction to the Great Creeds of the Church*)

Of all the creeds used in local churches, the one adopted in Rome began to be widely preferred. In A.D. 340 it looked like this:

1. I believe in God almighty
2. And in Christ Jesus, his only son, our Lord
3. Who was born of the Holy Spirit and the Virgin Mary
4. Who was crucified under Pontius Pilate and was buried
5. And the third day rose from the dead
6. Who ascended into heaven
7. And sitteth on the right hand of the Father
8. Whence he cometh to judge the living and the dead
9. And in the Holy Ghost
10. The holy church
11. The remission of sins
12. The resurrection of the flesh
13. The life everlasting.

> (from H. Bettenson, *Documents of the Christian Church*)

Several centuries of development yielded our present Apostles' Creed by about A.D. 700. (The last item to be added was "He descended into hell.) Since then, this Creed has enjoyed the status of being the most truly ecumenical creed of the West.

Structure and Content

Look at the Creed itself. It has traditionally (and somewhat arbitrarily) been divided into twelve articles because of the legend of its composition by the twelve apostles. But a more basic

CHOIR REHEARSAL
HIGHLAND CRC
11·13·78

division, as already suggested, is *trinitarian*. In fact, some people speak of only three articles, corresponding to the material about God the Father (old article I), about Jesus Christ (old articles II—VII), and about the Holy Spirit and His work (old articles VIII—XII).

Now the New Testament's most typical creed, we remember, is "Jesus is Lord," or "Jesus, the Christ, is Lord." The Apostles' Creed is of the same type. It is heavy and large in the middle; that is, it is *Christ-centered*. Moreover, like one of the most famous of the biblical creeds (Phil. 2:6-11), the Apostles' Creed gives an account of the vast sweep of the Son's career—from pre-existence ("only begotten Son"), through humiliation ("born of the virgin Mary; suffered under Pontius Pilate..."), to exaltation ("rose again from the dead; He ascended into heaven...").

The framework of the Creed includes the repeated preface, "I believe in," or "I believe." The "I" is a product of the baptismal use of the Creed in its infancy, and still today commits each of us to personal responsibility for his or her confession. This "I" must never be said, however, without a keen sense of the prior *community* "chosen for eternal life" of which "I am and always will be a living member" (Heidelberg Catechism, Answer 54).

The content of the Creed is well packed into the framework we have just sketched. The Trinity; creation; the virgin birth, passion, death, resurrection, ascension, session, and second coming of the Lord; the church; forgiveness; the life to come—all these things are simply affirmed.

One might wonder why the Creed bothers to rehearse all the events of Christ's life. Why, for example, is so homely an item as Jesus' *burial* mentioned? The answer apparently is that some early heretics called Gnostics denied Jesus' true humanity. (Note the concern already in I John 4:2 that Jesus' *flesh* be confessed.) Gnostics thought Jesus only "seemed" to be human, and did not *really* die, was not *actually* buried, etc. The Apostles' Creed wants to shut the door against this misunderstanding. If there is any polemical (argumentative) spirit at all in the Creed, it shows through here.

But some Christians still wonder about the inclusion of certain items. Is Jesus' descent into hell a truly central and biblical belief? Why does Pontius Pilate ("an otherwise unknown and trivial character in Roman history," as one writer has it) get precious space in the compact Creed?

Again, why are some important items missing? The most orthodox Christians have puzzled over this. Why isn't the fall mentioned? Why the yawning gap between the virgin birth and Pontius Pilate? Doesn't Jesus' *teaching* deserve to fill such a gap? Why isn't "the hinge of the Reformation," namely, justification through faith alone, somewhere asserted? Nobody has a sure answer to all these questions. Yet the Creed is still accepted as a biblical, trinitarian, and ecumenical rule of faith.

Uses of the Creed

The Apostles' Creed originally was used to help converts prepare for baptism. Later on, it was used to instruct the baptized children of believers, and to renew one's vows of belief in God—especially at public worship.

It has these same uses today. Instructional manuals for both children and adults are often based on the articles of the Creed. For example, these articles hinge together much of the great second section of the Heidelberg Catechism. Plainly, the Apostles' Creed is a summary of Christian belief, helpful for *teaching* that belief.

The Creed is, moreover, still regularly used in public worship. In medieval times, and in some of the Reformation churches, the Creed was seen primarily as an instructional tool; it was used at public worship only as a summary of the doctrine preached by the minister. Thus it was said at the close of the sermon—and said only by the minister.

But perhaps there is a more imaginative and satisfying use of the creed in public worship. Perhaps it is best used by the people as a *response* to what God has said and done. It could still follow the sermon, just as it used to. After the sermon, after God has spoken, the people give a joyous "Amen" by standing to say, "I believe in God the Father, Almighty...." And there is no reason why the Creed cannot be powerfully said at baptism and the Lord's Supper as well.

At any event, intelligent and faithful use of the Creed will mean that by saying these ancient words we not only affirm certain facts, but also retake our vow to commit our lives in gratitude to God. Saying "I believe" is like saying "I do" at a wedding. You want to do it carefully. After all, you are not merely *describing* a vow; you are actually *vowing*.

CHAPTER 3
The Nicene Creed

Introduction—Who Is Jesus?

In the summer of 1977, seven British theologians published a book called *The Myth of God Incarnate*. In this regrettable volume, these churchmen announce that what the church has always believed about Jesus Christ—that He is the very Son of God incarnate—is myth and pious nonsense. Six of the seven are Anglicans. Every communion service, Anglicans confess that Jesus Christ is "very God of very God...of one substance with the Father...Who, for us men and for our salvation, came down from heaven and was incarnate by the Holy Spirit of the virgin Mary, and was made man." According to one report, the seven theologians think such claims "should be relegated to the ash heap."

The claims are from the Nicene Creed. They have been disbelieved before. In fact, it was just this sort of controversy about Jesus Christ which gave birth to the Creed. What fascinated the big minds of the early church was the question of Jesus' *identity*. The main doctrinal disputes were over the question, "Who is Jesus?" As we can see, those disputes and that question are still with us.

In the first century, two sorts of people asked the identity question about Jesus and disputed its answer. The first sort was Jewish. And to the question "Who is Jesus?" the answer most likely to inflame Jews was "He is the Son of God." This title raised Jesus to the status of divinity—way above such heroes as Moses (a "*man* of God" in Deut. 33:1). That is why those Jews who heard Jesus refer to Himself as "*the* Son," and to God as "*my* Father," were enraged. They rightly discerned that Jesus was "making himself equal with God" (John 5:17-19). Jews are, of course, strict monotheists. Thus, to call Jesus "the Son of God," or especially, "the *only* Son of God," was from the start an abomination to them. They did not merely regard Jesus as a deluded fraud, as orthodox Christians regard Joseph Smith. The Jews regarded Him with horror as a blasphemer.

The other sort of people to ask the identity question was Gentile. Gentiles had a full stock of deities and many "lords," as Paul says (I Cor. 8:5). So the title given to Jesus which most interested them was "Lord." It was moreover among Greek-speaking Gentiles that the earliest creed ("Jesus is Lord") seemed most audacious and most puzzling. After all, they could read in their Greek translation of the Old Testament that "the Lord our God is one Lord" (Deut. 6:4). Yet here was another person called Jesus Christ who also asserted to be "one Lord" (Eph. 4:5), somehow alongside the "one God" (I Cor. 8:6). What's more, the Christian claim appeared to compete with the emperor's claim: "Caesar is lord."

We can now see something important. The question of Jesus' identity is hooked directly to the question of the Trinity. When the church identified Jesus as *Lord* and *Son of God*, and by those terms meant that He was *divine*, they faced a serious problem: How can both Jesus and God be divine without being two Gods? Eventually, of course, the church affirmed that not only God and Jesus, but also the Holy Spirit, *are* divine—but that, nonetheless, there is only one divine being, one God in three persons. Thus, at the root of the mystery of the Trinity is the mystery of the incarnation. And a central question of the incarnation, posed from biblical times to the present, is: "Who is this?" "Who is Jesus?" "Who do men say that the Son of man is?" (Matt. 16:13).

DENNIS ROOZEBOOM FAMILY
11-14-78

Arius

To this sort of question, there have always been answers. Not all of them have been right answers. One of the most important and interesting wrong answers of the ancient church was that of Arius. Arius was a presbyter of Alexandria, a keen scholar, and a popular preacher. Around 318 he began to teach some distinctive things about Christ, the Son of God. Arius said God had *made* the Son, just as He made us. The Son was God's first creation made before the world was created. Moreover, the Son cannot have the Father's godly essence or substance. No creature could have that. Hence the Son is decidedly inferior and subordinate to the Father. He is a *creature*— a higher creature, to be sure, than human creatures—but still only a creature.

Arius believed, then, that the Son had a beginning in time just as God's other creatures do. He taught that Christ was a "tertium quid" (third thing), neither fully God nor fully man. Deity is one thing (one *quid*), humanity is another thing (a second *quid*), and Jesus is a third (*tertium*) thing (*quid*).

Why did Arius say these things? Apparently he was no foolish or casual heretic, and no theological pushover. He took the transcendence and uniqueness of God so seriously that he could not conceive of God's sharing His divine essence with another. To suppose that someone else besides the Father is God, Arius thought, is to lapse back into pagan polytheism. Let God be God alone, said Arius. God is incomparable. He is high. He is absolutely other, independent, and self-contained. If he could have heard the twentieth century theologian Karl Barth talk of "the infinite, qualitative difference between God and man," Arius would have applauded.

The Nicene Creed

Arius was by no means the church's first heretic. Many others before him had held eccentric and unbiblical views. But Arius' case is special for two reasons: First, Arius forced the church to specify in what *sense* Christ is equal with the Father. As John Leith has observed, the church had all along been used to thinking of

12

Christ as both God and man. When other heretics denied it, they were condemned by local synods. It was not until Nicea that the relationship between Father and Son was actually defined.

Secondly, Arius' was the first heresy to be treated at an ecumenical council. Because Arius attracted powerful supporters, because his particular heresy seemed outstandingly dangerous, because it was disturbing the peace of the empire, the emperor Constantine called the first ecumenical council in the history of the church. It convened at Nicea in A.D. 325. Some 318 fathers of the church were present.

At Nicea, Arius was condemned with a series of pointed statements, each ruling out one Arian error. Most important among these were the phrases describing Christ as "begotten, not made," and "of one substance with the Father." Nicea also studded the end of its creed with a series of curses or anathemas:

And those that say "There was when he was not,"

and, "Before he was begotten he was not,"

and that, "He came into being from what-is-not,"

or those that allege, that the Son of God is "Of another substance or essence"

or "created,"

or "changeable"

or "alterable,"

these the Catholic and Apostolic Church anathematizes.

This studded tail of the Creed was intended, of course, to lash Arius and his followers. But you will not find it in your copy of the Creed. What we have is not the original Nicene Creed, but rather a Creed modified two generations later at the Council of Constantinople (381) and finally ratified by the church at the Council of Chalcedon in 451. The development of the Niceno-Constantinopolitan Creed, as our present version is more correctly called, was part of a whole process of trinitarian controversy marked, as E.A. Dowey has said, by "diversity of training and piety, suspicions about the use of words, imperial politics and regional rivalries, saintliness and cussedness...." Yet, from all this came the most truly ecumenical creed of the Christian church.

The Nicene Creed contains many significant phrases, but perhaps three might be lifted out for inspection. One of these, *homoousios*, is orthodoxy's largest trophy in the struggle with Arius.

"Begotten, not made"

First, note that the Creed says Christ was "begotten, not made." Here Nicea wanted to say, at least, that just as a human father produces a son of the same kind or generic essence as himself (a *human* son), and does not create something essentially different from himself, so, in some mysterious way, God begets a Son of *His* own essence (a Son of *God*). Indeed, the next phrase, "being of one substance with the Father," may simply reinforce the fact that the Son was "begotten, not made."

"One substance with the Father"

"Being of one substance with the Father" is the big phrase in the Creed. It translates a Greek word famous in the theological world, the word *homoousios. Homo* means "same," thus, "homogenize," "homo-sexual,"etc. *Ousios* means "substance" or "essence" or "being." The Son is said to be of the very *same* substance or being as the Father. He is *homoousios* (pronounced hoe-moe-OO-see-us) with the Father. We can see that by this phrase Nicea hoped to state the Son's equality with the Father as strongly as possible.

From the start there were two objections to this celebrated term. One was that the term is not scriptural. It comes from Greek philosophy. What was a term from pagan Athens doing here in the heart of the city of God? The second objection was that the term is ambiguous. Did Nicea mean that the Son somehow *is* the Father? Or did it only mean that the Son is of the same *essence* as the Father? (You can get a feeling for the ambiguity by reflecting on the expression, "Look! Those two women are wearing the same dress!") The latter meaning seems closer to the sense of the Creed, and has the virtue of being understandable, but many took it the first way. They thought the Creed took away all distinction between Father and Son.

"And the Son"

The third expression we consider comes from the section on the Holy Spirit, "...who proceedeth from the Father *and the Son.*" Strange to say, this one little phrase caused the main split in Christendom. The phrase "and the Son" is a single word in Latin: *filioque* (pronounced FEE-lee-oh-kwa). It was not found in the original Nicene Creed, nor even in the Niceno-Constantinopolitan Creed, but came into gradual use in the West between the seventh and eleventh centuries by those who followed St. Augustine's theology of the Trinity. In one of his analogies Augustine compared the Spirit to the bond of love between a lover and his beloved. Naturally, that love has to proceed from both. But the Greek East did not see it that way, and when the Western church persisted in using the *filioque,* these two great sections of Christendom pulled apart. This great schism, which occurred in 1054, remains unhealed to this day.

The East hated the *filioque* for several reasons: first, because in John 15:26, the key text, it is not present; second, because the whole Eastern trinitarian scheme located trinitarian unity in the Father (He begets the Son, and He generates the Spirit); third, because they thought Pope Benedict VIII (the Western pope who officially added the *filioque* in 1014) was utterly presumptuous. What right does a pope have to alter a creed set by an ecumenical council? (The trouble with being infallible is that you have to be so careful never to make a mistake.)

The West liked the *filioque,* and they also had their reasons. They believed *filioque* was important first, because Augustine taught it and second, because it introduced into the Creed a suggestion of the New Testament teaching that the Spirit is the Spirit of Christ, and the fulfiller of Christ's work.

Still, except for the *filioque,* the Nicene Creed has more use among Christians all over the world than either of the other creeds we are considering in this course. It remains, in a much-quoted expression, "one of the few threads by which the tattered fragments of the divided robe of Christendom are held together."

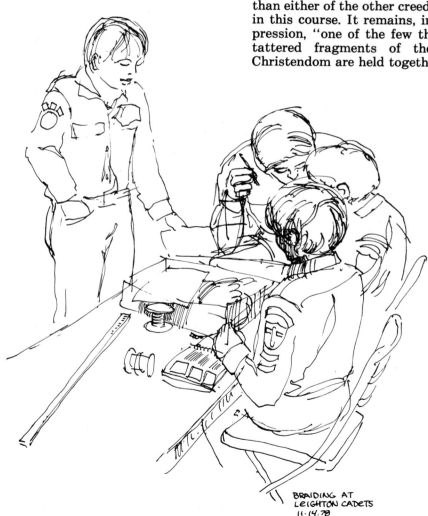

BRAIDING AT
LEIGHTON CADETS
11·14·78

CHAPTER 4
The Athanasian Creed

Introduction

"According to a well-known epigram, the only two assured facts about the Athanasian Creed are that it is neither a creed nor by Athanasius." Thus begins the best modern study of this ecumenical rule of faith, J. N. D. Kelly's *Early Christian Creeds*.

At least half the epigram is right. Athanasius, bishop of Alexandria from A.D. 328 to 373, almost certainly never laid eyes on the work which bears his name. For a thousand years (roughly 550 to 1550) Athanasius was set down as its author. But today nobody knows who wrote the Creed, nor exactly when or where it was written. The safest opinion is that some highly-skilled theologian composed it in southern France, or Spain, early in the sixth century.

But the other half of the epigram is wrong. This *is* a creed, and a most remarkable one. It is simply of a different sort from the other two we have studied. For example, it has no trinitarian structure, even though it treats the Trinity at length. It does not fit so well into a liturgy as either of the other two, and it was probably never used at baptism. Moreover, the Athanasian Creed has never had the same popular appeal. In fact, it has drawn a certain amount of abuse. Matthew Arnold (a nineteenth century British essayist) once described it as "learned science which has fought and got ruffled by fighting, and is dictatorial now it has won; learned science with a strong dash of violent and vindictive temper."

Why has the Athanasian Creed never captured the minds and hearts of believers? The answer is obvious to anyone who has given the Creed ten minutes' worth of inspection. It is long, dense, and technical. Most believers find it tedious until they read it closely. Then they may find it irritating. After all, the Creed lays out a lengthy series of highly refined and sophisticated theological propositions—and then advises that you are damned if you do not believe them!

Yet, to the intelligent and sympathetic reader, this intimidating Creed does offer several choice treasures. Mainly, it offers *a concise summary of five centuries' work on the doctrines of the Trinity and the incarnation*. This summary is so balanced, rhythmical, and efficient that the Athanasian Creed has been called "one of the most splendid legacies of the patristic age."

Structure and Purpose

Let us get a sense for the way this document is put together. It looks somewhat like a moderately long chapter of the Bible—one of forty-four verses. The body of the Creed is in two sections, a section on the Trinity (3-28), and a shorter one on the incarnation (29-43). You can see that verses 28 and 29 act together as a bridge between the two sections. A fast glance also reveals that the first two verses and the last together form the notoriously frightening outer skin or frame which stretches around the Creed. Nearly all the verses are carefully weighted and balanced with either three clauses or two. Often these alternate. Read verses 13-18, for example, to get a sense of this balance.

The careful and polished structure of the Creed has made scholars believe that a single hand composed it. It is also believed that the Creed was composed to educate clergy—not lay people—and that its "schoolmasterish" tone confirms this.

Content—The Trinity

In our last lesson, we were introduced to some features of the doctrine of the Trinity, and to Arius, a famous heretic. Like the Nicene Creed, the Athanasian Creed is *polemical*. It is intended to guard orthodox trinitarian doctrine. It does this in two ways. The first way is *positive*. The Creed simply affirms in repeating, balanced sentences the traditional doctrine. The heart of it is found in verse 3: "We worship one God in Trinity, and Trinity in Unity." For twenty-three verses this basic assertion is elaborated. Typically, the Creed attributes a godly characteristic to each person (that He is uncreated, incomprehensible, God, Lord, etc.), and then hastens to reassure us that it does not have in mind *three* uncreateds, three incomprehensibles, three Gods, three Lords, but only *one*. Yet this *one* does exist in three persons who each possess a distinct characteristic. Thus the Father is unbegotten (21), the Son begotten (22), and the Holy Spirit proceeds (23).

A theologian would tell you this is all straight, orthodox, Western trinitarian doctrine. Augustine talks like this. So does Thomas Aquinas. So does John Calvin. Perhaps the best summary of the positive doctrine is in verses 15 and 16: "So the Father is God, the Son is God, and the Holy Spirit is God; and yet they are not three Gods, but one God."

Thus the Creed positively reinforces orthodoxy. But it also has a *negative* function: It denies certain heresies. One of these, as in the Nicene Creed, is Arianism. Arius, we recall, said that the Son was of a different substance than the Father. The Son is a kind of junior-grade god who was made by the Father. Some later barbarian Arians worked out an interesting scheme in which the three persons are stacked in a hierarchy, like Roman clergy. Greatest is the Father. Next comes the Son. Lowliest is the Holy Spirit.

The Creed attacks these heresies. It refuses to "divide the substance" (4) of the one God we worship. It attacks again and again the tendencies toward tritheism (belief in three gods) which it discerns in Arianism (thus verses 11, 12, 14, 16, etc.). It similarly aims its guns at the Arian subordination of Spirit and Son to the Father by asserting (25) that none of the divine persons is "greater, or less than another." And, like the Nicene Creed, so the Athanasian Creed asserts that the Son was "not made nor created, but begotten" (22).

While Arianism had tendencies toward tritheism, and toward denial of "one God," another opposite heresy denied that there are really three distinct persons. This is the heresy of modalism. Modalists believe there is one divine being, one individual God, who shows Himself in three different *modes,* or roles. First, He appeared in the Creator role. Later, He revealed Himself in the mode of Son and Savior. Most recently, He has performed in the role of the Holy Spirit. He is like a single actor who plays different roles. Sabellius, a third century thinker, was modalism's best promoter. He denied that there are three distinguishable and enduring persons.

Orthodoxy, as is its habit, has always tried to steer between two opposites—in this case, tritheism and modalism. Orthodoxy wants to deny that there are three Gods. But it also denies that Father, Son, and Spirit are merely modes of the one Godhead. This last notion, the heretical doctrine of modalism, confuses the three persons.

The Athanasian Creed has modalism in view when, in verse 4, it warns against confusing or "confounding" the persons. Both positively and negatively, then, the Creed is a stalwart champion of traditional trinitarian doctrine.

Content—The Incarnation

The problem of stating the truth about the mystery of the incarnation has always been similar to the problem of stating the truth about the mystery of the Trinity. Just as in the doctrine of the Trinity there is the problem of stating that the Godhead is plural in some respect and singular in some other respect, so in the doctrine of the incarnation there is the problem of stating that Christ is plural in some respect and singular in some other respect. The solution in both cases has been to state the errors on both extremes and to opt for a middle position—but not to analyze the middle position very closely. That is left for theologians to puzzle over.

In the case of the incarnation, as we see in the Creed, Christ is plural in the respect that He is "God and man" (30). He is of God's substance and also of Mary's. Yet He is singular in being "one Christ" (37). Insistently (34-37) the Creed "hammers home in four successive clauses," as Kelly puts it, that "He is not two, but one Christ" (34). Chiefly in view here is the heresy of a certain Nestorius who so separated the divinity and humanity of Christ as to make Him seem like a sufferer of multiple personality. When we come to the relevant section of the Belgic Confession (Art. XIX), we shall have a closer look at Nestorianism, and at its opposite heresy. Like shoes, heresies always seem to come in pairs.

Assessment

What are we to make of all this? Especially, how are we to take the claim that unless a person believes this highly theological formulation of

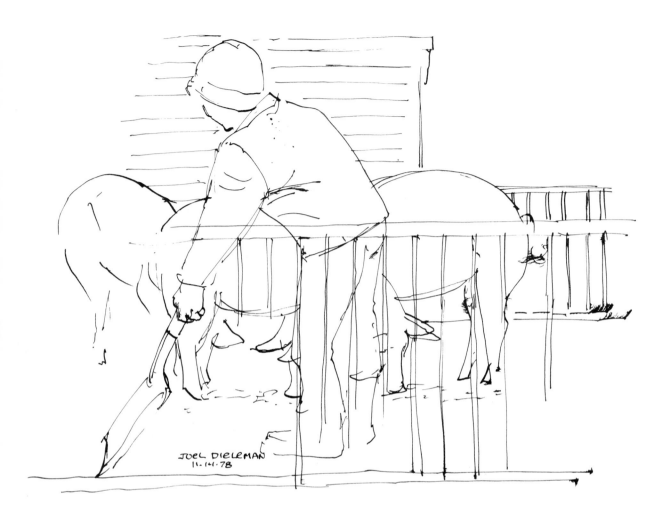

JOEL DIELEMAN
11-14-78

"the catholic faith," he cannot be saved? After all, many devout Christians cannot understand technical theology, and have no taste for it. Some die before they have ever had a chance to study it. Many faithfully trust Christ for their salvation, but dispute this or that point made by the Creed. Are they all hopelessly lost?

The Creed seems plainly to say that they are. It is hard to see how one could tinker with it to get a different conclusion. Admittedly, the damnatory phrases were a staple of the creedal diet in the ancient church. There was a ready dogmatism about what and how much a person had to believe lest he incur the everlasting wrath of God. But even though these curses were routine, they were seriously meant.

We rightly find this distressing. Still, in a time when many people think that sharing some feel-ings about Jesus is equivalent to believing the catholic faith, it does not hurt us to be reminded that correct belief is of great importance. And perhaps any who *do* understand the subtler doctrines have been called to a subtler belief than those who are not so burdened.

At any rate, the Creed repays hard study with real insight into what the church has said about the Trinity and Christ. It is too long, no doubt, to be used very well in public worship. It was not intended for such use. It is too technical for the average person to love it at once. But we would be very much poorer without it. We may even come to say with Kelly that "no other official...creed sets forth, so incisively and with such majestic clarity, the profound theology implicit in the New Testament affirmation that 'God was in Christ reconciling the world to Himself.' "

CHAPTER 5
Introduction to the
Heidelberg Catechism

Introduction

With this new unit, we move closer to home. We have just finished a unit of lessons on the ecumenical creeds. These, we recall, are accepted by Catholics and Protestants alike. The Nicene Creed (without the *filioque*) is even endorsed by the Eastern Orthodox churches. So we have been moving in a vast, ecumenical circle.

But now we turn to the first of three specifically *Reformed* creeds (or "confessions"). Every Reformed Christian is a member of at least five communities, large to small. (This way of putting the matter, and several observations of the lesson, are owed to John Leith's fine *Introduction to the Reformed Tradition.*) He is first a *Christian*—as opposed, say, to being a Jew, Muslim, or secularist. This is the largest group.

Secondly, he is a *Protestant* Christian—as opposed to being a Roman Catholic Christian. Here he stands with Luther and the Anabaptists (forerunners of modern Mennonites, Amish, etc.) as a son or daughter of the Reformation. This group is not as large as the first.

Thirdly, he is *Reformed*—as opposed to being Lutheran or Anabaptist (or Episcopalian, Methodist, Independent Fundamental, etc.). He is a product more of the Swiss than the German Reformation, informed more by Calvin's than by Luther's theology, and is a partaker in a massively important outlook and life-style which is distinctively Reformed according to the Word of God. This is the third largest group.

Then, fourthly, he is a member of some Reformed *denomination*—the Christian Reformed Church, for instance, or the United Presbyterian Church. There is likely to be both an ethnic origin and flavor to these denominations, such as Dutch, Scotch, Hungarian, African, Latin American, or the like.

Finally, he is a member of some *local congregation* of his denomination—let's say the Clarkson Christian Reformed Church of Mississauga, Ontario. However great in spirit, this is the smallest group of all.

A Reformed Christian, we said, moves in all these circles. But where in this series of concentric circles, largest to smallest, does the Heidelberg Catechism fit?

It fits right in the middle, in the Reformed circle. The Heidelberg Catechism is claimed not merely by one local congregation, nor by one Reformed denomination. It is larger than that. But neither is it used by all Christians, nor by all Protestants. It is smaller than that. Thus Lutherans and Anabaptists could not in good conscience own the Catechism. It opposes Lutheran theology of Christ (Q & A 48) and Anabaptist views of civil government (Q & A 101). The Heidelberg Catechism is clearly and centrally *Reformed*.

The real difference between Lutheran and Reformed branches of the Reformation was first one of separate starting points. Luther agonized personally over the question of salvation by grace and through faith. His whole theology was framed by the law-versus-gospel issue. But the Zurich Reformers were Christian humanists, much influenced by Erasmus. Their driving motif was a concern to get "back to the sources." The source in this case was, of course, the Bible. In this concern the German-speaking Zurich Reformers (Zwingli and Bullinger) were joined by the French-speaking Geneva Reformers (Farel

18

The Men's Society · Highland CRC
11·13·78

and Calvin). Calvin's Christian humanism has been the object of a great deal of scholarly work.

Origin of the Catechism

The Protestant Reformation began in Germany. Martin Luther was a German. But the Reformed strand of the Reformation, as opposed to the Lutheran, began in Switzerland. There it is an often-told tale of two cities, Zurich and Geneva. We need briefly to retell this much of it: Zurich was in 1519 the birthplace of the Reformed tradition. There, somewhat independently of Luther, Huldrich Zwingli, and later Heinrich Bullinger, so emphasized the return to the Bible as the source for reforming the church's life that they moved beyond the Lutheran reforms.

But for the long reach of the Reformed tradition, Geneva was to become even more important. There, in 1536 (when Zwingli had already been dead for five years) the Frenchman John Calvin began his successful attempt to make Geneva an embodiment of what we have come to know as the Reformed ethos or life-style. In that same year, just prior to his arrival in Geneva, Calvin published the first edition of what was to become for hundreds of years the definitive statement of Reformed theology: the *Institutes of the Christian Religion* (Basel, 1536).

It was quite late in the Reformation before this Reformed faith secured any foothold in Germany. Earlier on Zwinglians and Anabaptists had made some progress there, but the Peace of Augsburg (1555) divided Germany between Catholics and Lutherans only. Each prince was to decide for his own territory whether his people would be the one or the other. There was obviously little room here for the Reformed faith which had so dominated Switzerland.

But then, in 1559, Frederick III, a genuinely pious and fair-minded man, became ruler of that splendidly beautiful area along the middle Rhine River known as the Palatinate. This area had officially been Lutheran since 1555, but its Lutheranism was of a mild sort. Hard-line Lutherans opposed it. So, of course, did any resident Zwinglians and Anabaptists. Lutheranism had been established in the Palatinate according to the Peace of Augsburg, but as Jeremiah had said long before, people were saying " 'Peace, peace,' when there is no peace." In fact, practically nowhere in Protestantism was the intramural fighting fiercer than in the Palatinate.

It was Frederick's aim to help this situation. He thought he might do this by settling on sound, biblical answers to the hardest questions being disputed (especially the ones on the Lord's Supper) and then publishing them in a new general catechism of the Protestant faith.

So he did it. Or, rather, he sponsored some experts to do it. What is most important to see is that he did not sponsor Lutheran experts. Rather, because he privately believed the Zurich theology of Bullinger to be more biblical than Lutheran theology, Frederick looked for Reformed authorship of the Zurich type. Thus, to his gloriously scenic hometown, the capital of the Palatinate, Frederick invited two young Reformed thinkers whose names have since become firmly attached to Frederick's project. The town, of course, was Heidelberg; the men, Ursinus and Olevianus; and the project, the Heidelberg Catechism.

The first of these men was brilliant. His family name was Bear. While he was growing up, he was always known as a Bear. But when he came to the years of discretion, Bear fashionably adopted the more dignified Latin version of his name, a name more suited to an up-and-coming theologian, and became known as Ursinus.

Ursinus, so it is reported, was not only brilliant, but also extremely hardworking. He hated to waste time, or to have it wasted by others. Over the door of his study in Heidelberg he posted a sign which said the following:

FRIEND, WHEN YOU COME HERE,
EITHER BE BRIEF,
OR GO AWAY,
OR HELP ME WITH MY WORK.

A technically trained and very skillful theologian, Ursinus is thought by many historians to be the single person most responsible for the writing of the Heidelberg Catechism. He was twenty-eight years old at the time.

His associate, according to tradition, was a particularly likable, twenty-six-year-old pastor, Caspar Olevianus. Though other people, possibly a committee of Ursinus' colleagues at the University of Heidelberg, likely had something to do with the drafting of the Catechism, Olevianus' name has always been said in the same long breath as Ursinus' when authorship is mentioned. Like the great Calvin, Olevianus had once been a law student. But, much impressed with the grace of God—revealed during a boating accident, Olevianus turned, as one commentator has put it, from law to gospel.

He entered the ministry, and after having served a short stretch in prison for Protestantism (he had tried to preach the Reformed faith in his hometown—which was in a Catholic territory), he was invited by Frederick to take the pulpit of Holy Spirit Church in Heidelberg. In his role as pastor, preacher, and dealer with the aches of humanity, Olevianus is said to have developed the warm and personal approach to the Christian faith so often noted and so much loved in the Catechism. We may suppose that if Ursinus' head is in this document, Olevianus' heart is in it.

The "attractive" or "largehearted" tone of the Catechism is difficult to appreciate unless a comparison is made with the general literature of the period. We may simply recall that this was a period in which devout sons of the church did not hesitate to call each other "dirty, rooting swine" and "the devil's whore" in print, and a period in which slow torture was sometimes applied to heretics. Largely because of the Bullinger-led Reformation in Zurich (in whose atmosphere Ursinus breathed for at least five years and whose spirit also deeply influenced Olevianus), there was one large strand of Reformed orthodoxy in the sixteenth century which showed some grace in an often graceless time. Among the Lutherans, Melanchthon, who first brought the (Lutheran) Reformation to the Palatinate, gives evidence of this same mildness and generosity.

Although the Catechism was intended to make and keep peace in Frederick's Palatinate, during the years which followed it became a center of controversy and trouble. Certain German Lutherans regarded it as dangerous, even devilish. Later a group of Dutch Catholics burned the pest and are reported to have given it occasional public whippings

But on the whole, the Heidelberg Catechism has been much admired, often commentated on,

CHAD SWIER
11-16-78

and deeply memorized. Its famous first answer has been alive on many deathbeds. The fact that the Catechism has been so widely translated has moved one historian to remark that "it has the Pentecostal gift of tongues in a rare degree."

Structure and Content

This is a *catechism*, a confessional statement named with the Greek term *catecheo* meaning "to pass down information from above." Technically, any confession taught by one generation to the next is a *catechism*, though it has become popular to assign that title only to confessions using a question-and-answer format.

In the Heidelberg Catechism there are 129 questions and answers, and all but one of them (Q & A 80) date from the earliest versions. The catechism is further divided into fifty-two "Lord's Days." Very early in the Catechism's history this division into Lord's Days was made so that a section might be read and explained at Sunday worship services.

Yet another feature, familiar to generations of students, is the division of the entire Catechism into three sections preceded by a short overture of two questions (Q and A 1,2) which announces the themes to follow. Variously memorized as Sin-Salvation-Service, or Guilt-Grace-Gratitude, these three sections follow the general outline of Paul's Romans. They move in personal, "existential," autobiographical fashion from a person's misery to his rescue to, at last, his life of grateful service.

Finally, we note that there are various chunks of outside material incorporated into the Catechism. The third section, on the life of gratitude, contains the Catechism's treatment both of the Ten Commandments and the Lord's Prayer. (This is a most distinctively Reformed *placement* of these items, as we shall see in chapter 8.) Most of the second section is shaped by an exposition of the Apostles' Creed. These three items, together with a treatment of the sacraments, were standard in most catechisms of the period. How better could you instruct a beginner than by teaching him creed, law, prayer, and sacrament? Here the Heidelberger shows an unusually deft hand in so cleverly building these items into the structure of the document that you can hardly tell where the joints or cracks might be.

General Characteristics

Several features of the Heidelberg Catechism are always mentioned in the commentaries and largely account for the work's great popularity. We may mention six. The Catechism is—

1. *Scriptural.* It is intended, as someone has put it, to bind the believer to the Word. It is meant to summarize, illuminate, and apply biblical teaching.
2. *Ecumenical.* Inside the Reformed circle, the Catechism is unusually rounded and mild. Howard Hageman has stated the matter well by noting that the "angularities" of Reformed theology (a doctrine of election and reprobation, a statement of scriptural infallibility) are almost completely missing in the Heidelberg Catechism. This document is intended to be as peace-loving and quarrel-healing as possible.
3. *Christocentric.* Christ is the One who comforts, commands, redeems, rules, calls a church, communes with us, guards the kingdom, and prays the model prayer. All of the main items in the Catechism are somewhere related to Him.
4. *Devotional.* Much of this Catechism seems to have been written from bended knees. There is resident in it a clear sense of the presence of God.
5. *Autobiographical.* Practically all the questions are asked in the second person and answered in the first. The Christian faith and life is seen from a personal, almost an intimate point of view. It may be that in the actual order of God's dealings with me, His grace comes first. But in the order of *my* knowledge, I first know my sins and miseries—then grace and gratitude. Note also that again and again the Catechism *applies* doctrinal teaching: "How does this benefit *me*?"
6. *Addressed to the whole person.* The "I," of which we have just taken note, is body and soul, heart and mind. The "heart" knowledge of God is balanced with "head" knowledge, with real information. This is not a simple-minded document. Because the Catechism is doctrinally sophisticated and often subtle, it continues to reward those who read and study it intelligently.

As E. A. Dowey has pointed out, the Catechism does not fall victim to the modern fantasy that religion is simply everybody's personal feelings and shared opinions. From the time of Calvin on, Reformed people have always insisted that solid commitment to Christ must be doctrinally *informed* commitment.

The Heidelberg Catechism, it is safe to say, surprises an open-minded reader with its liveliness and interest. Part of the idea behind the chapters of this survey is that the Catechism's liveliness and interest are apparent only to those who see how it was prepared, and who taste its full flavor.

CHAPTER 6
Misery

Introduction

•A killer in a record shop stomps a ball-point pen down through a person's eardrum into his skull. •A fat woman on a water tower hesitates, while a gathering crowd screams at her to jump. In rage, the crowd pelts the firemen who rescue her. •A child sobs because someone has unmercifully teased him about the way he looks. •A dismally lonesome businessman spends Christmas Eve in a porno theater. •A mother sinks into depression because her daughter sends a bare greeting card with no note. •A tiny nation becomes a battleground for one horrible war after another.

Everybody knows that the word *misery* has an unpleasant ring. People use words in the misery family to describe their condition when they are feeling very bad. A person with a head cold claims to feel miserable. A person with a slipped disk may be obviously in misery. A person who has no physical pain at all, but who is afraid and depressed, suffers miserably as well.

Sometimes misery words are not for how someone feels, but for how he performs: A truly wretched violinist is said to play miserably. Sometimes they are used broadly for a whole state of affairs that is unusually bad: A person whose home and reputation and money have all been hopelessly lost is *miserable*.

It is along this last line that the Heidelberg Catechism moves. Part I is entitled "Man's Misery"; it is intended to describe "how great my sin and misery are" (Answer 2). But the Heidelberg Catechism is not talking particularly about *feeling* miserable. It is talking instead about the unhappy fact that we are in a miserable condition whether we feel it or not.

It is interesting to know that the German word which Ursinus selected for misery (*das Elend*) originally meant something like "exile" or "a foreign land." The suggestion is plain. By losing our home with God in paradise, because of Adam's sin, we have gone into exile. We have become foreigners to God and strangers to each other. We have become aliens. We have lost our estate. *In the Heidelberg Catechism "misery" stands for all of the desperate consequences of original sin.* It stands for the human situation or the human predicament after the fall.

The Heidelberg Catechism takes this situation with deadly seriousness. Questions and Answers 10 and 11, for instance, are blunt: Unless we are rescued, we will suffer miserably forever. Yet the Catechism does not linger over this suffering or this misery. In fact, the Misery section is the shortest of the three main sections of the Catechism. Its main point is this: The loss of our home with God has made our misery great. In making this point, the Catechism says three things. It says first that we know our predicament from the law of God (Answer 3). It says that we fell into this predicament by sinning in Adam (Answer 7). And it says, finally, that our misery is so great that unless we are somehow given new life, its last horror will be everlasting punishment (Answer 11).

Our Knowledge of Misery

3 Q. How do you come to know your misery?
 A. The law of God tells me.

When you come to think of it, what the Heidelberg Catechism actually says in Q & A 3 is a bit strange. Why should the Catechism think we need to be *told* we are in misery? Nobody needs to tell you when you have a splitting headache. Nobody needs to tell you you are in trouble when some disastrous sin has ruined your marriage and taken away your job. Nobody needs

PAUL BANDSTRA
11·15·78

to tell you things have gotten bad when all the sirens and children are screaming. After a time, a situation can become so dark and painful that nobody who has his/her senses can possibly miss it.

Why then does the Catechism suppose we need to be told that our misery is great? Why should we have (as the U.S. Pentagon might put it) a "need to know"?

The reason is that we may be miserable without knowing or feeling it. At the very least we may misunderstand the true nature of our misery. Consider, by comparison, a courtroom situation. The main interest is not whether a defendant *feels* guilty, but rather whether (s)he *is* guilty (and, perhaps, whether (s)he *pleads* guilty). Even if the defendant was ignorant of the law, people want to know whether or not (s)he has broken it. So here with the Heidelberg Catechism. We need to know the truth because part of our fallenness is that we are confused. We cannot get our bearings. We are so disoriented that we call evil good and good evil (Isa. 5:20). Strange to say, it is part of our predicament that we cannot even *recognize* our predicament.

We see examples of this all the time. Unsaved persons, using their own standards of what is true and false, right and wrong, are likely to be completely indifferent to God and deeply in love with themselves. They like to keep other things and persons in orbit around them. Such people do not find God very real, and regard all talk of prayer and repentance and salvation through Christ as something foreign and strange.

But look what has happened! Like us, these unsaved persons were meant to live in God's company and to breathe in God's atmosphere and to listen to God speak. But because of the fall, they have become confused. Instead of being at home with God and finding the fallen world a foreign place, they make their home in the world and find the things of God foreign and strange. They are completely disoriented.

We are all disoriented until we are set right again. What sets us right is nothing from the fallen world. That, after all, would not help matters. No physician tries to cure a patient with contaminated instruments, or to diagnose an illness with tools which are bent out of shape. Nor do we try to help our situation with personal conscience or the opinions of society—things which are infected with the very disease which needs curing. Instead, we need something clean and straight from *outside* ourselves. We need a standard which is free from our own confusion and sin. We need, says the Heidelberg Catechism, the law of God.

How, then, do I come to *know* that I am in a strange land? How do I tell that I have wandered far from home? How do I come to know, frankly, that I am a miserable sinner? "The law of God tells me." Even blind sins, secret sins, and happy-go-lucky sins are exposed by this law.

Ursinus did not make this up. He got it from the Bible, especially from Romans. Paul says that "through the law comes knowledge of sin" (3:20), and that "if it had not been for the law, I should not have known sin" (7:7). The law Paul has in mind is mainly the Ten Commandments. In its great third section on Gratitude, the Catechsim does comment richly on the commandments. But here in the section on Misery, the law which the Catechism quotes (Answer 4) is not the Ten Commandments, but rather our Lord's summary of them. This is worth noticing. After all, a poorly taught Christian might believe he or she is innocent of breaking those commandments which begin "Thou shalt not . . . ." Such a person might leave church like the cartoon sailor who says to his friend, "Well, at least I ain't made no graven images lately!" But the law of love, Christ's version of the law, reminds us that we are under obligation to love God with every part of our being—with heart and mind and soul and strength—and that we are to love our neighbor as ourselves.

With this form of the law, all of our gross sins of omission rise up to accuse us. We ought to love God and neighbor—but we do not. In fact, our tendency is to hate them (Answer 5). This is the root of our misery. And without the law to tell us, we might never have known our failure. We would be like some ignorant flyer who has set his automatic pilot and who thinks he can soar safely forever. Whether or not he knows it (or likes it), he may be headed straight for the side of a mountain.

So with us. Until we are arrested and turned around, we are steadily moving downhill, by inclination, toward that unspeakable alienation from God called hell. The law of Christ is used, in the first place, to alert us to our situation and to arouse us to seek salvation from it.

PART OF CONGREGATION
CHURCH OF THE SERVANT
9-10-78

24

Original Sin

"If misery loves company, misery has company enough."   Thoreau

The second thing the Catechism says in the Misery section is that our misery began with Adam. "In Adam's fall, we sinned all," as McGuffey's Reader had it. (McGuffey, obviously, had been brought up on Paul: Rom. 5:12.) Even now, we suffer not only from our own sin, but also—sometimes more—from the sins of others. It has been so from near the beginning. We should have had a rich estate and a great inheritance. Instead, through Adam and Eve's original sin, we have lost our estate and have received a foul inheritance.

The account of this original and disastrous sin is found in Genesis 3. We may note two features of this original sin which have come down to us. One is that, then and now, sin may consist in attacking God. We call this *rebellion*. The other feature is that sin sometimes consists in running away from God. We call this *alienation*.

Think it over. The sin of Adam and Eve begins with a willingness to entertain questioning of God's Word: "Did God say . . .?" (Gen. 3:1). The temptation here is to try to "be like God," to attack His lordship, to challenge His sovereignty. The first couple tries to step out from underneath God's rule. After they have done it, they find themselves fleeing and hiding from God. With that quiet, insistent voice, God calls into Adam's hiding place, "Where are you?" (Gen. 3:9). The man has attacked and then he has run.

We do the same. We rebel against God's rule of our lives. We hate to bow the head or bend the knee. We try to legislate for ourselves, to become autonomous. We can be very proud people. The result is always chaos and disharmony. As someone once put it: We are trying to run our lives on the wrong gas, and it is not working.

But sometimes we flee from God. Like the murderer Cain who became a fugitive in the land, or like the prophet Jonah who could not face God's plan for his life, so we wander in the dark places of the earth where we hope to be let alone. We learn what it means to be aliens. In fact, alienation, as we have already seen, is very close to the word which Ursinus chose for our predicament. By ceaseless work or ceaseless play, by drugs and sex, by drowning out that quiet voice which speaks our name, we try to escape. But there is no escape from God, as the psalmist knew (Psalm 139). Flight from God only brings us to a place where life is barren. Apart from acknowledgment of Him who made us and who wants us home, we are everlastingly vagrant and rootless. One of the world's most famous prayers says it powerfully: "Thou, O Lord, hast made us for Thyself, and our hearts are restless till they find rest in thee" (Augustine).

The Seriousness of Our Predicament

Our sin and misery are so great that they will kill us—unless we are born again. This is the third thing the Catechism says in this section. Our sin is an offense to the holiness of God and deserves "the supreme penalty" (Answer 11). We have a tendency to hate, and an inclination toward all evil (Q & A 5). Unchecked, this tendency and this inclination will finally remove us hopelessly from the sustaining presence of God. The Heidelberg Catechism, as we have seen, does not dwell on our sin and misery. Neither does it minimize them. Like a skillful physician, it makes a pointed diagnosis of our condition, no matter how unwelcome the news may be. It tells us that unless we get help at once, we are lost.

CHAPTER 7
Deliverance

Introduction—Debt and Deliverance

People sometimes earn less than they spend. It may not be particularly their own fault. Sickness, accident, rising taxes, and galloping inflation may enlarge the flow of cash out. Meanwhile, unemployment, relatively low pay, or retirement may narrow the flow of cash in. The result is almost unavoidable debt.

But often people are in debt by their own fault. They may have a decent enough income, but their spending is entirely indecent. A relish for fine dining, a reckless use of credit cards, a naive idea of interest rates, and a general financial slovenliness begin finally to bend them under an intolerable financial burden. They may seek to have it lifted by a "bill-consolidator." But because it costs so much to borrow money this way, the burden is cinched up even tighter. Finally, the people have to admit their inadequacy and visit one of those agencies where they ceremonially cut your credit cards to ribbons before your eyes and then help you plan a way to be free from debt.

It is in this last area of debt and freedom that Part II of the Catechism moves. We have just completed a lesson in which we saw our misery described as *das Elend*. Alienation is one description of our predicament. Like some prodigal son, we are wanderers in a far country. But there are other descriptions. One could talk, for example, as Jesus did when He described the miserable person who built his house on sand. Our trouble, like the foolish man's, keeps getting worse because our foundations are insecure. Or we might speak of our misery as a kind of slavery. We are bound by sin, shackled, enthralled. So St. Paul, in the well-known Romans 7 passage about the inner war between wanting and doing, speaks of being a *captive* to the law of sin. At last he virtually roars: "Wretched man that I am! who will deliver me from this body of death?" (Rom. 7:24).

Who will *deliver* me? Who will cut me loose? Who will spring me free? This is the question Ursinus raises early in Part II of the Catechism. The word he uses (*die Erlosung*) means "loosening," or "liberation," or "deliverance." These last two words come from the same root and have to do with setting free. Here, following a main line of theology, the Catechism is no longer thinking of our predicament as alienation. It has a new picture in view. It now sees us as staggering under a gross weight, a burden (14,17). What we need is to get out from underneath. What we need is to be loosed, liberated, delivered. We need *Erlosung*.

From what must we be delivered? What has us bowed and bent? Debt. Picking up the big medieval image from the world of commerce, the Catechism talks about our predicament as debt. Like reckless spenders, we have (by sinning) gotten ourselves hopelessly in debt. And like those who try to consolidate bills with a costly loan, we find our debt does not stay put. "Actually, we increase our guilt every day" (Answer 13). What we need is to be delivered. What we need is to become debt-free.

The middle section of the Heidelberg Catechism speaks of our deliverance from debt, and of the Deliverer. It does so in four ways. It says first that we must trust our Deliverer, Jesus Christ, to pay the debt we cannot pay for ourselves (Q & A 12-28). Secondly, it tells the events of Christ's career calculated to pay this debt (Q & A 29-52). Next, it speaks of the benefits of this payment applied on our account through the Holy Spirit (Q & A 53-64). Finally, the Catechism discusses the confirmation of these benefits through the use of the sacraments and church discipline (Q & A 65-85). The predominating imagery is financial. There is debt and there is payment on our account. But the credit is never our own.

The main image of our misery and deliverance in Part II of the Catechism is that of debt and payment. If it seems a bit crass to think of our obligation and Christ's deliverance in money terms, remember that the money imagery *is* biblical, as the parable of the unforgiving steward shows (Matt. 18:21-35). The comparison in the parable is between money debts and our religious debts to God. Jesus is really talking about our religious (or "life") debt. We owe "ten thousand talents"—that is, an infinite amount. Mercifully, our Lord forgives. But He expects us to forgive others too.

The Bible abounds in other images for our deliverance besides the debt-payment ones. Here are a few:

We were		But now are
slaves	(Gal. 5:1)	set free
slaves	(Gal. 4:7, Rom. 8:17)	sons
sick	(Mark 2:17)	cured
lost sheep, coin, son	(Luke 15)	found
hungry	(Luke 15:16,17, 23,24)	fed
dead	(Luke 15:24)	alive
cut off	(Rom. 11:17-24)	grafted on
enemies	(Rom. 5:10)	reconciled
weary	(Matt. 11:28,29)	rested
foolish	(Matt. 7:24-27)	wise
poor	(II Cor. 8:9)	rich
blemished, spotted, soiled	(Eph. 2:26,27)	cleansed
strangers, aliens	(Eph. 2:19)	citizens
in the dark	(I Peter 2:9)	in the light
sinners	(Rom. 3:23,24)	justified
sinners	(I John 1:9)	forgiven
hopeless	(Eph. 2:12, Col. 1:23)	hopeful

Faith in Our Deliverer (Q & A 12-28)

Part II, especially the early section on debt and justice, has often been regarded as the least attractive part of the Catechism. The warm, personal tone seems to cool here, the binding together of law and gospel to loosen. The Catechism here shows its Western theological inheritance. There is a distinctively legal mentality in Western theology, running from Tertullian through Anselm to Calvin. This legal mentality is especially reflected in Q & A 12-18, which state our predicament in terms of debt, punishment, guilt, justice, payment, and satisfaction.

However, already in the previous section (Q & A 9-11), God's justice plays an important role. Answer 11 contains the heart of the issue: We have by original and actual sin offended God. But this is not an ordinary offense. This is not like offending a human being. We have offended an infinite, supremely majestic Being. Because of the supreme dignity and honor of God, any sin against Him is a supreme sin. There are no trifles. There are no peccadilloes. The infinite weightiness of human sin requires an infinite satisfaction. That is what God's justice demands, and God must have His justice satisfied (Q & A 11,12).

But just here is our predicament: We are both obliged and unable to render infinite satisfaction. We must pay ultimately; yet we cannot. No creature could. The weight, the burden of this debt would crush any mere creature (Answer 14). Only a human being is obligated to bear this weight and pay this debt (Answer 16), but only a divine being *can* bear this weight and pay this debt (Answer 17). Hence, in a godly plan which combines justice and mercy, a God-man pays. Who in heaven's name, who on earth might this be?

Our Lord Jesus Christ,
who was given us
to set us completely free
and to make us right with God.

(Answer 18)

Cindy Mulder
2ND GRADE
ORANGE CITY CHRISTIAN
11-16-78

As C. S. Lewis once put it, in less severely legal language, when a person is badly in debt, "the trouble of getting him out usually falls on a kind friend." In the present case, because the debt was no ordinary debt, the "friend we have in Jesus" could be no ordinary friend.

How does a person take advantage of this saving plan? By using the gift of "true faith" to become so attached to Christ as to receive His benefits (Answer 20). Such faith combines a belief in the gospel (summarized for us in the Apostles' Creed) with a "deep-rooted" personal assurance that all it promises applies to me as well as others. This belief is so sure that it qualifies as knowledge, and this assurance so secure that it cannot be lost. I am *forever* "right with God" (Answer 21).

The Events of Christ (Q & A 29-52)

The Catechism now wants to say *how* Christ delivers us. It takes up the Apostles' Creed as a suitable tool for doing this because, as we remember, the middle section of the Creed includes a list of the historical events of Christ. It is through this cluster of saving events that our debt is paid and we become Christ's (Answer 34).

But the Catechism cannot simply plunge into the middle of the Creed where these events are recited. It does want to use the middle of the Creed to explain our deliverance (which is what Part II is all about), but it cannot begin there. What we see, then, is that the Catechism moves through some short preparatory stretches of material—like a train rumbling across a switchyard before it gets out on the main line. So something is said to introduce the Creed (Q & A 22-24) and the Trinity by which it is organized (Q & A 25). Something brief, but important, is also said about the first article of the Creed, about the creation and providence of the Father (Q & A 26-28). Then "God the Son" is introduced by means of His names (Q & A 29-34), and in Q & A 35 and following the saving events of Christ the Son are finally recited and discussed.

This discussion is carried on in a most distinctive way: The Catechism mentions an objective event of Christ's life, an event of history, and then turns back to ask how this event personally affects *us*. How does this benefit you? What "further advantage" do we receive from this? How does it comfort you?

The precedent is memorably set in Q & A 31 and 32. "Why is *he* called Christ?" is followed at once by the personal question, "But why are *you* called a Christian?" From then on, down the list of the events of Christ, this pattern continues until the summary question about the whole recital is characteristically and disarmingly asked: "What good does it do you, however, to believe all this?" (Q & A 59).

But that is in the next section. The climax of *this* section, of Q & A 29-52, comes in Q & A 52. Here the rhythm of objective event and subjective benefit concludes with a striking return to the Catechism's key concept. The question asked about the last judgment is not how we might fare in the face of this frightening prospect, nor how we can best prepare for it. The question, remarkably, is how Christ's final judgment *comforts* us! The judgment is seen as something *welcome!* The reason is that we do not have to face some "condemning conqueror who fulminates against sinners," as H. Berkhof observes. Rather, we face as judge the very One who has Himself delivered us. The judgment, therefore, is not some curse to be dreaded, but instead a part of the gospel to be craved.

The Benefits of Christ (Q & A 53-64)

The Catechism purposely uses the Apostles' Creed as its main teaching material in the Deliverance section. We have just seen that Q & A 29-52 include the first seven articles of the Creed. These articles talk about both God the Father and Christ. Now we turn in Q & A 53-64 to the last four articles, to the Holy Spirit.

At once we notice something odd. We notice that the Catechism, like the Creed it is discussing, strangely says very little about the Holy Spirit Himself. It rather quickly passes on to the holy catholic church, the communion of saints, and the rest. Of course these are all fruits of the sanctified life, and with this gradually sanctified life the Holy Spirit (or *Sanctifier*) has already been specially associated.

But it seems to be a kind of uneasy association. You see this particularly when you observe that the Catechism, as we just said, seems hardly to talk about the Holy Spirit. It mentions the Spirit briefly (Q & A 53) and then hurries on to talk some more about Christ. It is Christ who gathers a church (Q & A 54), Christ in whom the communion of saints shares (Q & A 55), Christ to whom my soul flees at death (Q & A 57), and in Christ that I become heir to "life everlasting" (Q & A 59). Why then is this section from Q & A 53-64 headed "God the Holy Spirit"? It's not about the Spirit at all. It's about Christ and His benefits!

Two things must be said about this. The first is that the Bible itself so closely unites Christ and

HAROLD BOER
11-17-78

the Spirit as to make them hard to distinguish. In the case of Christ and the *Father,* it may be easier. After all, Christ prays to the Father, claims to know less than the Father, and says that the Father is greater than He. These are clearly two different divine persons.

But the biblical material about Christ and the Spirit is not so clear. It sometimes seems difficult to make out the distinct person or personality of the Holy Spirit. In Paul's letters, being ''in Christ'' and ''in the Spirit'' (Rom. 8: 9,10) come to about the same thing. At one point (II Cor. 3:17), Paul flatly says, ''The Lord *is* the Spirit.'' Always the fellowship, life, and hope in the Spirit are fellowship, life, and hope in Christ. The Holy Spirit appears to be that personal power by whom Christ acts and in whom Christ is present to be experienced by the church.

Thus we can see that the Catechism is quite biblical in so closely yoking the Holy Spirit to the benefits of Christ. Communion of saints, forgiveness of sins, and the rest are gifts granted by the Son of God ''through his Spirit and Word'' (Answer 54).

The other thing to be said about the Catechism's treatment of the Holy Spirit is that it is not so slim as it looks. Because the Spirit is not an isolated person who has just one little section of work carved out for Him, but is rather the acting Spirit of Christ, His activity is quite widely mentioned in the Catechism. It is not limited to Q & A 53-64. Questions and Answers 35, 47, 49, 51, etc. all deal with the Spirit's work of applying to believers what Christ has done.

Sacraments and Discipline (Q & A 65-85)

After a solid review of salvation by grace and through faith in Q & A 60-64 (recall the earlier treatment, before the Creed intervenes, at Q & A 20-22), the Catechism moves on finally to a presentation of the sacraments and discipline. These are *church* matters. For all of their wariness about the hierarchical medieval church, the Reformers never abandon a high view of the church. The church is never simply a voluntary assembling of individually saved persons. In the gem-like Answer 54 (about as close as the Catechism comes to a statement of election) we discern instead that the ''I'' which is so prominently featured in the Catechism's answers is a living member of a prior *community* of those chosen by Christ. The Reformers never talk about Christ as a merely ''personal Savior.'' He *is* a personal Savior; that is, He does save persons. But the persons are saved only *as* members of a body, a communion, a fellowship, a church.

Now it is in this context that the benefits of Christ (one of which is the community itself) are confirmed and secured. Faith is produced by the church's preaching and confirmed by the sacraments and discipline (Q & A 65, 83).

We shall have to reserve our comments on the sacraments and discipline until the relevant lesson in the series on the Belgic Confession. For now, we may note only this much: The ''keys of the kingdom,'' namely preaching and discipline, are strategically treated by the Catechism, together with the sacraments, between the Creed of Part II and the law of Part III. The point apparently is that these marks of the true church—preaching, sacraments, and discipline— are all gracious means of confirming and nourishing that creedal faith and those assured benefits which must come to expression in the good works of the law. As we shall see in our next lesson, there is a thoroughly Reformed interest in doing good works, and in doing them according to the law. This is, in fact, the way we *show* that ''He has paid the debt and made us free.''

CHAPTER 8
Gratitude

Introduction—The Third Use of the Law

Howard Hageman reminds us of a story Abraham Kuyper, the great Dutch Calvinist scholar and statesman, told at Princeton Seminary when he gave his Stone lectures there in 1888-89. Striving mightily to identify part of the genius of the Reformed tradition, Kuyper told the story of the sixteenth century plague which ruined the Italian city of Milan. Cardinal Borromeo bravely stayed to help and pray for those who were dying.

> But when the city of Geneva was similarly afflicted not only did Calvin look after the spiritual needs of the sick and the dying, he introduced a whole new system of hygienic measures which stopped the plague and prevented any future recurrence.
>
> (*The Reformed Journal*, March, 1975)

John Calvin was the first great Reformed sanitation engineer! In this characteristic action, Calvin indeed exemplifies the unique contribution which the Reformed tradition has made to the world. It is the Reformed view that the gospel applies to political, economic, educational, recreational, and all other areas of human life. The gospel applies to sanitation and urban affairs. No Calvinist, no Reformed person would ever talk of Christians "sticking to the gospel and not meddling in politics." That is a repudiation of God's sovereignty! That is intolerable pietism. That is a wretched separation of Christ and culture.

Of course, Calvin did not fall victim, on the other hand, to the sort of classically liberal thinking which *identifies* the coming of the kingdom of God with this or that socio-political program. And no decently Reformed person today would do so either. We cannot look at a Marxist revolution in South America and say "Lo, *here* is the kingdom." Reformed people, as Richard Mouw

has observed, repudiate any "Lo, hereism." But they also reject the pietistic tendencies to flee the world, to let the world go to hell, to hide safe in the bosom of Jesus "till the storm of life be over." Between utopianism on the one hand, and escapism on the other, Reformed people have always sought to make their way.

Now, interestingly enough, one can see in this great, rich third section of the Heidelberg Catechism some of this enormous *ethical* interest which lies deep in the tradition. This interest is stimulated in the Reformed tradition not only by the doctrine of God's sovereignty, or by the doctrine of Christ's lordship over all areas of life. It is stimulated as well by a practical and very distinctive way of seeing the law of God. Above all, we must note this distinctively Reformed view of the law in the present lesson.

Luther believed that the law of God, the Ten Commandments, had two uses. It could be used, first, as a *civil* protection against chaos. The law is a dike against sin. Through the "order" of government, and the government's laws against stealing, killing, bearing false witness, and the like, God providentially prevents a fallen creation from sliding completely into chaos and ruin.

The second use of the law, in Luther's view, is its chief use. This is a *theological* or religious use. The law is a mirror in which the sinner sees his shabbiness, his misery, his desperate need of the Savior. The law strikes terror in him, and drives him to despair. Only in despair does he see his need of justification by grace.

Calvin and the Reformed thinkers accepted these two uses and made much of them. But they added a third—and made it primary. They saw the law as *a guide for the redeemed life*. The law is not merely a civil dike against sin. It is also a constitution for the city of God. It is not merely for sinners. It is also for saints. In fact, as is often

FIFTH GRADE
PELLA CHRISTIAN
11·15·78

remarked, what really connects salvation with our everyday lives in the world is the law. The question of newly delivered Christians is always, "How then shall we *live*?"

The Catechism has one answer: We are to live gratefully, thankfully. The great third part of the Heidelberg Catechism is concerned with gratitude, with what the German called *Dankbarkeit*. But there are two main ways in which we are to show this gratitude. One is to do good works according to the law. This lies at the heart of conversion itself (Answer 90). The other is to pray. The law and prayer together make up most of the third part.

The Shape of the Third Part

A fast look at Part III of the Catechism reveals, however, that there is a preface to law and prayer. Questions and Answers 86-91 raise and answer two questions preliminary to the entire third part.

The first question is very natural—especially considering the Reformational fear of good-works salvation. Its main answer has just been suggested above. The first question is: Why, if we are delivered, do we still need to do good works? Four answers are given. One of these ("so that we may be assured of our faith by its fruits") has always been controversial. But the main answer, the most general answer, is "so that in all our living we may show we are thankful to God for all he has done for us" (Answer 86). The idea here, of course, is that people who are deeply grateful will want naturally, inevitably, to show it. Even to other human beings, good people try to show their gratitude: "Look, isn't there something now that I can do for *you*?"

The second important preliminary question is not why we do good works, but rather *what* makes a work good. Here is the nub of that distinctively Reformed approach to the law: We are to do good works as the flower and fruit of our deliverance. But we are not to do just any good work which strikes our fancy. Rather, as the Catechism pointedly remarks, we are to do those good deeds which "arise out of true faith, conform to God's law, and are done for His glory" (Answer 91).

In this nugget, three qualifications are made on our good works. The first is that they must blossom out of belief and trust. That is their soil, their matrix. An unbeliever who helps an old woman across a street, for example, has done better than if (s)he were to stomp on her. Yet (s)he has not yet done what is really "good." For that, the deed must arise "out of true faith."

Secondly, good deeds must be formed, and informed, by God's law. The law has a *normative* use. Because this third use of the law is so distinctively Reformed, one wonders why those Reformed churches which still read the law do not do so after the confession of sin (as a guide to life) rather than before the confession of sin (as a call to penitence).

Thirdly, delivered lives glisten with good works not so that they themselves may be enhanced, but rather so that the Deliverer's greatness may be reflected from them. There is a magnifying, or an illuminating, of God's greatness when His people live as He intends. For this the Reformed slogan has always been *soli Deo gloria.* To God alone be glory.

Here in Answer 91, then, the Catechism gives a threefold qualification for good works. Immediately the central one of these, conformity to God's law, is selected for extended treatment. Thus, a striking, and sometimes virtuoso, interpretation of the Ten Commandments follows. The Catechism is simply saying what it means for good works to be conformed to God's law. The Catechism is simply exhibiting the profound Reformed interest in law-shaped gratitude.

But obedience to the Ten Words is not the only part of our *Dankbarkeit.* In fact, it is not even the chief part. That distinction is reserved for prayer.

Why do Christians need to pray?

Because prayer is the most important part of the thankfulness God requires of us.

(Q & A 116)

Almost at once follows the Catechism's deeply devotional treatment of the Lord's Prayer, a treatment which, as we recall, consists largely of answers which are themselves prayers.

So the Heidelberg Catechism thinks of the life of gratitude as combining work and prayer, good deeds and devout words. Both are necessary. Most heretical practices can be traced to a minimizing of the one or the other. There are the cold-eyed activists, going angrily and prayerlessly about the business of benevolence. And there are the self-indulgent pietists who have callouses on their knees, but none on their hands. Yet, according to the Catechism, gratitude will lead us to practice a combination of work and prayer.

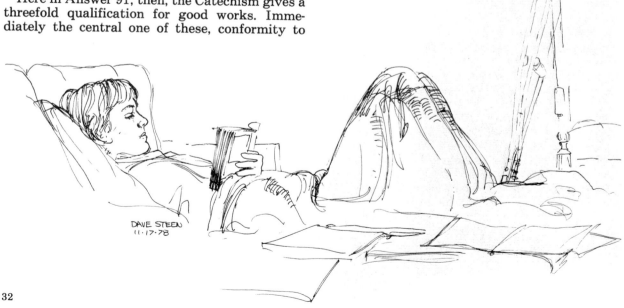

DAVE STEEN
11·17·78

The Catechism on the Law

Sad to say, we do not have room here to do justice to the truly interesting, and often very contemporary, commentary on the law. We shall have to be content to notice, with examples, four ways in which the Catechism goes far beyond the letter of the law to probe its spirit. As is sometimes observed by thoughtful readers, the Catechism treats the law in sermon-on-the-mount fashion when it—

1. *broadens* the range of a commandment, as in Answer 104 where the fifth commandment's range is extended beyond "my father and mother" to "all those in authority over me."

2. *deepens* the commandments, as in Answer 110 where the eighth commandment is deepened to forbid the attitude of greediness as well as the overt deed of stealing.

3. *positivizes* the commands, as in Answer 112 where the ninth commandment is seen not only to *forbid* (negatively) bearing of false witness, but also to *require* (positively) that I "love the truth, speak it candidly, and openly acknowlege it."

4. *applies* the commands, as in Q & A 98 where the second commandment is applied to an urgent Reformation concern. Note also in Answer 110 how sharply relevant to every age is the concern about the hand in the till, and the thumb on the scale. What a list of larcenous practices we have here! All of them are "schemes made to appear legitimate."

Now we are in a position to see something very significant. It might be thought that obedience to the Ten Commandments is an oddly narrow way to show one's gratitude to God for deliverance. Indeed it would be—if one conceived of the Ten Words narrowly, as a series of "thou shalt not" commands. Then the life of gratitude would consist merely in a scrupulous avoidance of "sins of commission," with little worry about the "sins of omission."

But the Catechism does not let us off so easily. Reformed writers had Ephesians 2:10 so constantly in mind that they attempted in every way to broaden, deepen, positivize, and apply the law which shapes those good works for which we have been saved. This is part of the glory of the Reformed tradition at its greatest. Unhappily, it has often gone unnoticed, or been perverted. Some Reformed people have let an interest in the law-shaped life curdle into legalism. Some others have been content with seeing our marching orders as purely negative. Avoid this! Don't do that! Obedience to the fourth commandment, for example, has sometimes been interpreted this way. But, as is typical, the Catechism is itself free from the sort of "fussy Sabbatarianism" which allowed Scottish divines to punish those who dared so much as to *smile* on the Sabbath. Note that in Answer 103 all the injunctions for our spending the "festive" day of rest are *positive*.

Thus we can see here what is true of the Catechism's treatment of the law in general: It is a rich, full, positive, life-related treatment. The Reformed Christian is faced not with some pinched and meager existence as a misfit in the world. Rather, in obedience to God, he takes a wholehearted joy and a hearty delight (*lust* in Answer 90) in doing good works. There is to be an openness, a healthiness, a heartiness about the activist life to which our gratitude stimulates us. We are to see before us the whole range of modern life as a field in which we are called to make visible God's sovereignty and to make viable His justice. Of this godliness we are to be agents, witnesses, and models.

The Catechism on Prayer

We have already noted that the Catechism calls prayer "the most important part" of our thankfulness. Why so?

We are not told. Indeed, after Q & A 116 not only is thankfulness scarcely mentioned again, but nearly all the interpretive little prayers (Q & A 122 ff.) are petitionary! They all ask, beseech, plead: "Help us...," "Do take care of...," "Do this...," "And so help us...." As E. A. Dowey has pointed out, "Thus conceived, the chief part of gratitude is asking for more."

This is at first surprising. But perhaps it reflects the Catechism's assumption that those who keep asking the Father for help are the ones who best acknowledge that He is "the giver of every good and perfect gift." As a matter of fact, in making all of its interpretive prayers petitionary, the Catechism is only following our Lord. The Lord's Prayer, on which this section comments, consists (except for the kingdom, power, and glory appendage) entirely in petitions. Thus thankfulness is assumed in those "who pray continually and groan inwardly, asking God for these gifts..." (Answer 116).

What is the range of Christian prayer? Can we pray to find a missing car key as well as a missing son? Indeed we can. In fact, we must. We are *commanded* to pray for "everything we need, spiritually and physically" (Answer 118).

We note that the Catechism does not see prayer as merely the outpouring of emotion. There will be times, of course, when out of our panic, or bewilderment, or ecstasy we will pray. But in the steady passage of ordinary days, in the rhythm of a stable life, there will be many other times when prayer is not fueled by an explosion of feeling. There is rather an exercise of the will that is required. Ursinus would almost surely have agreed with C. S. Lewis' speculation that God likes best those prayers we deliberately make when we don't feel like praying. Prayer is (let us say it) a duty. But it is a duty of the same sort as eating a meal. That is, regular prayer should build such communion with God that we miss it in the same way as we miss dinner—occasionally and with pangs. So when the Catechism emphasizes that we *must* pray, and that we are *commanded* to pray, it does not at all imagine that we will always do so grimly or resentfully.

Christian prayer has five qualities according to the remarkable Answer 117. It is—

1. "from the heart." It is sincere. The mumbling of prefabricated little strings of cliches from

RUTH STURSMA
11-15-78

which heart and mind are utterly disengaged is ruled out.

2. rightly directed "to no other than the one true God."

3. open, that is, we are to "hide nothing." There can be no waiting till every dingy corner of one's life has first been swept clean. That dinginess must itself be acknowledged.

4. humble. Prayer must always have that quality of quiet awe and reverence which befits an address to the majestic Sovereign of heaven and earth.

5. confident. We have, because of Christ, an "unshakable foundation" for the belief that we are heard.

This last quality leads us to the concluding Amen.

The Amen

Hendrikus Berkhof has alerted students of the Catechism to the fact that the little Answer 129, like the little word "Amen," contains an eloquent climax not only to the section on prayer, but also to the entire Catechism. What it says is this:

> It is even more sure
> that God listens to my prayer,
> than that I really desire
> what I pray for.

This must not be overlooked! The Catechism here assures us that our own feelings and desires are finally overwhelmed by the sheer reality and faithfulness of God. The point of prayer is never to crank up our own feelings or work ourselves into "the little engine that could" mentality ("I think I can...I think I can"). There are plenty of times in a Christian's life when (s)he must be steadfastly obedient to God even while (s)he feels dry, abandoned, and empty of any presence of God. It is the willingness to work and to pray even out of such desolation which builds strong faith and sturdy outposts of the kingdom. It may be only much later that a person comes to say,"Surely the Lord is in this place; and I did not know it" (Gen. 28:16).

So the Catechism progresses from the very personal, almost experience-oriented, Q & A 1 to this very objective, bedrock affirmation of Answer 129. The "I" which has spoken so eloquently for so many answers is at last completely surrendered to the One who is, and who was, and who is to come. Even when my grip on Him loosens, He never loosens His grip on me.

Amen. This is sure to be.

CHAPTER 9
Introduction to the Belgic Confession

Introduction—The Blood of a Martyr

Shortly before he was hanged for his Protestantism, the Belgian Reformer Guido de Bres (pronounced GEE-doe de BRAY) wrote to his wife Catherine from the foul dungeon in which he was imprisoned. Because the letter enlightens us both about de Bres and about the circumstances surrounding his Belgic Confession, we quote a part of it:

My dear and well beloved wife in our
Lord Jesus:

Your grief and anguish, troubling me in the midst of my joy and gladness, are the cause of my writing you this present letter. I most earnestly pray you not to be grieved beyond measure...If the Lord had wished us to live together longer, He could easily have caused it so to be. But such was not His pleasure. Let His good will be done then, and let that suffice for all reason. Moreover, consider that I have not fallen into the hands of my enemies by chance, but by the providence of my God, which guides and governs all things, small as well as great...I pray you, my dear and faithful companion, to be glad with me, and to thank the good God for what He is doing, for He does nothing but what is altogether right and good....

I am shut up in the strongest and wretchedest of dungeons, so dark and gloomy that it goes by the name of the Black Hole. I can get but little air, and that of the foulest. I have on my hands and feet heavy irons which are a constant torture, galling the flesh even to my poor bones. But, notwithstanding all, my God fails not to make good His promise, and to comfort my heart, and to give me a most blessed content....

I pray you then, to be comforted in the Lord, to commit yourself and your affairs to Him, for He is the Husband of the widow and the Father of the fatherless, and He will never leave nor forsake you....

Good-bye, Catherine, my well beloved! I pray my God to comfort you, and give you resignation to His holy will.

> Your faithful husband,
> Guido de Bres
> Minister of God's Word
> at Valenciennes, and at
> present prisoner for the
> Son of God.

In this moving attempt to console his grieving wife, de Bres shows some of the great personal courage and profound commitment to the providence of God which marked the noblest souls of the Reformation in the Netherlands. De Bres knew he was doomed. He knew that any day he would be forcibly compelled to meet the Lord who had been his guide through the valley of the shadow of death. Yet, remarkably, he surrenders not to self-pity, but to the everlasting arms which had all along been holding him up. Indeed, he speaks of his "joy and gladness." He speaks more than once of comfort. Up to his neck in trouble, he attempts to speak solace and strength to her who must soon discover whether God is indeed "Husband of the widow and the Father of the fatherless."

Of this sort of heroism most of us know very little personally. Yet without it, an important branch of the Calvinist Reformation could never have flourished.

The Netherlands Situation

Guido de Bres (1522-67) was a native of the area known as the Lowlands or Netherlands. In the middle sixteenth century, this area comprised seventeen provinces of territory in what is now Holland, northern France, and Belgium. It is simply because de Bres' confession of faith of 1561 originated in what is now Belgium that it is called the Belgic Confession.

After 1555, the Netherlands was under the sovereignty of Philip II of Spain. Philip, like his father Charles V, who had been Holy Roman Emperor and King of Spain from 1519 to 1555, was a fiercely loyal Roman Catholic. But the Netherlands Philip governed was openly hospitable to Reformation teachings, and had been for decades. Already in the 1470s, Wessel Gansvoort of Groningen had spoken out against masses, prayers for the dead, the sale of indulgences, and several other items which were to become famously sensitive issues in Luther's Wittenberg of 1517. In fact, Luther himself remarked: "If I had read Wessel before I began, my opponents would have imagined that I had derived everything from him, so entirely do we two agree in spirit."

Moreover, the Netherlands was the birthplace of the famous humanist Erasmus of Rotterdam—a truly significant figure in the preparation for both Lutheran and Calvinist Reformations. By his typically humanist interest in returning to the Scriptures, to the very origins of the church, Erasmus gave impetus to the great Reformation insistence on the reading of the Bible. By his attack on the excesses of the medieval church, he also fomented impatience with Roman abuses.

So the Netherlands had indigenous springs of reform. But it also had a door wide open to France in the sixteenth century, and France was alive with the teaching of Calvin. If the Heidelberg Catechism, however Calvinistic, has its roots ultimately in Bullinger's Zurich (from which both Ursinus and Olevianus had come), the Belgic Confession has its roots ultimately in Calvin's Geneva. In fact, just two years before de Bres' confession appeared, the French or Gallican Confession, authorized by Calvin, was approved by synod at Paris. Anybody who compares the French document with de Bres' will see how intimately de Bres knew Calvin's work. Look, for example, at the first articles of the two confessions:

The Calvinistic Gallican Confession

We believe and confess that there is but one God, who is one sole and simple essence, spiritual, eternal, invisible, immutable, infinite, incomprehensible, ineffable, omnipotent; who is all-wise, all-good, all-just, and all-merciful.

De Bres' Belgic Confession

We all believe with the heart and confess with the mouth that there is one only simple and spiritual Being, which we call God; and that He is eternal, imcomprehensible, invisible, immutable, infinite, almighty, perfectly wise, just, good, and the overflowing fountain of all good.

Thus both from its own soil and also from the Calvinist center of France, the Netherlands reaped a ripe harvest of Reformed ideas and practices. It was with this—and with a peculiar stoutness of heart among the Netherlanders—that Philip II was obliged to deal.

He did so with a particular forcefulness and cruelty. Philip's father, Charles, had been equally determined to eradicate every Reformed plant in the Netherlands, and to enforce Catholic orthodoxy; but Charles had the advantage of speaking Flemish and of having been raised in the Netherlands. Thus to the inhabitants of Flanders, especially, Charles was regarded with a certain amount of tolerant obedience. Roland Bainton reports that "there were tears at Brussels when he abdicated in 1555." But the tears for his son Philip were only born of anger and frustration. Philip was hated as a tyrant and an absentee landlord. Ruling by means of his sister, Margaret of Parma, Philip undertook to punish heresy in the Netherlands and to harass every exponent of reform.

Of course, Philip was driven by much more than his private religious preferences. He was not just *theologically* convinced of the rightness of Roman orthodoxy and the wrongness of Genevan, Parisian, and Netherlandish reform. He was trying to run an empire. He was trying to control Spain, the Netherlands, and some sizeable portions of Italy. Crucial to this control, so he understandably thought, was the squashing of that religious dissent which prevented political unity.

Hence he imported Spanish Inquisition to the Netherlands. What Charles had already declared in 1550 was reissued as an edict by Philip and enforced; namely (in the words of a nineteenth century commentator), that "no one should print, write, copy, keep, buy, sell, or give any heretical book or writing, or hold or be present at any heretical meeting, or read, teach, or expound the holy Scriptures, or preach secretly or openly, or entertain any heretical opinions . . . ." Those who dared to transgress this carefully worded prohibition were not spared. The same commentator remarks, "All the great elements of nature were pressed into service—fire for burning, water for drowning, air for hanging, and earth for burying alive."

MARGARET LITTLE
12-14-78

Naturally, such flaming zealots as Guido de Bres were always in danger of their lives and regularly obliged to flee their homeland for safer foreign cities. By 1568 the situation had become so serious in the Netherlands that many of the citizens became convinced that Philip meant to wipe them all out—men, women, and children. Charles had been accused by some of trying to quench the fires of reform by his subjects' blood, but Philip was feared even more. He is said to have vowed stubbornly to make a wilderness of the Netherlands rather than to allow it to be inhabited by heretics.

Yet the Protestant Netherlanders proved tough, wily, and just as stubborn as Philip. They were remarkably hard to intimidate. Often unusually literate, according to one historian, "it was their boast that . . . even the fishermen who dwelt in the huts of Friesland could read, and write, and discuss the interpretations of Scripture." The Netherlanders, especially the Reformed, did not give in. Some of them went "underground," others fled to towns just across the German border, particularly Wesel and

Emden. De Bres remained in the Lowlands, serving the Reformed churches in Tournai, Lille, and Valenciennes. It was for these churches that he prepared, in 1559, the first draft of the Belgic Confession.

A copy was sent to Calvin, who approved its contents. The preachers in Emden likewise approved it. A copy, together with a letter to Philip II, was tossed over the castle wall, but nobody knows whether the emperor ever read it. An underground synod, meeting in Antwerp in 1566, adopted it. And since that time the Belgic Confession has remained one of the three standards of faith of all Reformed churches of Dutch origin. Born in the fires of political and religious oppression, the Belgic Confession became the theological rallying point of the Reformed people in their heroic struggle against the Spanish Inquisition.

De Bres himself became one of an estimated 100,000 Dutchmen who lost their lives during the persecution, which scholars affirm to be more devastating than all the ancient persecutions by the Roman Empire. By the night of May 30, 1567, when Guido de Bres faced his killers, the Calvinist Reformation in the Netherlands was so deeply rooted it could no longer be eradicated.

A major modern historian of the Reformation, R. Bainton, has commented on why Calvinism gained the upper hand in the Netherlands:

> The success in the Netherlands may well have been due to the fact that Calvinism was better suited (than Lutheranism) to be the religion of a resistance movement. The activism of the Calvinists, their progress in France in divesting themselves of all of the earlier scruples with regard to the legitimacy of armed resistance to tyranny, their heroic devotion to the glory of God by erecting his kingdom upon earth made them just the group to "drive the Spanish vermin from the land."
>
> (*The Reformation of the Sixteenth Century*)

The Anabaptists on the Left

The Netherlands Calvinists inherited, then, an activism from Calvinist France which, combined with a native resourcefulness, made them hard to tyrannize. But in the same Netherlands was another group, or a number of groups, of activists. Their resistance to Spanish Catholic control was both less controlled and less successful than that of the Calvinists. Loosely called "Anabaptists" because of their belief in adult rebaptism, these people were keenly impatient with the reforms of Luther and Calvin, regarding them as half-baked and half-hearted reforms.

ELSON HAAN FAMILY
11·17·78

The Anabaptist movement began in Switzerland, in the 1520s, but soon spread across Europe. Always the movement spawned fringe groups and fringe individuals which mainline Anabaptists themselves repudiated. But, in the Netherlands as well as elsewhere, their opponents did not make nice distinctions and cruelly persecuted them all. Perhaps the main reason for their persecution was that various Anabaptists held what were thought to be radical views about the Christian's relationship to civil government. Anabaptist thought and practice was dominated by a doctrine of the "two kingdoms"—the kingdom of God and the kingdom of the devil, the kingdom of light and the kingdom of dark. Instead of thinking that Christians ought to reclaim culture for Christ, to transform it under the sovereignty of God (a Reformed impetus we saw in the last lesson on the Heidelberg Catechism), Anabaptists wanted to oppose and withdraw from most everything in the world. Separation from the world meant for them not only abandonment of the Roman Catholic Church—whose concessions to worldliness had returned it to the kingdom of darkness—but also separation from the (worldly) *government,* at least in its alliance with the church. Thus participation in military service was rejected, the taking of legal oaths refused, and, in some cases, taxes neglected.

Most Anabaptists practiced gentle nonresistance to evil. But some other radicals, often grouped under the same name, engaged in armed rebellion against their government. It was a group of these that Luther angrily denounced in 1527 as "*Schwarmer,*" (fanatics), and whose crushing he advised.

It is quite true that some of the radicals did bizarre things and held eccentric beliefs. They were regarded as an embarrassment by other Protestants, and as likely to wreck the whole cause by their excesses. In *The Church's Witness to the World*, P. Y. De Jong retells the dark story of Munster (1530s) in which the Netherlanders John Matthyszoon of Haarlem and John Beukelszoon of Leyden figured prominently. Polygamous, frenzied, desperately sure of the imminent end of the world, these Netherlanders were exceeded in their extreme views only by some of their countrymen who urged the killing of all Roman priests and monks—on the grounds that they were clearly the helpers of the devil's whore presented in the book of Revelation. De Jong summarizes:

> Amid this confusion many Anabaptists refused to be wooed from the ways of gentleness and peace. But so great were the disturbances that the magistrates were constrained to regard all those who had Anabaptist leanings as a pestilential crowd.

We can see, then, why the Reformed Christians whom Guido de Bres represented were not eager to be confused with Anabaptists. Indeed, as already noted, most Anabaptists themselves rejected the excesses of the fringe groups. But the upshot of it is that the Belgic Confession, unlike the Heidelberg Catechism, is stronger and more pointed in its rejection of Anabaptist positions than Roman Catholic ones. Many Roman Catholic positions are rejected, but the rejection tends always to be implicit and somewhat muted. Not so with the Anabaptists. They are mentioned by name, and together with their views said to be "detested." The readiness of de Bres to establish the sanity and balance of Reformed principles is largely due to his fear of being tarred with the same brush applied to Anabaptists.

Content of the Confession

A look through the Confession reveals some of the fear just mentioned. It is clearest, perhaps, in controversial Article XXXVI:

> Wherefore we detest the Anabaptists and other seditious people, and in general all those who reject the higher powers and magistrates and would subvert justice, introduce community of goods, and confound that decency and good order which God has established among men.

In the tense religious and political situation of the Netherlands, it was always the "seditious" people from whom de Bres took pains to disentangle himself. In a cover letter to Philip II, de Bres insists that he and his kind are not seditious, not revolutionaries. He assures Philip that prayers are offered for him. Taxes are paid. The Netherlands Reformed people are responsible. Yet, de Bres insists, they must witness to the Christ of the Scriptures and finally obey God rather than man.

Anabaptist positions are elsewhere in view as well. For instance, Menno Simons (the Netherlandish Anabaptist after whom modern Mennonites are named) held a Docetic view of Christ: He thought Christ only appeared to be human, but really was not. In Article XVIII the Confession rejects Menno's Docetism. Other instances in which Anabaptist views are in mind will be mentioned in later lessons.

But the Confession is not merely polemical, and surely not merely polemical against Anabaptists. The majority of the thirty-seven articles offer a straight reproduction of Calvinist orthodoxy, much of it apparently written with one eye on Calvin's Genevan Confession of 1559. The articles, like Calvin's, are traditionally shaped into a rough trinitarian pattern: God and how we know Him (1-9), Christ and how He justified us (10-23), the Holy Spirit and the sanctified life (24-37).

Four final comments could be made about the Confession's content. It will be helpful to make them by way of a comparison with the Heidelberg Catechism. First, the Confession differs from the Catechism in dealing so prominently with the Scriptures. The Catechism strikingly omits all reference to what the Bible is. In its early and prominent statements about the Word of God and the canon of Scripture, the Belgic Confession both follows Calvin and anticipates similar statements by the standard Reformed orthodoxy of the seventeenth century. Such statements (the Westminster Confession is a good example) first define God and then say how He is known.

Secondly, in another anticipation of seventeenth century confessional orthodoxy, the Confession deals with election and reprobation (Art. XVI). We recall that the Catechism, except for the phrase "a community chosen for eternal life" in Answer 54, says nothing about election and reprobation.

Thirdly, except for the doctrine of the sacraments, the Confession lavishes much more attention on the church than does the Catechism. The Catechism has only the splendid Q & A 54 which seems a bit slim by comparison with the Confession.

Finally, the Confession shows much more of an interest in the relation of church and state—a big social-ethical question—than does the Catechism. As we have seen, this may largely be owed to the Anabaptist background in de Bres' Netherlands, and the special circumstances of persecution there. On this difficult issue, Calvin had profound things to say, and since his time Reformed thinkers have always attempted to distinguish their position from those of Catholics, Lutherans, and Anabaptists.

Conclusion

The Belgic Confession is a highly Calvinistic document which breathes the spirit of courage in persecution. It must be understood in its context of persecution in the Netherlands. Perhaps it is this context, and what we know of Guido de Bres' personal bravery, which together make the article on providence speak to us so acutely even today. De Bres never thought of providence merely as the bringer of good picnic weather or the finder of lost wallets. He risked, and finally gave, his life under the firm conviction that nothing could ever tear him out of the grasp of his heavenly Father:

> This doctrine affords us unspeakable consolation, since we are taught thereby that nothing can befall us by chance, but by the direction of our most gracious and heavenly Father; who watches over us with a paternal care, keeping all creatures so under His power that *not a hair of our head (for they are all numbered), nor a sparrow can fall to the ground without the will of our Father*, in whom we do entirely trust; being persuaded that He so restrains the devil and all our enemies that without His will and permission they cannot hurt us. (Art. XIII)

CHAPTER 10
There Is One Only God

Belgic Confession, Article I

Introduction—The Question of God

Bertrand Russell, one of the best known of modern atheists, insisted that "the whole conception of God is a conception...quite unworthy of free men," and that he was hence ready to build life "only on the firm foundation of unyielding despair." The passage in which Russell says this is one of the world's most notorious statements of atheist philosophy:

> That man is the product of causes which had no prevision of the end they were achieving; that his origin, his growth, his hopes and fears, his loves and his beliefs, are but the outcome of accidental collocations of atoms; that no fire, no heroism, no intensity of thought and feeling, can preserve an individual life beyond the grave; that all the labors of the ages, all the devotion, all the inspiration, all the noonday brightness of human genius, are destined to extinction in the vast death of the solar system, and that the whole temple of man's achievement must inevitably be buried beneath the debris of a universe in ruins—all these things, if not quite beyond dispute, are yet so nearly certain that no philosophy which rejects them can hope to stand. Only within the scaffolding of these truths, only on the firm foundation of unyielding despair, can the soul's habitation henceforth be built.
>
> "A Free Man's Worship"

Surely, all Christian believers must deplore such eloquent error. And yet, there is a clarity here which we prize. Here is a *clear* statement of the alternative to belief in God, helping us to see exactly what we are rejecting with all our heart. Such clarity in discussions of the question of God is a rare commodity.

Regrettably, it is often *theologians* who try somehow to paper over the distinction between affirming and denying the existence of God.

Paul Tillich, for example, writes, "God does not exist. He is a being—itself beyond essence and existence. Therefore, to argue that God exists, is to deny him." Tillich, and certain theologians who agree with him, does not believe there is any personal, conscious, supremely great being who created the heavens and the earth. He denies there is anyone like that, yet says he is not an atheist. Instead, he claims to use the term *God* in a new way—for the finitude of *man* under certain conditions. But this new and confusing use of the term does not exempt Tillich and those like him from atheism. All it does is confuse discussion and mislead the unwary.

The fact that it is theologians who are doing this kind of misleading reminds one of the aptness of a remark once made by a distinguished British Christian. Addressing a young woman who was distressed and scandalized by her minister's doubts, this Christian said, "My dear, you must believe in God in spite of what the preachers tell you!"

Belief in God is what really matters. The restless heart of an ancient seeker such as Augustine, the yearning spirit of a modern seeker such as C. S. Lewis, the quiet reflection or desperate calling into the darkness of ordinary human beings everywhere—all such seeking, reflecting, and calling takes on meaning only with reference to God and the question of God. All thinking, loving, hoping, believing, planning, and living divide on this ultimate question. If God is, then all of these things must be referred to Him, seen in His light, shaped by His will. If God is not—if believers are of all men most to be pitied, then all human activity, all the hopes and fears of all the years must be taken up in a Fatherless world. So far as God is concerned, we are then alone in the universe and must pass through the days of our years accordingly.

The Attributes

Clearer than Tillich, less grandiose than Russell, and on the opposite side from both is the first article of the Belgic Confession. With Christian theists across the world and along the generations, the first article confesses the belief that there is one only God.

The whole article is a kind of description of God. It tries to say not merely *that* we believe God is, but also *what* we believe Him to be. We believe that God is a certain sort of being. *He* has a number of "attributes." Attributes are simply characteristics or properties of something or somebody. Thus, Jimmy Carter has the attribute of "being the 39th president of the United States." He also has the attribute of "being Billy Carter's brother." Some attributes are better than others. Kindness and compassion, for example, are attributes which we value in a person. Frivolousness and greed are ones we do not.

It is easy to see that the second half of Article I is taken up with a listing of ten important attributes of God. Until recent times, nearly every description of God by theologians or by confessional statements included a list like this one. There are several interesting things to note about the list. The first five attributes are negative and are referred to by words which have negative prefixes. Thus *e*ternal means not temporal; *in*comprehensible means not comprehensible; *in*visible, not visible; *im*mutable, not changeable; *in*finite, not finite. This sort of procedure in which one tries to describe God by removing from Him all human limitations is called the *via negativa*, or the "negative way" to God, and has been a staple of theology since the sixth century. The Confession here notes that God is a personal being, but unlike other personal beings, He does not suffer the handicaps of temporality, changeability, finitude, or the like.

The second five attributes are positive. The first four of these—namely, that God is almighty, perfectly wise, perfectly just, and perfectly good— are typical of another famous way of talk-

MENS SOCIETY
LEIGHTON CRC
4-14-78

ing about God. This way is called the *via eminentiae*, or "way of eminence," and seeks to talk to God by raising to eminence, to the highest degree, those virtues which even God's children possess. Samson, for example, was mighty. Solomon was wise. Mary's husband Joseph was "a just man," while Joseph of Arimathea was "a good...man." Yet Samson was not almighty, nor Solomon perfectly wise, nor Joseph perfectly just, nor Joseph of Arimathea perfectly good. None had his virtue to an eminent degree. This distinction is reserved for God alone.

The last of the attributes—namely, that God is "the overflowing fountain of all good"—is a particularly gracious way of referring to God's creative and lavishly providential care. This sort of attribute, a sort ascribed to God on the basis of the good things we see around us in nature and history, is typical of what has traditionally been called the *via causalitatis*, or "way of causality."

It is not important for us to stay in the Latin department for very long. But it is important to see what the traditional lists are trying to do. They are trying to describe God—a being whom some theology has thought to be properly indescribable. They are trying to speak truly of God—a being whom some theology has thought unspeakable. They are trying, within certain limits, to understand what sort of being God is—a being whom some theology has thought beyond understanding.

Thus these descriptions of God have often been thought to be a bit odd and delicate. To describe God, so many have said, is like trying to picture a bird in flight. You have to do as well as you can with "static" and "human" categories and terms when the fact is that God outstrips them all.

No doubt real humility in our speaking of God is right and proper. Still, we should not be at all afraid of firm attribution to God of all genuine virtues and excellences of which the Bible speaks. We must not become so squeamish in our talk of God that we dare say nothing about Him. It is an ironic and disturbing fact that some Christians try to make God so transcendent, so wholly "other," so mysterious, that they can neither know nor legitimately speak of Him. This is a grave mistake. In fact, as we can plainly see, this position is not so much pious as agnostic. The God who has spoken and acted both in creation and by His ambassadors, the God who has spoken and acted especially in Jesus Christ, has made Himself *known* (John 1:18). We have been allowed to have genuine, though not exhaustive, knowledge of what God really is like. We must

not apologize, then, for any serious and biblically informed attempt to state God's attributes.

The First Half of Article I

This list of ten attributes takes up only the second half of the article. The first half reminds us of several features of the whole Confession which we noticed in chapter 9. Let us take a close look:

"We all"

Here is the *communal* tone we have pointed out. Guido de Bres was making not merely a personal, but a communal, confession. He was representing "we all" who were being persecuted by Philip II. It is worth saying again that Reformed Christians are always uncomfortable with talk of a "personal Savior" or "personal faith" unless the person in question is a member of the church, the community for whom Christ died.

"believe with the heart and confess with the mouth"

Here, in a fine paraphrase of Romans 10:9, the confessional emphasis of the document is presented. In chapter 1 we distinguished between believing *that* God exists and believing *in* God. In the first case, you merely assent to the claim that there is a supreme being who made the world and possesses all perfections. In the latter case, you actually trust God, lean on God, depend on Him, refer all things to Him.

Now it looks as if the Confession merely wants to say *that* God exists. "We believe... *that* there is one only simple and spiritual Being, which we call God." And, of course, it is no small confession against the Russells (and Tillichs) of the world to say that you believe this.

But, interestingly, the Confession deepens and qualifies the statement by saying we believe *with the heart.* We are committed at the core, the center, the quick of our lives to the reality of God. Against every fool who says in his *heart,* "There is no God," we say, "There is."

But heartfelt belief must be expressed. Jesus made a most disturbing reference to those who refused to confess Him before men (Luke 12:9). The Old Testament people of God were likewise outside God's favor unless they "confessed His name" (I Kings 8:33-35). And, of course, Romans 10:9 (paraphrased here by de

Bres) names confession as one of two conditions for salvation.

What is needed is the combination of belief and confession. Plenty of people will say with their lips that they believe in God. Gallup polls in the U.S. still get a better than 90% affirmative response in the lip department to such questions as "Do you believe in God?" But that does not say much about the attitude of the heart. Our nations and our churches abound in *practical* atheists—people who willingly say "Lord, Lord" but who do not have the Lord at the center of their lives.

Not as common, perhaps, but just as real, are those who, like Joseph of Arimathea, are disciples secretly (John 19:38). Their heart is in the right place, but for the tallying confession of the lips one listens in vain.

To some degree, and under various circumstances, both of these faults plague us all.

"that there is one only"

Christians are not polytheists. We do not believe in many gods. We believe, of course, in three divine persons, but also believe that these three wholly possess one divinity. Sometimes we use the term *God* to refer to that commonly held divinity. And sometimes, as the New Testament does overwhelmingly, we use the term *God* as a proper name for the Father.

The Confession does not tell us which use it is employing here. Very likely, it is employing the former use. But the proof texts, as expected, all employ the latter use. Both Ephesians 4:4-6 and I Corinthians 8:6 pretty clearly have the Father in mind. I Corinthians 8:6 is particularly instructive. In the context of "many gods" and "many lords" of the idol-worshipers, "for us there is one God, the Father."

"simple"

This description, like spirituality which immediately follows it, is placed in a prime position before the list of ten attributes. To say that God is simple is to say that there are absolutely no differentiations within Him. The doctrine of simplicity is difficult to understand and seems to lack adequate biblical support.

"and spiritual Being"

In John 4:24, Jesus remarks that "God is (a) spirit." Both of the Westminster Catechisms, Longer and Shorter, follow this text in beginning their answers to the question "What is God?"

To affirm that God is a Spirit, or a spiritual being, is to affirm that He is immaterial. He has no body. He has no extension in space. Paul may have implied this when he said to the Greeks that God "does not live in shrines made by man," and that "we ought not to think that the Deity is like gold, or silver, or stone..." (Acts 17:24, 29).

"which we call God"

As already suggested, the Confession apparently means to refer to that "essence" of divinity possessed equally by Father, Son, and Spirit. That, at any rate, is to be inferred from the theological atmosphere in which this sort of description breathes.

Conclusion

One has to see this confession of heartfelt belief in God against the backdrop of a modern age in which secularism has disenchanted our world, blinded our vision, and made our hearts heavy and hard.

FRANK STEEN
11-17-78

Think it over. There have always been the exceptional, Bertrand Russell sorts of atheists. But we live in an age in which secularism and godlessness have made their way so generally and so deeply into our culture that they are merely taken for granted. In the sixties we even witnessed the absurd spectacle of theologians rushing to embrace secularism as the salvation of Christianity. Unsurpassed in blasphemy and confusion, "Death of God" theologians announced that God's demise is the triumph of Christianity. This, as one believer suggested, is like claiming that whoredom is the final flowering of chastity. Godlessness has obviously seeped into theology and the church as well as into the rest of society. Even in the seventies, when the Death of God theology is no longer talked about, there is still a great reluctance among academic theologians to affirm belief in God—however cleverly or confusingly they may still use the *word* "God"—and a lingering pride in that human freedom which knows and wants no God in our setup, and no divine will to which one must bow in humility and submission.

Atheism in its many forms finds God an impertinence. Not nearly all atheists say clearly what Bertrand Russell said, or say "I hate God as I do my personal enemies," with Nikolai Lenin. Most of humanity, and all of us at times, simply proceed godlessly. We live without thinking of God for days or weeks or months. It is quite possible for ministers and theologians to fall into the trap of an actual, practical atheism while speaking endlessly the name of God. We live *as if* there were no God.

It is this indifference, this deadly indifference, which we must fear. Very few of us will rant and rave against God. We will simply ignore Him. We will attempt to fashion comfortable, well-fed, purposeful lives for ourselves and to regard God only as a flier regards a parachute. He knows it's there, but he hopes he will never have to use it. It is a mark of how thoroughly secularism has smeared our souls and clogged our hearts that it takes a crisis, a border-situation, for the old words about God to mean anything. A dreaded report comes back from the lab; a loved and needed person inexplicably perishes; a child seems determined to kick to pieces all we hold precious. And then, it seems, the old truth comes home. We again believe with the heart and confess with the lips—and mean it. We begin once more to refer all things to God.

Robert Louis Stevenson, the Scottish poet and novelist, was raised to know and confess God. But as an adult, Stevenson lapsed into agnosticism. Only as he lay dying on his bed in Samoa did Stevenson rediscover the faith he had misplaced. Rheumatic and speechless, the forty-four-year-old man held a pad on his knees on which he scratched out a few words for those attending him. Shortly before he died, Stevenson reached for his pad, and with the pen held in swollen fingers he scrawled the words: "stately music; enter God."

LION WEDDING
9-30-78

44

CHAPTER 11
How God Is Known

Belgic Confession, Article II

Introduction—Knowing a Person

Knowledge comes in several varieties. All conscious, thinking humans know that some things are true and some false. We call things that can be true or false *propositions*, and the knowledge of them *propositional knowledge,* or "knowledge-that." For example, we know *that* racquetball is a fast-growing sport. That is, we know that the proposition, "Racquetball is a fast-growing sport," is true.

Another kind of knowledge is *know-how.* We say a person knows *how* to play racquetball. Obviously, this second sort of knowledge differs from the first. One could easily have either sort without having the other.

But there is a third kind of knowledge. We may call it *person-knowledge.* To know a person is very different from know-how, and is more than merely knowing some propositions about the person in question. To know a person is both to know some propositions about the person and also to have a relationship with him or her.

An example may help. What would it mean to say that you know Pierre Trudeau? If you know a long list of propositions about Trudeau, but have never talked with him, never corresponded with him, never met him, you can hardly say without qualification that you *know* the man—at least not "personally." You would rather be inclined to say that you know of him, or know a good deal about him, or (given enough hours of watching Trudeau on TV) that it "feels like" you know him. But even if you were a political scientist and Trudeau biographer, and were highly informed about all the events of his life and work, there might still be an important sense in which his barber knows him and you do not. For to know a person is to have a hybrid knowledge including both "knowl-edge that" and personal relationship. Some thinkers believe that even know-how may be involved, that at least part of the time you must know how to recognize, or pick out, the person you know.

Several twentieth century theologians have emphasized the encounter part of knowing a person. To know a person, they insist, includes entering into an "I-Thou" relationship with him. These theologians, we may add, have not been slow to apply the encounter requirement to our knowledge of God.

But, already in the sixteenth century, John Calvin had a rich, personal knowledge of this sort in mind when he talked about our knowledge of God the Creator and God the Redeemer. For Calvin, knowledge of God is a full, multi-faceted sort of thing, including perfect trust, obedience, and even worship. "For we cannot with propriety say, there is any knowledge of God where there is no religion or piety."

Calvin must be mentioned, of course, because his voice was almost surely in the ear of Guido de Bres when he wrote Article II about the means by which we know God. The two means he mentions are the same ones named by Calvin. Calvin says that God is manifested "both in the structure of the world and in the general tenor of Scripture." De Bres mentions "the creation, preservation, and government of the universe" and "His holy and divine Word." "Universe" (including both creation and providence) and "Word"—these are the two means by which we know God.

Though one cannot tell merely from reading Article II, the Confession moves onto a theological battleground with its two means—especially with the first. From the Reformation period to the present, some of the fiercest and most interesting of all theological battles have been fought here. Let us have a look.

Knowledge of God by Means of the Universe

Practically every Christian can think of a particular feature of God's creation which seems to manifest the divinely creative hand. A climber finds mystery and majesty and terror in the mountains at dawn; a gardener breathes deep in his summer's garden at twilight; an autumn traveler comes upon a sight of deep blue waters ringed with trees of salmon pink, apple red, and fiery orange. In such cases, a believer's thoughts turn to God. C. S. Lewis, a believer and a veteran walker, talked of times when a person who sees a particular landscape under just the right conditions yearns somehow to get *inside* it—so powerfully does it mediate the presence of Him who made it.

Such is the creation. Believers have long been under the deep impression that the universe cannot have come accidentally, or purposelessly, into being. To the eye of faith that seems absurd. M. D. Landon tells of a time when the notorious agnostic, Robert Ingersoll, came upon a splendid globe which beautifully portrayed the constellations and stars of the heavens.

"Who made it?" he asked. "Why colonel," replied Henry Ward Beecher, "nobody made it; it just happened."

But de Bres, like Calvin before him, wants to include more than creation under the heading of God's "general revelation," as it is sometimes called. He wants to include that providence of God which embraces both the preservation and government of what He has made.

How is God known in providence? Let us pick just one example: God's preservation and government of the universe, without which it would collapse like a lung without air, is marked by a kind of *orderliness* which we take for granted even when we are not aware of it. Without such orderliness, all science, for instance, would be impossible. If, as Wittgenstein speculates in *On Certainty*, we sometimes "saw houses gradually turning into steam without any obvious cause, if the cattle in the fields laughed and stood on their heads and spoke comprehensible words, if trees gradually turned into men and men into trees," several of the natural sciences would become considerably more difficult.

These things, as a matter of fact, do not happen. And it is a testimony to the general regularity and order of God's providence that when God *does* act irregularly, unusually, extraordinarily—that is, when God performs miracles—people are surprised and afraid. Biblical accounts of a miracle quite commonly include a report that those who witnessed it were filled with fear and wonder.

All these things—creation, preservation, and government—together make God known. Picking up a famous image from Calvin, de Bres suggests that they are a "most elegant book." In this book, all things bright and beautiful, "all creatures, great and small" (Ps. 104:25) are "characters" or marks which lead us "to see clearly the invisible things of God." Which things are these? Here de Bres simply turns to the central biblical passage on our natural knowledge of God. What is seen by means of God's general works is His "everlasting power and divinity" (Rom. 1:20).

We might note that when Calvin discusses all creatures great and small, he always includes *us*. Humans, says Calvin, "even to their very toenails," are themselves the acme of God's creation and the highest example of His creative wisdom. Infants, "while they nurse at their mothers' breasts, have tongues so eloquent to preach His glory that there is no need at all of other orators." In fact, it is not merely in such *outer* respects that humans show signs of God's presence. There are also *inner* signs—the "sense of divinity" in every human, no matter how confused, and the "seed of religion," no matter how deformed or idolatrously cultivated, and conscience, which witnesses to the moral law built into the very structure of human existence. In one great burst, Calvin points to the "sparks of [God's] glory," both outer and inner:

> . . . the little birds that sing, sing of God; the beasts clamor for him; the elements dread him, the mountains echo him, the fountains and overflowing waters cast their glances at him, and the grass and flowers laugh before him. Truly, there is no need for long searching, since everyone could find him in himself, because every one of us is sustained and preserved by his power which is in us.
>
> ("Preface to Olivetan's New Testament")

But since the Reformation, as suggested above, there has always been trouble and controversy over this natural knowledge of God. The controversy swirls around the question of the fall—how the fall affects human ability to know God through His works, and how, indeed, the fall affects those works themselves.

Look again at the passage from Calvin quoted above. Little birds do sing—but some are also torn to shreds by cats. Beasts clamor—and also fight to the death. The elements which "dread God" are themselves dreaded by man—air, for instance, in the form of a tornado funnel, air and

BILL GREVENGOED
AND HIS JR. HIGH
BASKETBALL TEAM.
ROSELAND CHRISTIAN
11-13-78

water in the form of a hurricane, and fire when it burns people and their habitats to ashes. Mountains can be dangerous and eruptive; overflowing waters drown people and ruin their food sources. Every one of us "sustained and preserved by his power" also dreads the powerful, uncontrolled multiplication of cells we call *cancer*.

Now do all these "natural" things speak of God? Or of the devil? Are these signs of God's creative power? Or are they signs of the power of the evil one, who is given some freedom by God in a fallen world? L. Berkhof (*Systematic Theology*) claims that "as a result of the entrance of sin into the world, the handwriting of God in nature is greatly obscured, and in some of the most important matters rather dim and illegible." This "elegant book" is not entirely clear any longer, says Berkhof.

Surely Berkhof is right. A gardener who "breathes deep in his summer's garden at twilight" has had to bend and sweat to uproot the thistles which a cursed ground now brings forth, and Calvin's nursing infant with the eloquent tongue has been born from hard labor and hard labor pains. These things, according to Genesis 3,

are to be assigned to our fallenness—a fallenness which has spread throughout nature and natural processes. So when we read God's "elegant book," we shall have to read even those pages which are smeared with blood, sweat, and tears.

A second, even more hotly disputed, question has to do not with the effects of the fall on the book of nature and history, but rather with its effects on our ability to *read* that book. Calvin said that the creation was like a glorious theater. The only trouble, he added, is that all of us spectators who patronize the theater are *blind*. The splendor and magnificence of what God has made are there. It is just that our receiving apparatus is no good.

If we jump ahead to Article XIV of the Confession, we notice that de Bres follows Calvin in using visual imagery for the blockage in our ability to read creation: "All the light which is in us is changed into darkness." For both Calvin and de Bres, the trouble we have in reading the book of nature is helped by another book! Book I is no longer any use to us because of our sinful blindness. What we need is Book II—the Word of God written—so that, fallen and enslaved, we may be raised to the full stature of sons and daughters. Moreover, Book II not only addresses our need for redemption and introduces God's plan of redemption, but also clarifies our original vision of God the Creator and Provider.

Yet this scheme does not answer all the questions. If "natural man" as *fallen* (whom Paul clearly has in mind in Romans 1) can know enough from nature and providence to "convince" him, and to leave him "without excuse," he apparently knows quite a lot. Paul flatly says that (at some time) the natural man "knew God" (Rom. 1:21). Yet, because he is perverse and sinful, he resists this knowledge, refusing to honor God or to thank Him. Eventually his knowledge, or his ability to gain it, deteriorates: "They became futile in their thinking and their senseless

minds were darkened." So there is, or at least was, some real knowledge of God in unbelievers. But, like an unwelcome thought, such knowledge has been repressed—only to reappear later in strange and idolatrous forms.

The question for Christian theology—often debated with more heat than light—is whether there is enough natural sense of God left among the unredeemed for believers to appeal to. May missionaries assume some "point of contact" in unbelievers? May Christian philosophers seek ways to make explicit for unbelievers some portion of their implicit natural knowledge of God? May they try to prove that God exists, for example?

To take just this last case, Calvin and (especially) Luther were not enthusiastic about it. It is not clear, however, exactly why. Usually it is said that they knew what Thomas Aquinas (the great Catholic arguer for God's existence) overlooked; that is, they knew that even our *reason* is crippled by sin and is therefore unable to ascend Jacob's ladder to God.

But that hardly seems enough to dispose of all arguments for God's existence. It is not as if, in natural theology, some unbeliever were trying to storm heaven with his puny, finite mind. Unbe-

GENE PROCTOR
12·14·78

48

lievers have in fact traditionally shown little relish for taking up the task of proving God's existence. It is rather *believers,* redeemed people, those who have had their blindness healed, who argue for God's existence. And here the wise thing is to wait and see whether any of their arguments are sound—instead of presumptuously ruling out all of their attempts from the beginning. Here the wise thing is to wait and see whether such arguments might be used by God to persuade an unbeliever of His existence. Admittedly, to believe that God exists is only a beginning. Nobody, surely not Thomas Aquinas, ever dreamed that such belief was enough. But from that it surely does not follow that such belief, or an argument which may be used to induce it, is useless.

Knowledge of God by Means of His Word

We may be very brief about this second means, often called "special revelation," since we will deal with it more fully in the next lesson.

We referred earlier to this second means as "Book II." That is not exactly accurate. As Article III makes clear, when de Bres speaks of the Word of God, he is not in the first place referring to the Bible. He is referring to what God *said* by means of His prophets and apostles. At first what He said by way of what they said was not written down. Later it was. When it was written down, the early church recognized certain books as containing this very voice of God. These were assembled into what we call the Bible.

What is the relationship between the knowledge of God by means of the creation and that by means of His Word? The Confession is very plain on this. God's Word makes God "more clearly and fully known to us." God's Word is addressed to us specifically in our fallenness and in our blindness. Because of sin, our natural knowledge of God has become confused and bedimmed. But God provides us with the means to read the "elegant book" of nature again. It is as if the Word were eyeglasses, Calvin says. The Word reassures us that "in the beginning God created the heavens and the earth" (Gen. 1:1) and that all creatures great and small (see especially Ps. 104) are now provided for by God's hand.

Moreover, since we are fallen, we need redemption. And this is something about which we cannot get even a hazy idea from creation alone. To know God the Redeemer, and the Redeemer's plan of redemption, we need Scripture and Scripture alone. That is why in the section on God's Word, de Bres speaks not only of God's glory, but also of "our salvation."

You notice that de Bres has one interesting provisional phrase in this second part of Article II. We know God, he says, "more clearly and fully" in His Word, "that is to say, *as far as is necessary for us to know in this life....*" It is an important phrase. Even the Word does not answer all of our questions. Calvin, who held that the Word is perspicuous, or clear, still acknowledged that it is not *absolutely* clear. Surely it does not satisfy our curiosity completely. As it has often been said, there are many things we should like to know when we get to heaven. No doubt the Word is not meant to answer all our questions. It is meant to tell us enough, to tell us what is necessary "to His glory and our salvation."

Conclusion

So by universe and by Word we know God. We do not merely know *about* God. Let it be said again: True knowledge of God includes the encounter in which, with bowed head and bended knee, we address Him as "Thou." God is not merely an *it,* but a *Thou*—a person, and a person with whom, by His grace, we have to do.

For a Christian, the works of God are means, avenues, channels for meeting God Himself. As A. Plantinga put it:

> To the believer the entire world looks different. Blue sky, verdant forests, great mountains, surging ocean, friends and family, love in its many forms and various manifestations—the believer sees these things as gifts from God. The entire universe takes on a personal cast for him; the fundamental truth about reality is truth about a *Person.*
>
> *(God, Freedom, and Evil)*

For salvation, however, we would never see and hear enough about this person unless the person Himself should speak to us "more clearly and fully." And so by prophets and apostles, God speaks. And, in these latter days, God has spoken by a Son. God's greatest and clearest Word is to be found in the life and words of Jesus the Christ. If we wonder where or how to know God by means of His Word, we must behold the answer given one night to a couple of peasants in a cowshed. That answer has gone out to all the world.

> And the Word became flesh and dwelt among us...No one has ever seen God; the only Son, who is in the bosom of the Father, he has made him known.   (John 1:14,18)

CHAPTER 12
The Bible

Belgic Confession, Articles III - VII

Introduction—The Strange Status of the Bible

The Bible is by all accounts the most important book in Western Civilization. Even those who cannot say they believe what the Bible says still must acknowledge its massive influence. Apart from its specific, and divinely intended, role in making believers wise unto salvation, the Bible's general role in shaping our culture is undeniable. Much of Western literature is hardly understandable without some knowledge of the Bible. The same goes for art, architecture, and music. Civil law, politics, education, even the movies, have felt the Bible's impact.

Yet, the often-mentioned irony remains: The most important book of our civilization, an all-time best-seller, is suprisingly little read. During the height of American church membership and church attendance (the 1950s), one Gallup poll showed that over 80 percent of adult American people believed the Bible to be "the revealed Word of God" instead of just "a great piece of literature." "Yet," as Will Herberg reports, "when these same Americans were asked to give the 'names of the first four books of the New Testament of the Bible, that is, the first four gospels,' 53 per cent could not name even one" (*Protestant, Catholic, Jew*).

We have sometimes been amused at the innocent misunderstandings of our children who picture "the flight into Egypt" as a Boeing 727 aloft (with Pontius the pilot), or of those who accept a reference to the book of "Hezekiah" without batting an eye, or of those who somehow suppose the epistles are the wives of the apostles.

But gross ignorance of the Bible among those who should know better—people who have been church members a long time—is not funny. Ignorance of the Bible makes us weak, soft, and vulnerable. Ignorance exposes our flank to those who battle against the faith by battling the Bible, and their number is increasing. Of course, there have always been skeptics outside the church who ridiculed the Bible. (Madalyn Murray O'Hair, for instance, was launched on her dismal career as an atheist by the conviction that the Bible was so full of myths, contradictions, and barbarisms as to be ludicrous.) But recently the Bible has been undermined by the unbelievers *within* the church. The church has been confused and weakened by those who assert that we cannot depend on the Gospels to tell us anything about the historical Jesus, by those who take their sermons from self-help philosophies instead of from the Bible, by those who in their small groups read and study everything but the Bible on the grounds that they are "way beyond the Bible."

What is the antidote for this malady? Surely it is not idolizing the Bible. We do not enhance the reputation of the Bible by telling old tales about men saved from speeding bullets by a pocket Bible perfectly positioned over the heart. We are not being faithful to the Word by regarding the Bible as a magic book. Some people have gotten their "text for the day" by closing their eyes, letting the Bible drape open where it will, and then letting a finger drop to the page. Under the finger is today's text. Never mind the fact that it says only that Uz is the brother of Buz, or that "Moab is my washpot." This is the tag for today's comfort and inspiration.

Of course this sort of "Bible roulette" is nonsense. It is an old trap. Let a book be regarded as holy, and little abuses and superstitions begin to creep in. Some of them (deriving comfort from the word "Selah") may be relatively harmless. Others are not. In any event, the first remedy for ignorance and disbelief of the Bible is to *read* it—and to read it heartily, mindfully, and searchingly. The Reformed faith made one of its greatest contributions to the broad church with its rediscovery of the centrality of the Word.

Luther, we may remember, had been restless and uneasy as a Roman Catholic monk. Why? He had been studying Romans. Luther had been reading and studying the *Bible*. Something there in Paul's talk of grace and faith cut Luther like a two-edged sword. Reading Romans and then remembering Tetzel (the seller of red-hot indulgences), reading the Bible and then examining church tradition—reading and comparing, Luther came to the terrible conclusion that something was desperately wrong in the church he loved, that it had badly strayed from the clear teaching of the Word. The church needed, with Luther, to recover the Bible it had mislaid.

Luther's discovery was deeply woven into the fabric of the later Reformed community. The church (to change the image) had to get back to its sources, its roots, and it had to make those sources and roots available for growth in all its people. The Bible needed to be translated and placed in the hands of the enormous priesthood of believers.

Reformation and the binding of the people to the Word have always gone together. Even today, every serious Reformed church will steadfastly seek to be reformed, again and again, by the Word of God.

The Confession on the Bible

The specifically Genevan Calvinist strand of the Reformation was especially eager to mark out the place and function of the Bible. (We recall that the Zurich-influenced Heidelberg Catechism has nothing to say about the Bible.) So Guido de Bres, heavily influenced by Calvin and by the Gallican Confession, provided an early and prominent treatment of the Bible in his Belgic Confession. The treatment takes up five articles, and is filled with rich and significant issues.

Article III—The Written Word of God

In the previous lesson, mention was made of the distinction between the Word of God *spoken* and the Word of God *written*. That distinction was made with reference to this article.

As Nicholas Wolterstorff reminds us: Basic to the whole biblical notion of how God acts is the idea that God often acts by way of, or by means of, certain human beings' acting. Not always, of course. God's mighty creation was not accomplished via the acts of human beings. But many of His other acts were and are. Moses, for exam-

ple, led the people of Israel out of Egypt. But Moses was actually acting for God. Moses, Joshua, Gideon, Samson, David, Samuel—all the "heroes of faith"—were God's *agents*. They acted for Him. We may point to many, though not all, of their acts, and say, "That was God's act." From Abraham to the apostles, the Bible shows us God's agents. And in Jesus we see One in whom God acts not just occasionally or sporadically; in Jesus we see One about whose *every* act we may say, "That was God's act."

HOWARD DE JONG
1-15-78

CATECHISM CLASS
HIGHLAND CRC
11·13·78

All of God's acts are speech-acts. God speaks. He has no lips, no vocal cords, no body. Yet He speaks. The Bible bears ample testimony to the fact that God commands, asserts, questions, and the like.

How does He do this? Typically, He does this by authorizing certain human beings to speak for Him, to speak on His behalf. A messenger or prophet in the Old Testament, and an apostle in the New, are people who are authorized, warranted, commissioned by God to speak for Him. Deuteronomy 18:18,19 is a classic place for seeing this:

> I will raise up for them a prophet like you from among their brethren; and I will put my words in his mouth, and he shall speak to them all that I command him. And whoever will not give heed to my words which he shall speak in my name, I myself will require it of him.

So what God's spokesman says is to be regarded as what God says. God commands, asserts, and questions by way of His ambassadors' commanding, asserting, and questioning.

All these things—commands, assertions, questions—together make up God's Word. Together they make up what God says.

Now Article III says two things. It says first that no human being invented this Word of God. Rather, the Word was sent from God and delivered by way of the speaking of men. Nor was this human speaking self-motivated. Rather, "*men* spake from God, being moved by the Holy Spirit." They were Spirit-possessed men.

The second thing Article III says is that by the providence of God His Word was inscripturated, or written down. This was a way of preserving what God had been saying via His messengers. For years, in some cases for decades or even longer, what God said was passed on orally. Hebrew fathers told their children what God had said and done. Those children told their children. But this oral tradition, this "handing down," was finally secured by writing. God authorized, indeed commanded, this writing.

Why? We recall from the previous lesson that God's Word is specially addressed to our fallenness. We are stubborn in our sin, but God is even more stubborn in His intent to redeem. Hence the written Word was inspired by God's "special care which He has for us and our salvation." The overarching purpose of the written Word is *redemptive*. We do not go to these writings with some eccentric, manufactured interest in "whatever became of the Jebusites." We attend to these writings to discover how we may become wise—wise unto salvation, instructed "for salvation through faith in Christ Jesus" (II Tim. 3:15).

Article IV—Canonical Books of the Holy Scripture

Article IV tells us which books constitute the "holy and divine Word" mentioned in Article III. The bulk of the article, then, is a list of the books of the Old and New Testaments. The Old and New Testaments are themselves "two books," according to the Confession, and are "canonical."

A *canon* in Greek was a carpenter's measuring rule or ruler. A canon by extension is any guideline, boundary line, or rule by which something is measured and judged. So the church has long called the sixty-six books of the Bible canonical. These are the ones the church recognizes as authoritative for its faith and life.

The New Testament canon was formed by applying two prior canons or rules. One was that a book had to have apostolic origin, broadly understood. The other was that a book had to be widely used and recognized in the churches. It was not until the late fourth century that the New Testament, as we have it, was fixed. Along the way, there were always some "problem books." Hebrews, James, II Peter, II and III John, Jude, and Revelation were all questioned at one time or another. As late as the Reformation, Luther said, pretty baldly, that he found the first two and last two of these "inferior." Like many others, Luther operated with a "canon within the canon." He was simply more open about it than some others.

The Old Testament canon was taken over by the church from the Jewish council of Jamnia (A.D. 90) which excluded the Apocrypha and settled on the thirty-nine books we now have in our Old Testament. That is, the *Reformation* church took it over. The early and medieval church continued to incorporate the Apocrypha into their Bible, following especially Augustine. In fact, the Roman Catholic Council of Trent (1546-63) declared "anathema" or "accursed" whoever did not accept these extra books. The Catholic church still accepts them today.

Article IV has lately raised some scholarly eyebrows. For one thing, Lamentations is strangely missing from the list of Old Testament books (though it may be implicitly listed under Jeremiah—who was long thought to be Lamentation's author). For another, the article lists Paul as the author of Hebrews. Practically no scholars, not even the most conservative, believe that Paul wrote Hebrews. It also affirms the Mosaic authorship of the Pentateuch ("the five books of Moses"), lists the three books of Solomon, and describes the Psalms as "Psalms of David." All of these authorships have been questioned by believers. However, "it is a patent fact that this article does not intend to bind us on detailed problems of Biblical Introduction," as P. Y. De Jong has observed. "Its aim is to acknowledge and define the canon for us."

Article V—Dignity and Authority of the Scriptures

Article V contains the heart of what the Confession has to say on Scripture. In this article we can see especially clearly the Calvinist influence.

After all, one of Calvin's great contributions to the Reformation was his doctrine of the *testimonium Spiritus Sancti internum*—"the internal testimony of the Holy Spirit." Calvin, we recall, claimed that no sinful human being could rightly read nature, nor rightly discern and appropriate the promise of Christ for redemption, without *Scripture*. Scripture embodies what God says to fallen and desperate people.

Yet, as Calvin and all of us recognize, the Scriptures do not seem to "take" with everybody. Some people, like Madalyn Murray O'Hair, or like Peter De Vries' Andrew Mackerel ("The Bible is at worst a hodgepodge of myths, superstitions and theologies so repugnant to a man of taste and sensibility, let alone a true Christian, that its culmination in the latter ethic is perhaps the greatest miracle we know." *The Mackerel Plaza)*, find in it only something to scorn or twit. They do not hear what believers have always heard—the very voice of God speaking.

Calvin and de Bres both firmly believed that the prophets and apostles were inspired by the Holy Spirit to speak for God. But they also believed that the objectively inspired Scripture does a person no good unless the divine character of Scripture, the fact that God actually speaks in the writings of the human authors, is attested or confirmed by the same Spirit who inspired those authors. So Calvin:

> For as God alone is a suitable witness for his own word, so also the word will never gain credit in the hearts of men until it is sealed by the internal testimony of the Spirit. It is necessary that the same Spirit who spoke by the mouth of the prophets should penetrate our hearts in order to convince us that they delivered faithfully the message which was divinely given. (*Calvin's Institutes* I, vii, 4)

Thus the outer Word is confirmed by the inner witness. The situation is akin to that in nature. There too the effects of God the Creator, pointing back to Him, are actually, objectively present. Yet it takes the eye of a biblically informed, faithful looker to see them clearly. So in Scripture. The objective, self-authenticating, God-breathed nature of Scripture is real whether you and I see it or not. Yet, for us to see it, for the Word to take root or "to be impressed on our hearts," we will need the testimony of the Spirit.

This combination of Word and Spirit, neither sufficient by itself, is a consistent Reformed emphasis. And, as we might expect, de Bres has it firmly in the heart of Article V. Certainly, he allows, the church officially receives the Word and approves these books as "holy and canonical"; certainly the books are self-authenticating, carrying "the evidence thereof in themselves" that they "are from God." But "*more especially*" we regulate, establish, and confirm our faith by these books "because the Holy Spirit witnesses in our hearts that they are from God."

Article VI—Apocryphal Books

The books listed are all Old Testament Apocrypha, written (roughly) between 200 B.C. and A.D. 100. There are, incidentally, also some New Testament Apocrypha, which are not listed. These include spurious gospels which fill in the boyhood years of Jesus with super-boy legends. But since no Christian church accepts these, the Confession does not find it necessary to list them as extra-canonical.

The Old Testament Apocrypha are far from worthless. No biblical scholar could get along without them. They fill in much of the void in our knowledge of the intertestamentary period, and some of them—The Wisdom of Solomon, for example—shed considerable light on our understanding of certain themes in the canonical books.

The term *apocrypha* originally meant something like "secret things," and referred to those books which had the inside, precious materials too rare for the run-of-the-mill believer. Later, the term took a darker meaning, suggesting those books whose value for faith and life was questionable. For Protestants, "apocrypha" now simply refers to extra-canonical books.

The Westminster Confession of 1648 insists that these books are "of no authority in the Church of God, nor to be in any otherwise approved, or made use of, than other human writings." The Belgic Confession, we note, is less severe. So far as these books agree with the canonical ones, "the Church may read and take instruction from" them.

Article VII—The Only Rule of Faith

In the last article in this section on the Word of God, the Confession emphasizes the *sufficiency* of the Word. Cultists and sectarians have always been tempted to add revelations, to claim "latter day" communications from God now binding on all believers.

Appealing to Scripture itself, the Confession rules out such additions, inferring from Scripture that we already have all we need, that the Scriptural doctrine "is most perfect and complete in all respects." We need no Book of Mormon, no writings of Sun Myung Moon, nothing by Mary Baker Eddy. We may not elevate Augustine, Calvin, nor even C. S. Lewis to scriptural status. We may not bind ourselves by church tradition, nor by church confession in the same absolute way that we are bound by Scripture.

Scripture is the only infallible rule. Its main function is not to satisfy our curiosity about the "beyond," nor even about God. Certainly it is tragic to search the Scriptures, as did many in Jesus' day, without coming to Christ (John 5: 39,40). These writings, so diverse, so rich, so multi-faceted, often so puzzling, are intended and are sufficient to give "whatsoever man ought to believe unto salvation."

CHAPTER 13
The Trinity

Belgic Confession, Articles VIII - XI

Introduction

Imagine:
Your dentist is tinkering with a particularly sensitive tooth. He has cotton, hooks and mirrors, a small vacuum cleaner, and both his hands in your mouth. Your eyes wander to his name tag: "Abraham Weinstein, D.D.S." He probes a place where the pain is most exquisite. "Tell me," he says, "Do you really think Jesus was divine?"

Such mixing of business and religion rarely happens in the twentieth century. Theology is hardly a topic for casual conversation. But it was in the fourth century when the church formulated the great doctrines of the faith. Theological argumentation was a street-corner affair and part of the menu at the family dinner table. As E. T. Thompson has written,

> The debate was conducted with the violence of a political convention. Everybody entered into it. Men who met to transact business neglected their bargaining to talk theology. . . .Arius put his doctrine into verse, to popular tunes, and it was sung and whistled in the streets. The arguments were punctuated with fists and clubs. *(Through the Ages, A History of the Christian Church)*

The fists and clubs were a bit excessive, but intense concern is understandable. People were trying to agree on one of the most basic doctrines of the faith—the holy Trinity.

In his classic study of the rise and fall of the Roman Empire, the English historian Edward Gibbon derides the church for making much of nothing in its controversy about whether Christ is God or is only like God—a difference expressed by the single letter *i* in Greek. But one letter does make a world of difference in some cases. A theist is worlds apart from an *a*theist. A Christ who is fully divine is vastly different from a Christ who is only semi-divine. We may deplore the sinful extremes to which debate often led. Yet, out of such controversies came the definitive statements of the Christian doctrines concerning Christ and the Trinity.

Reflecting the outcome of those ancient debates, Guido de Bres confesses: "We believe in one only God, who is the one single essence, in which are three persons, really, truly, and eternally distinct according to their incommunicable properties; namely, the Father, and the Son, and the Holy Spirit." With de Bres, all Reformed churches (in fact, all Protestant, Roman Catholic, and Eastern Orthodox churches) confess the doctrine of the Trinity.

But the doctrine of the Trinity has recently fallen on hard times. Many Unitarians who, like Thomas Jefferson, deride "the incomprehensible jargon of the trinitarian arithmetic," deny the doctrine outright.

Schleiermacher, the father of modern liberalism, relegated the doctrine of the Trinity to the very last chapter of his 750 page treatise on *The Christian Faith*. Almost a postscript, the chapter does little more than call for a "thorough-going criticism of the doctrine in its older form, so as to prepare the way for, and introduce, a reconstruction of it."

Julian Huxley, a scientist who philosophized about religion, attempted such a reconstruction: "As I see it broadly," he writes, in *Religion Without Revelation*, " 'God the Father' is a personification of the forces of non-human nature; 'God the holy Ghost' represents abstract ideals; and 'God the Son' personifies human nature at its highest."

But what is perhaps even more regrettable than outright denials, scurrilous ridicule, and unbiblical redefinition, is the sheer boredom which sincere Christians sometimes feel about the doctrine of the Trinity. More than time separates the modern Christian who confesses this doctrine with a yawn, and the ancient Christian who formulated it with his fists!

Biblical Basis

The Bible never uses the word *Trinity*. Nor is the confession that there is "one single essence, in which are three persons" (Article VIII) found explicitly in the Bible. In fact, the sort of technical statement we find in the Belgic Confession was not officially settled in the church until the fourth century—after several hundred years of doctrinal trial and error.

Did the fourth century church council make up the Trinity doctrine, then? Is the central dogma of Christian theology a creation out of whole cloth by the councils of Nicea and Constantinople in 325 and 381?

No. These councils were merely trying to state technically what the biblical authors state nontechnically. The councils were trying, in a context of multiple heresies (see the end of Article IX for a rogues' gallery of trinitarian heretics), to use precise theological language to state the truth about the Trinity. The biblical authors, in a context of worship and devotion, bear witness in less official language to those events and truths on which all later trinitarian reflection is based.

In Article IX the Confession reviews some of the most central biblical materials. As we learned in the lesson on the Nicene Creed, trinitarian thinking was originally kindled by the fact that in Jesus Christ believers saw someone who was, and who deserved to be called, "Lord" and "Son of God." They saw someone who, besides the God whom Jesus called "Father," deserved to be *worshiped!* And, interestingly, some of the clearest trinitarian passages in the New Testament have a worship context. At our Lord's baptism (the beginning of Matthew), for example, there is a trinitarian revelation—the Father's voice is heard, the Son is baptized, and the Spirit is present in the symbolic form of a dove (Matt. 3:16,17).

At the end of Matthew's Gospel, and at the end of Jesus' earthly ministry, it is again in the context of a *baptismal* command (". . . baptizing them in the name of the Father and of the Son and of the Holy Spirit") that the three persons are distinguished. We still follow this command and make this distinction in the church today. In fact, in most Christian churches one of the questions at issue when a person wants to confess faith or transfer membership is whether he has been baptized according to the trinitarian formula.

A third example: It is to the worshiping community of Christians that St. Paul writes what our ministers now use as a benediction to close our own worship: "The grace of the Lord Jesus Christ and the love of God and the fellowship of the Holy Spirit be with you all" (II Cor. 13:14).

Obviously these are not the only important biblical texts for trinitarian understanding. Nor are they the only ones mentioned by the Confession. The Confession also presents, for instance, the remarkably suggestive plural pronouns of Genesis 1 and 3 ("Let *us* make man in *our* image. . .Behold, the man has become like one of *us*"). Still, it is helpful for us to see the setting of worship and liturgy as a main context, worth emphasizing. The Trinity was worshiped, celebrated in baptism, experienced, and even sung before being theologically analyzed or dogmatically described.

Safeguarding the Doctrine of Christ and the Holy Spirit.

Why did it take the church hundreds of years to produce a doctrine of the Trinity? Because the church was preoccupied with another doctrinal controversy which had to be clarified and settled first—the one concerning the identity of Christ. Christians were struggling mightily to say as exactly as possible who Christ is. (See chapters 2, 3, and 4 on this Christological controversy.) Article X of the Belgic Confession reflects the outcome of that struggle: "Jesus Christ is true and eternal God"; He is "co-essential and co-eternal with the Father."

The question of the identity of the Holy Spirit stirred up far less trouble, but was equally important to the doctrine of the Trinity. Article XI of the Confession represents the position of the ancient church when it states that the Holy Spirit is "of one and the same essence, majesty, and glory with the Father and the Son."

It takes but little reflection to see how these conclusions compelled the church to formulate a trinitarian dogma. Beginning with the belief in the single God of the Old Testament, how could the church say that Christ was also God without saying there are two Gods? Given the Holy Spirit, how could Christians avoid tritheism? How can one conscientiously hold that the Father is God, that Jesus Christ is God, and that the Holy Spirit is God—and still maintain there is only one true God?

Yet, remarkably, that is exactly what the church did. The church refused to succumb to pressures from various non-biblical sources which would have made both Christ and the Holy Spirit

LION WEDDING
9 30 78

HOLY BIBLE

less than fully divine. No doctrine of the Trinity would have been necessary or possible if Christ were not fully equal with the Father, "of the same substance." But once this full equality was accepted, the church had to say how that belief avoided polytheism. Thus, by developing its doctrine of Trinity in unity, and unity in Trinity, the church attempted to safeguard both the doctrines of the full deity of Christ and of the Holy Spirit, while at the same time avoiding the charge of tritheism. Perhaps the most representative statement of the church's position is the formula from the Athanasian Creed: "So the Father is God, the Son is God, and the Holy Spirit is God; and yet they are not three Gods, but one God (vss. 15, 16).

Anyone who takes the trouble to think seriously about the doctrine of the Trinity will soon discover frustrating questions and problems. Competent theologians have struggled with trinitarian questions ever since the doctrine was first defined, but none has gained the widespread acceptance enjoyed by the original formula itself.

Properties and Offices

The Belgic Confession elaborates on the Creed's simple formula. Some of what it says is positive, but there is also much that is negative. Article VIII, for example, contains many negative statements:

> God is not by this distinction divided into three...the Father is not the Son, nor the Son the Father, and likewise the Holy Spirit is neither the Father nor the Son...these persons thus distinguished are not divided, nor intermixed;...the Father has not assumed the flesh, nor has the Holy Spirit...The Father has never been without

His Son, or without His Holy Spirit.... There is neither first nor last.

But there are also positive statements; for example:

> ...the Holy Scriptures teach us that the Father, and the Son, and the Holy Spirit have each His personality, distinguished by Their properties. (Art. VIII)

The negative statements warn against heresies, while the positive statements summarize what the Bible teaches. In describing what the Bible teaches about the three persons of the Trinity, the Confession distinguishes between what the three persons have, and what they do not have, in common. Each of the persons shares alike in "truth, power, goodness, mercy." But there are

RICHARD VELDMAN
11-13-78

other qualities (properties, or attributes) which are not shared. These distinguish one person from the others. The Confession calls these distinguishing traits "incommunicable properties."

The "incommunicable property" of the Father is that He, and He alone, is the "cause, origin, and beginning of all things visible and invisible." Similarly, what is unique about the Son is that He is the "word, wisdom, and image of the Father," terms which the Bible uses only for the Son and not for the Father or the Holy Spirit. What then is the "incommunicable property" of the Spirit? He is the "eternal power and might proceeding from the Father and the Son." Each person of the Trinity has at least one unique property. Otherwise the persons would be indistinguishable.

Notice something interesting about these "properties"; they speak more about who the persons *are* than about what the persons *do*. But the doctrine of the Trinity is not complete without showing how the persons work, and the Confession does not neglect to speak about that important aspect of the doctrine. Each of the persons has an office or work peculiar to Him. Article IX describes these "offices" as follows: "The Father is called our Creator, by His power; the Son is our Savior and Redeemer, by His blood; the Holy Spirit is our Sanctifier, by His dwelling in our hearts."

Scholars have devised two other technical, theological terms to describe these major aspects of trinitarian doctrine: "ontological Trinity" and "economic Trinity." *Ontological* (that which has to do with *being*) refers to relational properties within the Trinity—what the Confession calls their incommunicable properties. Thus, the Father is unbegotten, but the Son begotten. *Economic* (that which has to do with *working*) refers to what the persons do with respect to us—what the Confession calls their offices and operations.

The Economic Trinity

The matter of what the persons do (economic Trinity) is worth pursuing farther. It will help us see part of the central importance of trinitarian doctrine for our faith and life.

Begin with the first chapter of Genesis. We are told that "in the beginning God created the heavens and the earth." In these words we read of *creation*, the work ascribed by the Confession to God the Father. We also find throughout the chapter a formula repeated for each day of creation: "And God said..." This formula shows us God in the act of "speaking" (*word*), a work which the Confession specifically attributes to God the Son. And verse two of the chapter tells us "the Spirit of God was moving over the face of the waters." Here we read of the *power* of God, the specific work attributed to the Holy Spirit.

Continue the same pattern as you examine the Bible's description of the creation of Adam and Eve: *Creation* is described in the words, "The Lord God formed man of dust from the ground"; *word* is seen in the passage, "Then God said, 'Let us make man' "; and *power* is seen in the statement, "God breathed into his nostrils the breath of life" (incidentally, the word "breath" in Hebrew is the same as "Spirit"). Human beings exist by the work of God the holy Trinity.

Consider what difference that makes for understanding ourselves. The Bible says we are created in God's image, in His likeness. How do we reflect the trinitarian nature of God? How do we "image" the Trinity? God gives us the responsibility to create civilization ("subdue the earth"), He gives us the wisdom or word to do it, and He provides the power to accomplish it. Thus, when humans build up a civilization according to God's word and by His strength, they are truly "imaging" God. Over and over again the pattern of the Trinity is shown in the pages of Scripture, in the work of the trinitarian God. And when we seek to be godlike, it is the Trinity we must imitate.

Conclusion

It is a part of our Reformed heritage to be wary of religious experience as a guide to the truth about God and about His will for us. Liberals in the nineteenth century celebrated experience and wanted to study it. Indeed, they studied little else. Even fundamentalists in our own time exalt experience as the heart of the Christian life. Schleiermacher, the father of modern liberalism, could have been speaking for many fundamentalists when he said that preaching is a kind of sharing of one's own experience "which shall arouse in others the desire to have the same experience."

But Reformed Christians have usually regarded this sort of thing as subjective, and dangerously undisciplined by the Word. As Richard Mouw has observed, Reformed Christians would rather sing

> Jesus loves me! this I know,
> *For the Bible tells me so.*

than

> You ask me how I know he lives?
> *He lives within my heart.*

Yet, at the beginning of Article IX, the Confession says something which sounds at least as much like the latter song as like the former. It says that we know the doctrine of the Trinity "as well from the testimonies of Holy Writ as from their *operations*, and *chiefly by those we feel in ourselves.*"

Can we "feel in ourselves" the operations of the holy Trinity? Yes. In some profound and mysterious way, believers feel and experience the operations of the Trinity. The first of these operations is creation. Of course, no human being was present at the creation of the universe. Still, when we see the result, when we now see the works of God's hand, when we marvel at the intricacy of a new, well-born child, we experience the creative work of God. This is the chief work of the *Father*. "The Father is called our Creator, by His power" (Art. IX).

Again, when from all of our wandering and wasting ourselves in some far country we come home—when we consciously feel that we have been saved from ruining ourselves and redeemed from selling ourselves out to the highest bidder—then we experience the redeeming work of the Son. "The Son is our Savior and Redeemer, by His blood" (Art. IX).

Finally, when against all the secular propaganda that life is bearable only when we are young, we notice that the flow of Christian life, and of our lives as we grow older, is rather one of advance, of progress, as we grow in grace and knowledge of God—then we experience the sanctifying work of the Holy Spirit. "The Holy Spirit is our Sanctifier, by His dwelling in our hearts" (Art IX).

And at the same time we experience the work of the persons of the Trinity, we acknowledge that all these are fully divine, together making up the one Trinity. The same Trinity of persons which creates us also redeems and sanctifies us. "And although this doctrine far surpasses all human understanding, nevertheless we now believe it by means of the Word of God, but expect hereafter to enjoy the perfect knowledge and benefit thereof in heaven" (Art. IX). "For now we see in a mirror dimly, but then face to face" (I Cor. 13:12).

CHAPTER 14
Creation and Providence

Belgic Confession, Articles XII and XIII

Introduction—We Are Not Alone

One of the most interesting features of our culture since 1971, or thereabouts, has been the transfer of a sense of *wonder* from religion to Hollywood. The seventies brought back through movies and best-sellers a part of what the church had abandoned. As Andrew Greeley wrote in the *New York Times* in 1977, "When religion cast off wonder, Hollywood seized it." In the churches, belief in the Lord was shaky enough, but belief in the Lord's *hosts* had collapsed. Surely, wise theologians said, angels and demons are of all things the remnants of a superstitious and pre-scientific mind. The infamous "death of God" theology was only the dismal climax of a general tendency to see as myth what we used to see as fact.

Especially during the late sixties, one got the impression that in mainline Christianity all the heart had gone out of a dwindling church. People still worshiped and tried to pray, but their sense of the supernatural had evaporated. What had been enchanting became disenchanting. Even for many Christians, the world had been emptied and flattened. Faith had lost its spine and clerical collars all of their starch. For the two or three who still gathered together, disheartened ministers still said, "Holy, holy, holy is the Lord of hosts; the whole earth is full of his glory." But they did not believe it. Intimidated by secularism, paralyzed by identity crises, depressed by their loss of prestige, many Christian ministers lived with the sinking feeling that *we are alone.*

Then, in 1971, William Peter Blatty published *The Exorcist* and reintroduced demons into North American culture—with a vengeance. In 1977 *Star Wars* offered a kindly Alec Guinness giving the benediction, "The force be with you,"

and spines, which had not known the contours of a church pew for years, began to tingle in movie theaters. In the same year *Close Encounters of the Third Kind* replaced the demons of *The Exorcist* with angels from outer space, moving and beckoning in an atmosphere of music, light, and aching wonder. The universe, it turns out, is alive with presences—and they are not bad. Billy Graham could write of *Angels: God's Secret Messengers,* but only Hollywood could captivate the masses with an ancient thought: *We are not alone.*

Creation

Nobody who reads Article XII of the Belgic Confession can fail to notice that it gives angels, good and bad, a lot of space: Two thirds of the article is concerned with these extra-human beings. What do we make of this? Why so much fascination with angels? Are they real, or are they merely the ancient world's version of Superman, Batman, Spiderman, and Wonder Woman? How important is angel belief for our authentic Christian commitment?

The Confession speaks of angels in the context of creation doctrine. Creation, the Confession says, is "by the Word"; it is "of nothing," it includes "all creatures," and it occurred "when it seemed good" to God. *Service* is the central theme. Everything, Article XII emphasizes, was created to serve its Creator.

Of course, in our society the concept of service lacks much of its old luster. People say things like this:

> You call this a *service* station?
>
> That woman has no life of her own; she does nothing but *serve* her husband, hand and foot.
>
> As your elected representative and public

servant, I will bring more of everything to everyone.

Dr. Hartshorne lifts faces. Therefore he is not in business, but in one of the *service* professions.

Our company is in business only to *serve* you, the customer!

But before the idea of service got tinged with contempt, irony, or sheer humbug, it could still bear the weight which the Confession gives it. The Confession sees the created universe as a setting for that mutual and joyful service which can make relationships both tender and strong. Note how often the words "serve" and "service" appear. God made creatures to "serve" their Creator. His power is for "the service of mankind" so that, in turn, "man may serve his God." Meanwhile, neither human nor divine, angels serve God as His "messengers." But they also "serve His elect."

Thus, there is service all around. Service in the Confession is something good, something not to be scorned, but valued. And the angels, like us, were made to serve the Creator in freedom and joy. The Confession does not mention blond hair and birds' wings, on the one side, nor dark hair and bats' wings on the other. Not a word is said about red tights and pitchforks. The Confession simply assumes the existence, and describes the function, of angels and demons.

In this it follows the Bible. Angels, like humans, are *created* beings, part of "all things . . . invisible" (Col. 1:16). They serve God as messengers, protectors of other creatures, and as general agents to act on God's behalf. For example, angels announce Jesus' birth, resurrection, ascension, and return. An angel strengthens Jesus in the garden. Both Old and New Testaments offer numerous examples of angel visitants. Summing up the biblical testimonies, Calvin says that through angels God declares His power, provides for the safety of believers, and communicates His gifts (*Institutes* I, xiv, 11).

Did biblical people take angels for granted? Did they calmly expect close encounters with this kind of heavenly creature? No. It is important to remember that people in the Bible typically react to an angel visitant just as *we* would expect to react. They are afraid. They tremble. They are filled with wonder. For them as for us, angels are alien and unfamiliar creatures. It is not because they are naive or primitive that biblical people report encounters with angels. It is because they *have* been encountered.

Two passages of Scripture (II Pet. 2:4 and Jude 6) reveal that not all angels have remained loyal servants of God. Some sinned. Some "did not keep their own position." These are now residents of the "pits of nether gloom." They are not free. God has them, so to speak, on a tether. Yet, as the Confession says, these demons, of whom Satan is chief, desperately do what damage and wreak what havoc they can.

Belief in angels and demons was common in church and society until the modern period. Some of the world's greatest art and literature expresses the deep human interest in them. Milton's *Paradise Lost*, for example, makes so much of Satan that he tends to overshadow all other figures. The church fathers all wrote about angels—about their existence, their nature, and their ways. In the thirteenth century, Thomas Aquinas developed a full-blown angelology. Angels, he said, are "pure spirits, subsistent separated substances, forms not joined with bodies." Detailed and confident in their assertions about angels, Aquinas and others provoked the modern claim that the medievals debated endlessly—"how many angels could dance on the head of a pin."

Calvin, as we have already noted, surely believed in angels. Yet he wrote about them cautiously, warning that "here, as in all religious doctrine . . . we ought to hold to one rule of modesty and sobriety: not to speak, or guess, or even to seek to know, concerning obscure matters anything except what has been imparted to us by God's Word." Following his own warning, Calvin does not dare say that we each have a guardian angel, because the Scriptures do not plainly say it. And he assesses one confident and famous book on angels as "nothing but talk."

Until just recently, except for the flutter of wings at Christmas, angels were scarcely mentioned in our churches. Preachers did not preach much about them. Lay persons did not know what to make of them. Everyone was somewhat embarrassed by them. But fashions change. In a culture which has recently been obsessed with astrology, numerology, reincarnation workshops, and advanced Voodoo, belief in the biblical hosts of heaven and hell seems almost chaste and restrained.

Is belief in angels and demons part of our authentic Christian commitment? No doubt. Is it central in the way that belief in Jesus Christ is central? No. Still, there are not good reasons for denying the existence of angels and demons, and there is one good reason for affirming their ex-

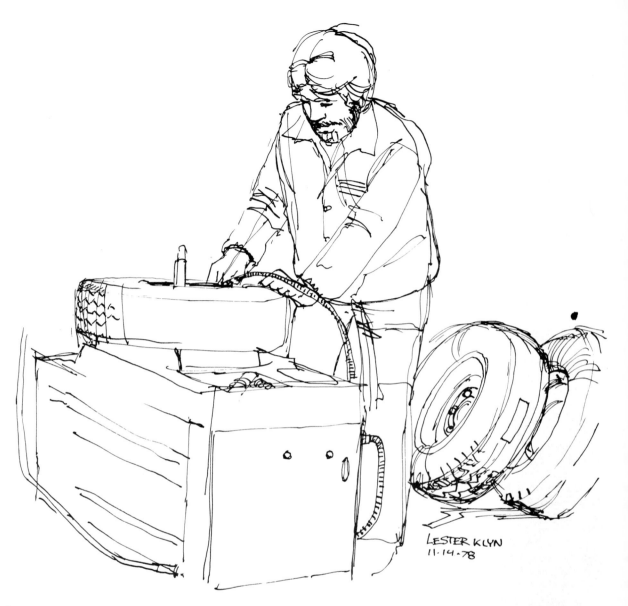

LESTER KLYN
11·14·78

istence: The Bible does so. You will notice that when people balk at angel-belief, they usually have some uneasiness about the supernatural in general. It is not that they confidently accept the existence and works of the members of the Trinity, for example, but worry about angels. Often they doubt both.

Perhaps we do best to follow Calvin in acknowledging the existence of angels and demons—but also in speaking cautiously of them. The Confession closes Article XII by warning us to err neither on the Sadducee side in denying the existence of a spirit world (Acts 23:8), nor on the Manichean side in overestimating its status and importance. That seems to be sane and balanced advice. We may observe that in any case our first loyalty is not to Gabriel or Michael, but to Christ.

Providence

In Article XIII of the Belgic Confession, Guido de Bres tells us (and King Philip II) what Reformed people believe about providence. The article is deeply pastoral in tone—almost a sermon in miniature. De Bres begins by explaining what we understand by the doctrine of providence. He continues with a denial of a common error, affirming that God is not the author of sin. Finally, he mentions the "unspeakable *consolation*" which this doctrine provides. The following paragraphs examine each of these three points in detail.

First, how do we explain providence? This doctrine is intended to deny the tyranny of chance or fortune. De Bres mentions Epicureans as damnable in this respect because they "say that God regards nothing, but leaves all things to chance." In fact, Epicurus (341-270 B.C.) did not believe in God, but only in " the gods," and then only in a strange way. The gods have nothing to do with his world. They exist tranquilly on their own, calmly talking things over in Greek. What humans must do in this life (for there is no afterlife) is to imitate this tranquility. We must be unbothered, unruffled, unfearful. The best recipe for this hassle-free existence, according to Epicurus, is to deny all providence and fate. We live on our own—self-reliant, self-assured, self-saved—and we are not interfered with by anything from beyond. It is this Epicurean doctrine which has recently been revived in secular "self-realization" movements.

So much for Epicurus' opinions. De Bres, with all biblical Christians, asserts the contrary. God actively rules our world. All the days of our lives and the events of our world are woven into His plan. In fact, "nothing happens in this world without His appointment."

All the Reformed confessions deny randomness in the world and in our affairs. We are not at the mercy of the wheel of fortune but walk under the guiding hand of our heavenly Father. Answer 27 of the Heidelberg Catechism describes providence in a particularly powerful way:

Providence is
    the almighty and ever present power of
    God
        by which he upholds, as with his hand,
        heaven
        and earth
        and all creatures,
    and so rules them that
        leaf and blade,
        rain and drought,
        fruitful and lean years,
        food and drink,
        health and sickness,
        prosperity and poverty—
    all things, in fact, come to us
        not by chance
        but from his fatherly hand.

Once we have explained and defined providence, we encounter a difficult question. De Bres was as acutely conscious of it as we are. The question has to do with sin and with evil generally. If "nothing happens in this world without His appointment," then how can we avoid admitting that God causes sins and other evils?

This is a very old and agonizing question. It had been asked and debated for many centuries by the time de Bres had to face it. The question is sharpened in the lives and thought of Christians who confess a strong doctrine of God's sovereignty and providence. Calvin worried about it. Seventeenth century Reformed theologians employed subtle philosophical concepts to deal with it.

How does the Belgic Confession handle this troublesome question? It simply affirms two aspects of biblical teaching (what God "has revealed to us in His Word") and refuses to go further. It says both that "nothing happens in this world without His appointment" and also that God is not the "author" of sins committed by us or the devil. Beyond that, it warns against inquiring too "curiously," exceeding human "capacity," and transgressing biblical "limits." Thus, as is typical of confessional documents, Article XIII only lays out boundaries on either side of the doctrine of providence. It does not attempt a theological construction in between. It does not say how these boundary confessions (God *appoints* all things; yet God does not *author* all things) are related or how they are to be technically understood.

Nor can we attempt here a technical examination of these sensitive issues. Yet, perhaps *something* can be said. First, sin and evil are not unattended by or independent of God's providence. In the great Joseph stories of Genesis, for example, we see Joseph's brothers intending evil by their actions, but God intending good to come from them. Even from wrong acts, God "brings about" His good (Gen. 50:20). Again, in the book of Job we read of demonic sins which cause human suffering. Satan hurts Job and his family. But Satan does not have unlimited reign over Job. He is allowed to go only so far. He is on a tether. He is not on his own. He is never out of control. God's providence reins him in, cuts him off, "restrains the devil and all our enemies that without His will and permission they cannot hurt us."

Every evil thing which comes into our lives must pass God's scrutiny, get through His filter, pass His screening test. None of it is out of His control. And all of it is turned, directed, redeemed so that good may be brought out of evil. "In everything God works for good with those who love him . . ." (Rom. 8:28). God averts all evil—or else turns it to our profit.

But we must not think that God authors, or originates, or causes sin. That is, in fact, a blasphemous idea. When a gas station robber in Rochester, New York, gouges out the eyes of the teenaged attendant to prevent his victim from later identifying him, *God* does not do this wicked deed. When an African dictator massacres his political opponents, *God* does not cause the massacre. However those biblical passages which describe God's "sending" various evils are to be understood, they are not to be understood as teaching that God causes, authors, or originates such evils. God causes, authors, and originates only *good*. As the last sentence of Article XIII suggests, evil things may be permitted by God (else they would not occur), but He is not their author. That is the unspeakable error which Article XIII and many other Reformed confessions pointedly reject.

Those are the boundaries set by the Confession. Inside them we have our questions. Some of them seem to defy all human understanding. An old Christian, already far advanced in sanctity, is wasted by cancer and sickened by its intended cure. In what way does God turn this to her/his profit? Could it be that He sometimes allows Christians to suffer vicariously—as our Lord did? Could it be that a single word of faith from the lips of a dying Christian can do more for a skeptic than all the cliches of some well-fed preacher?

A child dies piteously from leukemia. Somebody's precious daughter is raped. Somebody's precious son has become the sort of person who rapes. Where do we look for the good in these things? Why are some Christians battered by one seemingly senseless tragedy after another? Why do some knock on the door of heaven until their knuckles run with blood? Why is *this* pious soul a target?

We do not know. The fact is we simply do not know. We know that God loves every one of His children and we know that He has His reasons for permitting evil—and for permitting *this* evil in the life of *this* person. But we do not often know what His reasons are. God's work, as the Confession says, sometimes agonizingly surpasses human understanding.

So we need to know how providence can be explained. And we face, with de Bres, the question: "If nothing happens in this world without His appointment, then how can we avoid admitting that God causes sins and other evils?" But those aren't the only questions involved. In a striking, unexpected turn, the Belgic Confession stands up to answer the Heidelberg Catechism's question, "What is your only comfort in life and in death?"

Says de Bres, the doctrine of providence "affords us unspeakable consolation."

Here the Confession stands with those centuries of Christians who have been shaken, wasted, or pursued; and who, through it all, have still been able to talk about the providence by which they were supported. In their darkness they were given to see light. In their walk through the valley of the shadow of death, they discovered to their astonishment that they were not walking alone. In the grip of stubborn pain they also felt—even more stubborn—the grip of God's fatherly hand. Such people can talk of consolation.

So St. Paul speaks—from experience of distress, famine, peril, and sword. From the same experience he affirms for all the ages that "nothing" will be able to separate us from the love of God in Christ Jesus our Lord" (Rom. 8:39). And so Guido de Bres. From prison, with manacles cutting him to the bone, waiting for the ugly ones to come in and finish him off, Guido de Bres writes to his wife:

> ...I have not fallen into the hands of my enemies by chance, but by the providence of my God, which guides and governs all things...I pray you, then, to be comforted in the Lord, to commit yourself and your affairs to Him, for He is the Husband of the widow and the Father of the fatherless....

Immature Christians sometimes speak too quickly about God's ways with the distress of others. What kind of sensitivity would speak of someone else's throat cancer as "all for the best"? How does a healthy Christian dare to quote Romans 8:28 glibly to a shrunken and miserable acquaintance? Those who comfort others ought themselves to show some scars and to know when it is time for silence.

But it is also a tragic mistake to minimize or wave away the firm consolation which is provided by a loving Father. It is a hopeless secularism which says with Gail Sheehy (the author of *Passages*, a 1976 best-seller on aging) something like this: "No one is with me. No one can keep me safe. There is no one who won't ever leave me alone." That is the statement of a derelict.

Out of his grief and anguish, Guido de Bres says something quite stunningly different: We are embraced. We are not held aloof from trouble and pain, but still in trouble and pain we are held. What de Bres is saying, against all the Gail Sheehys of the world, is that for life and death our unspeakable consolation is that we are not alone. We are in the hands of Him who does all things well.

CHAPTER 15
The Human Tragedy

Belgic Confession, Articles XIV and XV

Introduction

On February 20, 1978, *Time* magazine published a cover story on "The Computer Society." While admitting some of the limitations of the new "microtechnology," *Time*'s general account of life in the computer age was exhilarating; the computer revolution may make us wiser, healthier, and even happier:

> The microelectronic revolution promises to ease, enhance and simplify life in ways undreamed of even by the utopians. At home or office, routine chores will be performed with astonishing efficiency and speed. Leisure time, greatly increased, will be greatly enriched. Public education... may be invested with the inspiriting quality of an Oxford tutorial... It will be safer to walk the streets... the home will again be the center of society.

Such promises are enough to brighten the tattletale gray in the soberest soul.

Quite an opposite view of our human prospects was taken by Mark Twain in his later years. The aging humorist, badly hurt by personal tragedy, turned not mellow, but sharp and cynical. Some of what he said is funny: "Man is the only animal that blushes. Or needs to." Some of what he said is not:

> A myriad of men are born; they labor and sweat and struggle for bread... they scramble for little, mean advantages over each other. Age creeps upon them and infirmities follow... Those they love are taken from them, and the joy of life is turned to aching grief... At length ambition is dead, vanity is dead; longing for release is in their place. It comes at last, the only unpoisoned gift earth ever had for them; and they vanish from a world where they were of no consequence, where they achieved nothing, where they were a mistake, a failure and foolishness.

> (from Twain's autobiography, quoted in Osterhaven, *Our Confession of Faith*)

How do we appraise our human prospects? Are we the engineers of a glorious future or are we a poor, scrambling, sweaty, and meager little race? Shall we devise ways to "ease, enhance and simplify life in ways undreamed of even by the utopians"? Or shall our burdens grow heavier year by year until we topple over into the grave? Who is right—*Time* or Twain?

Neither. One of the most important positions which Reformed Christians take is the one on our humanity. And the Reformed position as taken in the Belgic Confession is in between *Time* and Twain.

Take *Time*. *Time* is too optimistic. It does not admit our fallenness. It overestimates sinful human nature. What it does not see is that technological advance, as H. B. Miller has rightly said, "...changes man's tools, but not man himself. The ancient rule of power and greed never alters; the greedy and powerful simply grasp each technological innovation and turn it to their own purposes" (*The Trentonian*, Feb. 26, 1978). C. S. Lewis has made the same point: "As long as men are twisters or bullies they will find some new way of carrying on the old game under the new system." Indeed, as *Time* itself reports, computer information theft has become a growing concern to industry and law enforcement. So *Time* does not have the right picture of our humanity.

But Twain is not right either. His picture is far too pessimistic. It knows nothing *but* our fallenness. It underestimates the possibilities for strong, purposeful, divinely redeemed human life.

When Twain wrote, "Damn these human beings; if I had invented them, I would go hide my head in a bag," he overlooked both creation and redemption. He saw only fall. But the fact is that we are not simply bad. We are not simply a "damned human race." We are good creatures *gone* bad. And for such creatures as we there is a provision in all the counsels of God and the reaches of heaven to remove what has spoiled us. Twain, then, has too low a view of our humanity.

In this chapter, we must confine ourselves to seeing why *Time* is wrong. We must see why no parade of human inventions leads to heaven. We must understand why no steam engine, no discovery of electricity, no invention of television, no harnessing of nuclear energy, no computer gadgetry—ingenious as all of it is—can possibly save us. We cannot be saved by the works of our hands. For those hands are stained.

Articles XIV and XV of the Belgic Confession describe the human tragedy. There would be no tragedy, of course, if we had always been corrupt and worthless. What is tragic is our *fall*, our loss, our miserable exchange of birthrights. Thus, these articles describe our creation, our fall, and the result of our fall.

The Creation of Humankind

We remember that Article XII has already introduced us to the biblical teaching on creation. It has, however, little to say specifically about the creation of *man*. That lack is supplied by Article XIV.

The first thing to see is that when Article XIV speaks of the creation of man, it means man and woman. It means "mankind" or "humankind." As we know from reading Genesis 1-3, both man and woman were formed by God, and both fell. Even though Adam was formed first, and then Eve—even though Eve was formed from the rib of Adam—the biblical account of our genesis does not feature man as the main event and woman as merely a sideshow. They are wonderfully, communally, fittingly, nakedly *together* in their creation. And they are tragically, brokenly, lonesomely together in their fallenness.

How were they—and we in them—created? The central thing of interest is that we were created in God's "own image and likeness." Theologians have argued for centuries about the precise meaning of "image of God." They still do not agree. Some theologians have pointed out that we are like God, and unlike stones and toads, in being *rational*. We can think, plan, remember. Even our children can show and tell. We are capable of reflection—and of reflection *on* our reflection.

Other theologians have argued that we are like God, and unlike the rest of His creation, in being *non-material*. That is, we *have* bodies, but it is not the case that we *are* bodies. These views about the image of God are taken, you notice, not from anything the Bible specifically says about the image, but rather from a process of simply thinking over the manifest differences between God and man—that is, from using the rational part of the image. Rationality, non-materiality, and other things of that sort are sometimes said to be the "broad" aspect of the image of God, and are said to remain after the fall. We are fallen, but we can still think, and we are still non-material.

But, especially just recently, many theologians have become very impatient with such "speculative" talk about the image. Karl Barth, for instance, has directed our attention back to the main verse in Genesis 1: "So God created man in his own image, in the image of God he created him; *male and female* he created them" (1:27; italics added). Look! says Barth. The clue is right there before our eyes. The image of God obviously has to do with our being created male and female! Barth goes on to develop the view that our sexuality, our being fitting and complementary to each other, is what the image means. The problem with Barth's view is, of course, that God is *not* male and female. Moreover, toads and cows are. How sexuality therefore marks man as like God and unlike animals seems hard to understand.

What does the Belgic Confession do in trying to settle on the meaning of the image of God? It suggests that God's image in us consists in our being created "good, righteous, and holy, capable in all things to will agreeably to the will of God." These gifts make up what is called the "narrow" aspect of the image and were lost at the fall. Where does this way of construing the image come from? "Good" comes from the end of Genesis 1 where God declared that everything He has made is "very good." But where does the Confession get "righteous and holy"? Genesis, after all, does not say anything like that.

Here, following the well-practiced move of Augustine and Calvin, de Bres turns to the New Testament where Paul describes a "new nature, created after the likeness of God in true righteousness and holiness" (Eph. 4:24). So de Bres, following the long tradition, finds the image of God in what we *regain* through conversion. When we are converted, we regain the old image of God which had been lost. Thus, putting together Genesis and Ephesians, the Confession has "good, righteous, and holy."

The last part of the description—"capable in all

things to will agreeably to the will of God"—again owes much to the pioneering theological work of Augustine. Augustine was positively fascinated with what Paul says in Romans 7 about the *will* ("For I do not do what I want, but I do the very thing I hate...."), and developed from it an enormously perceptive and influential account of sin. We have a *divided* will, said Augustine. On the one hand, because God made us, we can never quite forget our home and birthright. We have seeking souls, restless hearts. We have a God-shaped vacuum in our lives. Yet, because we are miserable, fallen creatures, we do not turn to God—who alone can satisfy us. We turn dismally to things *below* God. We seek to quiet our restless hearts with sex, money, power, status. Even when we know that these things cannot save us, they fatally attract us. Divided creatures that we are, we sin with sinking heart—drawn to what will hurt us—at the same time that our restless hearts seek God.

Now the point is that we were not always so divided. In paradise there was perfect harmony between will and deed, and between God's will and man's will. Thus de Bres includes as part of their original image of God the ability "in all things to will agreeably to the will of God."

Fall

The Confession says very little about the fall itself, about that awful moment in which man stepped outside the embrace of God and earned a foul inheritance for all of his successors. Much is said about the *result* of the fall and the nature of inherited sin, but about the first sin itself, the Confession is very restrained. There are, however, at least three interesting remarks which the Confession makes almost in passing.

The first is that though man in paradise was created in God's image, and was therefore "in honor," he did not realize this fact. According to de Bres, he "understood it not, neither knew his excellency...." What does this mean? That man was a kind of primitive? A naive human child? Did God build in every excellence except the *knowledge* of excellence?

Perhaps de Bres does mean something like that. Man in the garden is good in an innocent,

CHUCK KORT and WILLIAM AGGEN   11-13-78

unreflective, uncalculating way. He is in honor, but he does not think about it. He does not think about himself at all. In fact, "the knowledge of good (and evil)" is withheld for him. It is only later, when man's eyes are opened, that he *knows* not only the new evil he has found, but also the old good which he has lost.

The second remark is that man "willfully subjected himself to sin." Here the Confession insists on the *voluntary* character of the first sin. Nobody outside of Adam and Eve caused it. Nobody else obliged or forced the act. It was willful and free. The Confession is following Augustine in saying man in paradise was not content with his creaturely good. His sin, stemming from pride, consisted in "disobedience," (see the opening of Article XV). He reached above himself to grasp the forbidden fruit and fell. He fell below himself. Wanting to be "like God," he showed that he did not understand his own excellency as man. He wanted to be more than man, and as a result became less.

The third remark is that this overreaching, this *superbia* of pride, this discontent with creaturely status, was occasioned by "giving ear to the words of the devil." In the first recorded practice of hermeneutics, the serpent asks the woman, "*Did* God say, 'You shall not eat...?' " As Richard Mouw has pointed out, Satan's success (the serpent is identified with Satan because of Rev. 12:9 and 20:2) depends on getting the woman to accept a revised view of God! God is presented to Eve as a tyrant and liar, a being who unreasonably wishes to keep all the power and privilege for Himself. It is only with such thoughts insinuated into her mind that Eve sees the forbidden fruit as goodness, beauty, and wisdom. The organ of deception is the *ear;* a false word is introduced into the ear and the word is heard and accepted. Then, as now, trouble began when God's word was rejected in favor of a lie. In an apt comment, Bernard of Clairvaux once noted that just as the ear was the organ by which sin and death gained entrance into our lives, so the ear is also the organ by which faith and life may now gain entrance when we *hear* and believe the gospel.

The Result of the Fall—Original Sin

The serpent questioned God's word: "Did God say, 'You shall not eat or you will die?' Actually, of course, you will not die. God knows you will not die. Here; take, eat, remember and believe that your eyes will be opened, and you will be like God, knowing good and evil."

In an upside-down communion, a communion

with the evil one, primal man is attracted by the possibility of advance, of getting ahead, of moving up to the top of the ontological heap. And the tragic irony of it all was that in a perverted way the serpent spoke the truth: After the fall Adam and Eve *did* know good and evil. The intertwined love between them, the innocent sexuality and mutuality they had enjoyed, was now recognized for the first time as being a true good. Shame and cover-up were introduced because of the loss of good. They knew good now—but only by memory. And they knew evil. The evil which had been only a word had become an unspeakable reality. Moral existence had been turned inside out, and what we know of human living testifies to the ageless result. Fellowship was broken; barriers went up; flight from God followed the attack on God. First we rebelled; then we fled. That was the fall, says C. S. Lewis, and out of that fall "has come nearly all that we call human history—money, poverty, ambition, war, prostitution, classes, empire, slavery—the long terrible story of man trying to find something other than God which will make him happy." (*Mere Christianity*).

Many of the dimensions of our fallenness are known to anyone who has been alive. The Confession speaks of our light having been changed into darkness, of the loss of our excellent gifts (goodness, righteousness, and holiness, for instance), of our present liability to corporal and spiritual death, of our slavery to sin. As we saw in chapter 6, all the dismal results of the fall are comprehended under the concept of "misery." The continuing *source* of such misery is the moral corruption of our human nature—the corruption we call "original sin."

Article XV compares original sin to three things: a hereditary disease, a root, and a fountain. The first is by far the most important historically and has been the center of much controversy. The comparison of sin with hereditary disease was already deep in the theological tradition by the sixteenth century, and Guido de Bres simply adopts it.

How are we to understand it? We will most likely be wrong if we imagine that de Bres has in mind a specific theory of the transmission of original sin—by genes, for example. Almost surely he did not. Rather, what he wants to emphasize with this teaching is that there is no time when any one of us is free from sin. We are "infected" already in the womb. The generic human nature in which we all share has been corrupted in such a fashion that all new instances of it, that is all new human beings, are inevitably affected. Calvin, who also employs contagion, infection,

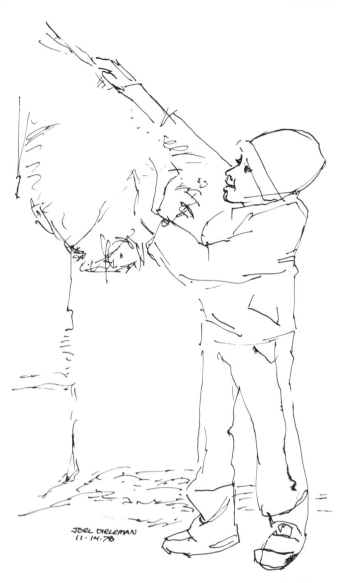

JOEL DIELEMAN
11·14·78

and disease imagery, combined it, as de Bres does, with root and water images:

> Hence rotten branches came forth from a rotten root, which transmitted their rottenness to the other twigs sprouting from them... That is, the beginning of corruption in Adam was such that it was conveyed in a perpetual stream from the ancestors into their descendants. (*Institutes* II, 1,7)

That stream, Calvin and de Bres both say, has become polluted. Every child is born with a taint. He does not learn how to sin by imitating his parents and friends as Pelagius thought. Rather he sins by second nature. Sin comes naturally to him. He is *inclined* to do wrong; he has, as the Catechism puts it, "a natural *tendency* to hate God and [his] neighbor" (Answer 5). Born in sin,

he needs to be born again. For the stark truth is that the guilt of original sin is by itself weighty enough to condemn us. Even after this guilt is forgiven, even after the washing with baptism and the renewal of life, the internal fountain of corruption within still emits a flow of sin, however restricted. One might think of sanctification as the gradual process by which this inner flow of corruption—whatever makes us proud, cold, grasping, self-righteous—is more and more overwhelmed by the grace of Him who is "the overflowing fountain of all good" (Article I).

Conclusion

The Confession, as we can see, offers a sober assessment of both our human tragedy and our human hope. On the one hand, the Confession tolerates no romantic nonsense about the goodness of human nature or the likelihood that we human beings can somehow construct and manage a city of brotherly and sisterly love on our own. If the Bible had not burst that balloon, our long and sad human experience would have. Christians, accordingly, must never suppose that *any* human plan will bring in the kingdom of God. Always we must have a sense of irony about every "road home," every "new deal," every "final solution." All of them are infected with us and with our fatal disease.

But, on the other hand, the Confession offers the sort of hope Mark Twain could not bring himself to embrace. True, we will not engineer a brave new world by our own efforts. But that does not mean that we are left only with despair. The next articles of the Confession speak of election and of recovery. Even Article XV, which speaks sternly of the seriousness of original sin, already mentions the forgiveness of guilt by the grace and mercy of God. The Confession, in other words, sees both the depths of our misery and the heights of God's grace. They go together. And because Christians believe in the height of God's grace, they never abandon this world as hopeless. They never suppose that the flawed character of all attempts to bring justice, peace, and hope into human lives lets us off from making the attempt. For if it is true, as Article XIV concludes, that without Christ we can do nothing, it is also true that we are not without Christ. The second Adam, the new Man, has taken on our corrupt nature and has led the way from Eden through Gethsemane to a heavenly city (Rev. 21:2). In Adam we have all fled from the presence of God. But in Christ, once more " the dwelling of God is with men" (Rev. 21:3).

CHAPTER 16
Election

Belgic Confession, Articles XVI and XVII

Introduction

In his provocative and important book, *The Freedom of God,* James Daane notes the strange silence on the doctrine of election in our Reformed churches. We do not deny election. We just never mention it from the pulpit. The doctrine is being silenced to death:

> Sermons on election are so rare that even a regular churchgoer may never hear one. Through the years I have asked many church people when they last heard a sermon on election, and with rare exceptions most answered that they could not recall. Many believed that they had never heard one.

How has this odd thing happened? After all, as Daane and others readily point out, the doctrine of election is not peripheral. It is not out on the circumference of the Reformed faith. Rather, the doctrine is central. For it speaks of mercy for sinners. It speaks of God's gracious plan for recovering His children and forging again those bonds of communion which were broken by the fall. This plan, as it historically unfolds, and is biblically described, turns out to be thoroughly *elective.*

Abram, for instance, is chosen to be the father of an elect nation—so that "by [him] all the families of the earth shall bless themselves" (Gen. 12:3). Jesus Christ is elected (I Pet. 2:6), and we "in" Him, to be agents of God's plan to reconcile and unite all things now hostile and at odds (Eph. 1:4-10; 2:11-22). Christ's church, the new Israel, is "a chosen race" and "God's own people," not for feeling warm and well-chosen, but for *declaring* the great deeds of Him who saves (I Pet. 2:9).

Here is a concept of election as *calling to a task.* We are called to be agents, witnesses, and ex-amples of God's reconciling work in Christ. Even when we shrink from this high calling, or flee from it like some desperate Jonah, we know it to be God's normal method for getting His redemptive work done. God elects a nation, a Christ, and a church to extend His claim on rebel territory and to declare His intention of rooting out every sin, so that one day again there may be a garden in which the tree of life flourishes—with its leaves "for the healing of the nations" (Rev. 22:2).

The trouble for our minds and hearts and pulpits is not with this task-election. Our trouble is, and always has been, with what might be called salvation-election. It is a biblical and confessional teaching that the elect are chosen not merely for work, but also to *be* saved; not merely to be graced with common sunshine and soft rains (Matt. 5:45), but also to be loved specially with that redeeming grace by which God lifts some of His creatures from the dirt, washes them in the blood of the Lamb, and bestows on them everlasting life. Here, as Article XVII puts it quite beautifully, God makes His way into our wreckage to "seek and comfort" those trembling ones whose sin has made them fugitive and "wholly miserable." Already at this early stage God promises not a woman made of a man, but a "Son (who would be born of a woman)." This is the God of grace who gently clothes the shameful creatures in His garden and promises a *person* who, in some wonderful way, can one day be "put on" like a garment (Rom. 13:14). It is only in Him, with Him, by His benefits, through His sacrifice—in general, by being attached to this Son through faith—that God's creatures can be rescued.

What is discomforting about salvation-election, of course, is that not all of God's fallen creatures are to benefit from it. Only some are elect, as Article XVI makes painfully clear. Adam's posterity is in ruins. All are equally broken and to blame. In this situation God manifests both mercy and justice. He shows mercy by delivering, and then preserving, some. He shows justice by leaving others in ruins. He abandons them to their own devices. He lets them sleep in the bed they have made. They are no more guilty than the elect. Yet for them there is to be no Christ, no Deliverer, no Savior. They are derelicts—left "in the fall and perdition wherein they have involved themselves."

It is this everlasting division of equally fallen creatures into these two groups which has troubled every thoughtful Christian. It is this human-destiny method of displaying justice and mercy which we find puzzling. In fact, *puzzling* is much too mild a word. We find the whole doctrine of election, put this way, deeply distressing. Could it be that some member of our own family will be among those abandoned? Could it be that someone we love shall have the distinction of exhibiting God's justice rather than His mercy? Do we dare say, meanwhile, that *we* are among those whom God, "In His admirable wisdom and goodness," has condescended to save, but that many others—through no fault of their own exceeding ours—shall never know deliverance and the surprise of joy and the deep, aching recognition of Him who made us? The thought seems intolerable and the very idea unpreachable. How could any preacher of such things avoid sounding smug, fatalistic, or both?

In this lesson we will want to think over three things the Confession says on election. First, we will want to say with de Bres that election can joyfully be confessed as God's *mercy* for sinners. Second, we will stress the context of election as being *in Christ*, and therefore in Christ's community. Finally, we will have to face up to the problem of *justice* in this doctrine.

Election as Mercy for Sinners

The confession that God mercifully elects sinners is the confession that salvation is by grace alone. Grace is unmerited favor, unearned benefit, undeserved kindness.

Suppose, for example, that you must be on time for an appointment or with a payment. There are rules about such things. But, as you gratefully discover, there is also a ten minute—or ten day—grace period. Suppose, more seriously, that you treacherously betray a person who loves you. Someone trusts you. But you betray the trust and bring disgrace upon yourself and humiliation to the one who loves you. Yet, astonishingly, the person, though shaken and hurt, takes you back. This stubborn lover tries mightily to understand and forgive and deal with you again. Somehow overcoming disgrace by God's grace, he or she turns to you afresh. And with humility and gratitude, you attempt to face and to serve so fierce a lover.

Of course, the lover's grace is not cheap. Anyone who loves, and therefore makes himself vulnerable, forgives only with pain and risk. Grace in real life is never magic, glib, fast, or easy. A child erases all of his doodling with a simple flip of his Etch-A-Sketch. But grace does not work like that. For grace must deal with sinners, with people whose violation of divine and human relationships can be persistent, elusive, and cunning.

So the Confession speaks of God's "mercy," of His "mere goodness," of His "most gracious" pleasure only against the dark backdrop of human sin. To such trembling, exposed, shameful creatures as we comes God with His graceful clothing, His gracious promise, and His merciful Son. Here de Bres, drawing upon the mature resources of the Reformation, anticipates some distinctive themes of the Heidelberg Catechism—misery, comfort, sheer grace. Behind all of it, of course, is this last and main theme of the Reformation: salvation by grace alone "without any respect to...works." What liberated Luther from his personal agony and launched the Protestant Reformation was the stunning rediscovery of a central biblical truth misplaced for centuries: God saves by grace alone. He saves not by, but for, good works. His mercy is for *sinners*. In fact, Luther insisted on this point in a way that is as entirely relevant to our own situation as it was to his. Luther warned against our persistent attempts to "clean ourselves up" before making profession of faith. People keep supposing that before they can come to God, they have to get their wayward sex lives, their flaring tempers, or their somewhat doubtful minds under control. No! said Luther. You do not come to God with your little compartmental housecleanings! Never! God comes to you where you are. His mercy, His grace, His election is for sinners. How do you dare—why do you presume—to do His work? Are *you* a savior for the likes of you?

The whole Protestant Reformation followed Luther in stressing the idea that God stoops in His mercy to the level of sinners. He saves by electing Christ to bear our cross and to be striped with our punishment. He does this because in His mere goodness He freely loves us. There is no reason

LYLE VANDE GRIEND
11·16·78

we know of to explain it. Nothing in it can be precisely calculated or reckoned in advance. Before we have done any good works at all, or blurted out any words of repentance, He comes to embrace us, and be with us, and show us the way home. This is salvation by grace, mercy for sinners, good news. This is the gospel! And insofar as any member of the church confesses such a gospel, he confesses the heart of election. However we formulate the doctrine of election, the central and non-negotiable idea in it is this: Whatever choosing and loving of God we do is made possible only by God's first choosing and loving us.

This we can preach and believe.

Election in Christ

The Confession states that election is "in Christ Jesus our Lord." This is not just a pious or rhetorical flourish, but a crucial statement of election's *context*. The elect individual is never a mere, isolated individual. He or she is always *in*. In the old covenant, (s)he is a member of Israel. There is an Israelite context. In the new covenant, (s)he is a member of the new Israel and of the new Israel's head. There is a Christ context. In this new era, as Paul cannot say often enough in Ephesians 1 and 2, we and all that graces us are "in Christ." We are *elect* "in Christ" (1:4). Lewis Smedes observes that Paul's rhapsody here is not a carefully worked out philosophy about "the eternal plan of an absolute diety" but rather

> ...a song, a confession, a hymn of wonder...We are elect *in* Christ. How hard it is to *say* what this means! Christ and His Christians, the Lord and His subjects, the King and His kingdom, the Reconciler and the reconciled, the Leader and His followers, the Head and His body are elect together.
>
> (*All Things Made New*)

Perhaps it *is* hard to say what it means that we are elect in Christ. But, practically speaking, it means at least that our election, both as task-election and salvation-election, comes when we are joined to Christ's body, the church. Admittedly, the last thing de Bres and the Reformers wanted was for us to be swallowed up or dissolved into the church. We have personal responsibility to repent and believe the gospel. But, on the other hand, we never have *merely* a personal faith or a personal Savior. For to be in Christ is to be part of a whole new creation inaugurated by His saving death and resurrection. And of this new creation, the church is the indispensable agent, witness, and example. We recall how impressively the Catechism declares the church context of our election in Answer 54. There it is "the Son of God" who gathers and chooses for eternal life. But it is a *community* which He chooses. Each of us as individuals is elect only insofar as (s)he is a "living member" of this community.

Later on we will have occasion to see that the Belgic Confession is no less insistent on the centrality of the church. Because most of us are so influenced by various fundamentalistic and nationalistic individualisms, we often overlook the thoroughly Reformed, communal, catholic, and church context of our election. Our election is deeply, mysteriously, intricately tied up with the election both of Christ (God's anointed) and of Christ's other followers. Task-election is assigned, and salvation-election mediated, by the preaching, sacraments, and discipline of the church.

Justice and Our Difficulty with Election

The Confession speaks not only of God's mercy, and of God's mercy *in* Christ, but also of God's justice. Simply, tersely, and yet terribly, Article XVI concludes that God is "just, in leaving others in the fall and perdition wherein they have involved themselves." This is non-election, the shadow of election, and de Bres did not make it up. From the Pauline material in Romans 8 (especially vss. 29, 30, 33, and 34), Romans 9, and Ephesians 1:3-14, centuries of Christians (Augustine, Aquinas, Luther, Calvin, and, in his own way, Barth) have derived the doctrine that God has chosen some, and only some of His creatures for redemption and forgiveness of sins, and that He has "passed by" or "left" the others.

As we have noted in the Introduction, this is not just an intellectual puzzle. This is no subject for idle chatter. We cannot, except in crude and insensitive moments, blithely assume that millions of pagans have been passed by, and that to us alone—and to people like us—has deliverance come. For we are soon sobered and corrected if by nothing else than the thought that God "has mercy upon whom He will" and that His passing by in justice might have its awful instances in our own church, our own children, our own marriage.

And so, inevitably, we ask our questions: How can this be? Why must God show His justice farther than in the death of Christ? If that death was fully and justly sufficient for the sins of the whole world, then why cannot the whole world be saved? Meanwhile, if the whole world is not saved, how do we dare to be consoled or comforted with our *own* election? Is it not simply smugness and elitism to claim that while God has passed by many others, He has seen fit to elect us—and that this thought ought to comfort us? What about those *others*? What about the ones who were no more guilty than we, but who never received the gift of deliverance?

May we speculate that in the next life, because of some probationary or purgatorial scheme of God's, their chance will still come? Are we allowed to guess, as C. S. Lewis apparently does in *The Great Divorce*, that hell is called "Purgatory" by some who make the "trip to heaven" and stay? And, if we do not dare say or preach these things, if we cannot find solid biblical support for them or for any notion that there is probation in the next life, what are we to say about the "passing by"? God wants to manifest both mercy and justice, we say in our Confession. But we cannot help privately thinking that it is far more blessed to be a mercy-exhibit than a justice-exhibit.

How are we to understand God's passing by? Nobody knows. Nobody can say. It is at this point that Paul, Augustine, Calvin, and all the saints after them, throw up their hands and say, "Who are you, O man, to question God?" And, of course, we cannot question God. We know that whatever God does is right, fair, and just.

The trouble is that the election and non-election doctrine does not *look* right, fair, and just. Of course, no one who is passed by has a claim on God. Each person is, after all, a sinner and does not deserve grace. But then, neither do the elect. And *they* receive it. In other words, some persons in this scheme seem to be favorites—through no merit of their own. They get to be the mercy-exhibits. Others seem everlastingly at a loss for the only thing which could save them and has saved others—the grace of God.

Perhaps our best posture in all of this is not to question God, but to question our *understanding* of God and His ways. Have we got it all perfectly straight? Could it be that God is here "accommodating Himself" to us, as Calvin always liked to say, so that we have a very incomplete picture? Could it be that God has let us hear, by way of Paul and His other writing deputies, only part of the story?

It surely seems possible. It surely seems that we may be missing some key part of God's overall plan which would allow us to understand election somewhat better. Meanwhile, we are wise to embrace all humility and resist all glibness—surely all pride—in these things. As Calvin said, we must not be ashamed of "a certain learned ignorance" where the doctrine of election is concerned. Moreover, to return to the place where this chapter began, we must not be ashamed of a similar learned silence in our pulpits.

There is some *reason* why our pulpits have been silent on the subject of election. For no matter how often we say that salvation is by grace alone, no matter how rightly and biblically we insist on the Christ-and-church context of election, someone will still ask: "But are *all* God's fallen creatures saved by this grace and in this context? And if not, why not?" And then we are rightly silent. We do not know what to say.

We are safest in confessing and preaching salvation by grace alone and in steadfastly obeying the Great Commission to preach this gospel to the ends of the earth. Let God have His way with His creatures, and let us be slow to speak of His final plan with respect to those "others" about whom we worry. Of two things we may be utterly confident. One is that for any of us concerned about his own election, the thing to do is to repent and believe the gospel. As Bullinger said: "For the preaching of the gospel is to be heard, and it is to be believed; and it is to be held as beyond doubt that if you believe and are in Christ, you are elected" (Second Helvetic Confession). Moreover, once we are delivered, we are also preserved, as Article XVI attests. Nothing can *separate* us from the love of God in Jesus Christ our Lord (Rom. 8:39).

The other thing of which we may be confident is that however election finally works out in the "eternal and unchangeable counsel" of God, it does not work out unjustly. Being very wary and reticent about what we say of God's election and non-election—lest we attribute to Him actions of which we ourselves would be ashamed, let us remain convinced that God deals in just love, and that if it sometimes seems that He does not, then the trouble is not with God but with our understanding of Him and His ways.

CHAPTER 17
Incarnation

Belgic Confession, Articles XVIII and XIX

Introduction

There are two main errors which people are always tempted to make when they think or talk about Jesus Christ. One is the denial of Christ's full divinity. The other is the denial of His full humanity—and already in the New Testament there is a stern reminder to confess that "Jesus Christ has come in the *flesh*" (I John 4:2,3; italics added). The reminder is still needed. In some popular orthodox Christianity, even today, the true divinity of Christ is rightly recognized, but His humanity is practically rejected. Certain hymns, for instance, are notorious for this:

> The cattle are lowing, the Baby awakes,
> But little Lord Jesus, no crying He makes.

The Jesus who wept as an adult is strangely silent as an infant!

Articles XVIII and XIX have to do with the incarnation. That is, they have to do with the fact that the second person of the holy Trinity assumed our human flesh. At the center of our confession is a great mystery of the Christian religion—that "He was manifested in the flesh," that "the Word became flesh and dwelt among us" (I Tim. 3:16; John 1:14). The God of grace comes to His rebellious children with graceful clothing (Gen. 3:21) and a gracious promise (Gen. 3:15). Then, at last, "...when the time had fully come, God sent forth his Son, born of woman..." (Gal. 4:4).

Earlier, the Confession solidly affirmed the full divinity of Jesus Christ as second person of the Trinity (chapter 13). Now we turn to Christ's humanity. Just mentioning that Christ is God's "only-begotten and eternal Son," and "God with us," Article XVIII insists that He became "a real man." Then Article XIX proceeds to the difficult task of trying to say how these two beliefs—in both Christ's full divinity and full humanity—can be combined. The summary statement is at the end: "Wherefore we confess that He is *very God* and *very man*...."

Let us look more closely at these articles and this summary.

Article XVIII—The Incarnation

The early church was set within two broad cultural communities. The smaller of these, but perhaps the deeper, was *Jewish*. Look at the end of Article XVIII. You cannot miss the Jewish connection. De Bres piles up the scriptural testimonies linking Jesus with David, Jesse, the tribe of Judah, the seed of Abraham, and, of course, the Jewish virgin, Mary. "Salvation is from the Jews," Jesus Himself said (John 4:22), and the Savior is born in a very Jewish history and lineage.

But salvation is also for the Gentiles, as Peter painfully learns in Acts 10. In the New Testament, *Gentile* mostly means "Greek." By 331 B.C., the great Alexander the Greek had conquered the world and begun to plant Greek culture in it. So, for example, in such cosmopolitan centers as Alexandria, in Egypt, exiled Jews soaked up Greek philosophy, language, and religion. There, three centuries before Christ, the Old Testament was translated into Greek for Jews who could no longer read Hebrew. Even after Greek political decline, and the rise of Rome, Greek language and culture long held its massive influence. In Palestine such influence was so old and deep by Jesus' time that the rudest fisherman had to be bilingual. Peter, for instance, although a Jew, almost surely spoke Greek to his first convert, Cornelius, who was a Roman! And when the New Testament came to be written, the chosen language was common Greek.

Why is this double context important? Because it helps us understand the two common errors about Jesus' identity. Remember our lesson on the Nicene Creed? Jews were expecting a Messiah, or "anointed one," but not clearly a *divine* Messiah.

Most Jews in Jesus' day probably thought of the deliverer as a political champion—someone to get Rome off their backs and Caesar out of their hair. The Jews had no problems with Jesus' humanity. "Is not this the carpenter, the son of Mary and brother of James?" (Mark 6:3). It was rather the claim of divinity in Jesus which offended and enraged the Jews. They believed in one God—who was high and holy and not to be confused with carpenters from Nazareth.

The Greeks made the opposite error. Their tradition included many divinities and lords. Hence, early Greek Christianity, once it accepted Christ as the "one Lord" alongside God the Father (I Cor. 8:6), tended to disbelieve not His divinity, but His *humanity*. Greek thought had always taken a somewhat dim view of the material world because it was fleeting, unstable, and liable to death.

Of course the material world included such things as human bodies and flesh. Thus the proclamation that He who is Lord had been crucified was folly to the Greeks (I Cor. 1:23). Likewise, the resurrection of the *body* seemed outrageous to them. We may note that Paul was doing rather well in his speech to the Greek philosophers of Athens until he came to the part about Jesus' resurrection (Acts 17:31,32). And we remember that John's writings (see John 1:14 and I John 4:2,3, quoted above) were sometimes pointedly aimed at Greek prejudice against the real incarnation, the real "enfleshment," of a divine being.

So the problem for Greek converts, as opposed to Jewish ones, was that of accepting Jesus' full humanity. Wherever the gospel fell on Greek ears there was a tendency to think that the Son of God did not really assume flesh, but only *appeared* to do so. People with this idea are called "Docetists," from the Greek word which means "to appear," and Docetists have appeared in every era of the church. Just as youngsters believe that Superman is only *posing* as mild-mannered reporter, Clark Kent," so Docetists think the Son of God is only *posing* as "gentle Jesus, meek and mild."

In the early church, the straight biblical doctrine of the full humanity of Jesus Christ was constantly being watered down by various sorts of Docetists. Some had been influenced by Gnosticism, a pre-Christian mystery religion which featured salvation by supernatural insight, or "gnosis." Others fell under the sway of Marcion, an important second-century Docetist who thought of Christ as a sort of phantom. Later, the third-century Persian blend of religions, Manichaeism, pictured Jesus with a kind of heavenly air-body.

Because these Docetisms were in the atmosphere, early Christian creeds included a confessional section on the very human events of Christ's life. As we have learned, both the Apostles' and Nicene Creeds insist that Christ was incarnate, born, made to suffer, crucified, and dead. They add pointedly that He was "buried." Moreover, the ecumenical councils of Constantinople (381), Chalcedon (451), and Constantinople again (680) all used technical language to rule out certain subtle forms of the ever-recurring Docetism. These official rulings became part of standard Christological orthodoxy in the Middle Ages, and were simply fed into the Lutheran and Reformed churches in the sixteenth century. Thus, when Guido de Bres sat to write Article XVIII of the Confession for Netherlanders, he had a long tradition to follow.

We see that he followed it faithfully. Chalcedon, the most important of the early councils for defining the person of Christ, had said with Nicea that Christ is "*homoousios* with the Father as to his Godhead," but had also added that Christ is "*homoousios* with us as to his manhood; in all things like unto us, sin only excepted." De Bres says the same, ". . . really assuming the true human nature with all its infirmities, sin excepted; being conceived in the womb of the blessed virgin Mary by the power of the Holy Spirit without the means of man." He says it in opposition to his contemporary Docetists.

In chapter 9 we saw how prominently Anabaptists and other radical reformers figure in de Bres' life and mind. Here is the first place in which he clearly calls them heretics. Exactly which radical reformers did he mean? We cannot tell. We do know that some radicals believed that the Son descended from heaven already equipped with a "celestial body" (a belief akin to the Manichaean one, as Calvin notes), and that others—the famous Menno Simons, for example—were afraid to say that Jesus was really born from the virgin Mary. What troubled this latter group was the thought that if Jesus were really "from," or "of" Mary, if He actually received human nature from a human mother, then He could not be utterly sinless. For our human nature is fallen, and each new instance of it bears the taint of original sin.

ED KRUID
11-16-78

Calvin deals with this objection by affirming that the Holy Spirit miraculously cleansed Christ's human nature of original sin. De Bres simply affirms the true humanity, "sin excepted."

He stresses that this humanity is not merely a bodily affair. Rather, taking the Reformed position that our whole humanity has been corrupted, de Bres emphasizes that Christ needed to assume our nature not only "as to the body," but also as to "a true human soul, that He might be a real man." This emphasis is meant to ward off such views as that of Appolinaris in the fourth century. Appolinaris had devised an ingenious way of relating the human and the divine in Christ. His proposal was that Christ had an ordinary human body and soul but not a human mind. In its place He had the second person of the Trinity. This idea struck the fathers at Constantinople as quaintly Docetic and entirely condemnable. So it strikes de Bres.

Article XIX—The Relation of Natures and Person

The orthodox Christian doctrine of the Trinity is that there are three divine persons in one Godhead. One of those persons, of course, is Jesus Christ. And the orthodox doctrine of the person of Jesus Christ is that He is a single person who unites two distinct natures, divine and human. This orthodox doctrine comes from the Council of Chalcedon (451), and was agreed upon as the church's answer to the two main schools of thought.

The problem for thoughtful Christians always had to do with the relation of the human and the divine in Jesus Christ. If we think of the sort of puzzles which intrigue any reflective person today, we will almost surely be thinking of the same ones which intrigued the reflective Christians of the early centuries. How does one wrap his mind around the idea of a person who was simultaneously fully divine and fully human? If He were fully divine, then why did He get tired? Why did He weep? How are we to understand His *temptations*? Was evil attractive to Him? If so, how could He be truly sinless? If not, how could it tempt Him? Was He tempted in *every* respect as we are (Heb. 4:15)? Our temptations—to pride, lust, tyranny, folly, laziness, despair—are, after all, so emphatically unholy.

Other questions occur to us. Was this Jesus of Nazareth omnipotent? Think of Jesus in the Garden of Gethsemane, or walking the Via Dolorosa with the cross lashed to His back, or thirsting and agonizing on the cross. "Even youths shall faint and be weary," said Isaiah, "and young men shall fall exhausted" (40:30). But can this be true of the divine Son of God?

Was Christ omniscient? Did He know everything? Did He know that the earth was round? Did He know relativity theory? Did He ever answer a difficult question with a thoughtful, "I don't know for sure about that"? Or, take the most controversial of the texts in the New Testament with respect to Jesus' knowledge. Talking about the time of the end of the world, Jesus said: "But of that day or that hour no one knows, not even the angels in heaven, *nor the Son*, but only the Father" (Mark 13:32, italics added). One long tradition of medieval interpretation tries to make out that Jesus really *did* know when the end of the world was coming, and that this text merely says that the Son's knowledge of that event cannot be given to others. Such readers as Calvin, on the other hand, insisted on taking the passage very straightforwardly—but as referring "solely to Christ's humanity" (*Institutes* II, xiv, 2).

These are some of the traditional puzzles. They seem sterile and fruitless to some Christians, but they are born out of a genuine attempt to understand our confession that this one person is *very God* and *very man*.

In the fourth and fifth centuries the attempts by various thinkers to relate the humanity and divinity of Christ fell into two main classes, or were represented by two main schools of theology. One of these was the school of Nestorius. Nestorius so emphasized the *separation* of the two natures in Christ, that his opponents charged him with teaching that there are in Christ two different persons—a divine one and a human one. This view allowed Nestorius to attribute some biblical attributes of Christ to the human person (being the son of Mary, for instance) while reserving others ("Before Abraham was, I am," in John 8:58) for the divine person.

Nestorius' position did not allow for any real unity of the one being, Jesus Christ. His view is really similar to what a modern psychiatrist would call "neurotic multiple personality." Here two quite distinct persons (Dr. Jekyl and Mr. Hyde, to use a fictional example) use the same body.

The other school of thought, best represented by Eutyches, so stressed the *unity* of the two natures that opponents charged Eutyches with confusing the two natures and particularly with teaching that the human nature was fused into the divine. As opposed to modern liberals who make of Jesus Christ simply a human being, Eutyches appeared to make Him simply a divine being, thus denying Christ's true humanity.

What was the church to make of these opposing views? The Council of Chalcedon made heresy of both. Chalcedon insisted that there is one person, "one and the same Son." He is however made known in two natures which are neither confused (thus ruling out Eutychianism) nor separated (thus ruling out Nestorianism). This one person has both divine and human attributes.

Like the trinitarian formula of Nicea, the Christological definition of Chalcedon occupies middle ground between two extreme views. On the one side, Chalcedon did not want to think of Christ as a pair of persons using the same body. On the other, it did not want to think of Christ as simply divine—or as a third sort of being, a *tertium quid*, between God and man. A fast look at Article XIX of the Confession shows, once again, that de Bres is following the Chalcedonian tradition.

Thus (against the like of Nestorius) the Confession denies that there are "two Sons of God" or "two persons." But (against all Eutychians) it also claims that each nature, divine and human, "retains its own distinct properties." This is said because Eutychians sometimes talked as if the human nature was simply absorbed, or changed, into the divine nature—yielding just one final nature.

There are, unfortunately, too many subtle and tangled issues in this article for us to do justice to them all. But note just these three points.

First, de Bres clearly intends to preserve the ancient Chalcedonian distinction of the two natures in Christ: "each nature retains its own distinct properties"; one nature has no beginning or end, the other has a "beginning of days." But some of his language is not so clear, giving occasion to Lutheran theologians to say that the Reformed position on Christ is Nestorian. For example, de Bres at times seems almost to be talking about two *persons* rather than two *natures*: one nature is "uncreated," the other a finite "creature"; the divine nature fills "heaven and earth," the other retains "all the properties of a real body." It is wise for us to keep in mind that when we talk about two distinct natures in Jesus Christ, we are not talking about two different persons. We are only talking about two distinct sets of properties or attributes, a set of divine properties and a set of human ones.

Secondly, note again how much de Bres makes of the "real body," the "real human spirit," the "reality of His human nature." He does this because of the ancient orthodox conviction that the whole person—body, soul, and mind—is corrupted, and that hence the Savior had to be wholly human. God "sent His Son to assume that nature in which the disobedience was committed, to make satisfaction in the same . . ." (Art. XX).

Finally, observe that de Bres wants very much (in spite of the Lutheran criticism mentioned above) to keep divine and human natures united in the one person, Jesus Christ. Even when He was an infant, even when He was in the grave, Christ was wholly divine, says de Bres. Why then does Luke report that the young Jesus "grew in wisdom" as well as in stature? Because, though "the Godhead did not cease to be in Him . . . it did not so clearly manifest itself for a while."

Conclusion

What can a reader who does not care for technical Christology get from all this? What must we remember from Articles XVIII and XIX? Reinforcing what is mentioned above, perhaps two things.

ROBIN STOUB
9-12-78

First, because of the tendency toward pious Docetism in our orthodox Reformed tradition, we must deliberately think of Jesus Christ as fully human. Even when we rightly think of Him as wholly divine and as sinless, we must not forget that His disciples knew a Man of a certain height and weight and physical appearance. Perhaps they knew Him when He had a head cold or a toothache. His father trained Him as a carpenter's apprentice, and probably knew Him when He had carefully cut a board three inches too short. He was sinless, but He was not naive. When the youths of Nazareth snickered about the village prostitute, He did not think instead that she was merely a nice lady with eccentric visiting hours. Jesus "knew what was in man"—and in woman (John 2:25). To think of Jesus as "gentle Jesus, meek and mild," who is forever clasping children to His creamy white toga is to miss much of the biblical picture. He could be fierce, angry, and terrifying. He could be afraid. He wept.

Secondly, we must root out of our minds every tendency to think of Jesus as a multiple personality who switches, like Superman, from one identity to another. Jesus of Nazareth is the Son of God (*that* person of the Trinity) who entered our human flesh. He did not then somehow become a different person. Rather, one divine person preexisted, became incarnate, ministered, died, was resurrected, and ascended. This one divine person took on a human nature: Things true of humans became true of Him. The union of divine and human in Christ was not such as could be tuned in and out like channels on a television set.

This is the mystery of the incarnation—that the one person was *very God* and *very man*. That is a theological and metaphysical mystery. But perhaps a greater mystery—a "wondrous love"—is that the very divine Son of God became "very man that He might die for us according to the infirmity of His flesh."

So Christians have always celebrated with thoughtful joy the advent and career of God's Son. Both at Christmas and communion we remind ourselves that God gave—and then gave up—flesh and blood for us. Here is a loving Father who was not determined to search and destroy a miserable human race, but who was "pleased to seek and comfort" us first with promise and then with fulfillment. Recognizing both grace and mystery in the incarnation, Christians have always said, "Thanks be to God for His unspeakable gift!"

CHAPTER 18
Atonement

Belgic Confession, Articles XX and XXI

Introduction

Much modern and liberal thought about God is vague. It has all the definiteness of a fog bank. It makes God a kind of oblong blur. Even where the idea of God does begin to take definite shape, the picture is incomplete. It does not include the righteous anger of a God who hates sin and is determined to punish and destroy it. Rather, the idea is that God has only one attribute: God is love—and nothing but love. He does not particularly hate sin because He does not hate at all. He does not get so excited. He is good-natured and easygoing. He smiles endlessly. He is a universalist. And He tends to be something of a romantic.

Orthodox and neoorthodox theologians strongly object to this (admittedly, exaggerated) liberal notion of God. They observe that the Bible allows for no such sentimental or cheap grace in God. Instead, at the heart of the biblical account is the insistence that God's love comes to us with blood on it, and is held out to us in scarred hands. This is the God who is terrible in His anger and an everlasting foe of all those forces of evil which have dug in against His coming. Emil Brunner once said that when we lose this idea of God's wrath, when we forget that sin is a personal affront to God's holiness, then we help the decay of the Christian faith and the decline of the church. For then, obviously, the whole notion of painstaking *atonement* for sin becomes an impertinence.

Brunner is on target. The modern liberal idea of God is unbiblical and leads to the yawning irrelevance of the Christian faith.

But there is another false idea of God. This one is not liberal. In fact, it has flourished most where liberalism was liked least. Those who accept this idea of God go to the opposite extreme. In their eagerness to teach God's justice and wrath, they seem to lose sight of His love and mercy. Their God is an absolute Lord of vengeance—quick to anger and abounding in steadfast hatred of evildoers. He wipes out sinners on the merest provocation, and enjoys it. He looks for chances to destroy things and let off steam.

In this awful caricature, *Christ* is the merciful one. He sees both God's wild anger and humanity's bottomless misery, and attempts to mediate. It is as if an aging and angry landlord wanted to destroy all of his unprofitable servants, but his kindly son intervened. He tries to placate his father and step in between. As one theologian put it, Christ says something like this: "Look, you get so angry all the time. Everything sets you off. Do you have to beat on somebody? All right, then beat on me. Get it out of your system! Clear the air! Then we can have peace again."

Of course this too, if seriously proposed, would be a blasphemous and unbiblical idea of God. It is not a liberal, but a *pagan* heresy. It is pagan deities who are wild, merciless, and capricious like this. It is they who have to be propitiated and appeased, or they start to smash things. As G. C. Berkouwer noted in *The Work of Christ*, this pagan idea, when introduced into Christianity, suggests terribly "that God is a person against whom we must be protected by Christ." God wants to get at us, but Christ holds Him off and takes on His own head and shoulders all the blows aimed at us. Before Christ offered Himself as a scapegoat, God had no mercy for the world at all.

The Reformed idea is neither liberal nor pagan, though it has sometimes been confused with the latter. On the one hand, against all sentimental ideas of God and His love, Reformed doctrine takes sin, and God's wrath against sin, with utter seriousness. On the other hand, against all pagan ideas of a tyrant-god, the Reformers bowed humbly before the God whose mercy is *from the beginning*. God the Father has not just lately had a change of heart because of what Christ did. Within the holy Trinity there is a mutual and concerted intent to redeem, to "seek and comfort" a fallen and trembling humanity (Article XVII). The Reformed view is that the same God who hates sin, fiercely loves His sinful children. He wants them back. Getting them back is hard and costly. Within God is the sort of justice which will not allow the gaping wound in the universe to be closed without cleansing it first. Yet God has mercifully provided the means for such cleansing and closing. *Reconciliation* is the broadest word for this gracious scheme; and the source of all Christian faith, religion, and theology is that "God was in Christ reconciling the world to himself" (II Cor. 5:19). He does it by atonement. That is what this chapter is about.

Cur Deus Homo?

Citizens of the United States sometimes complain that their government is not so much by law as by lawyers. A similar complaint has been heard in the church about Christian theology. Much of our doctrine and theology has been framed by people with legal training. Tertullian and Calvin are notable examples. The Western theological mind has always been a legal mind, and is instinctively attracted to religious theories which can be framed with legal terms and concepts.

This is impressively true with respect to atonement doctrine. We recall from chapter 7 on "Deliverance" that there are many biblical descriptions of God's reconciling work in Christ. Most of them are not particularly legal. Some are pastoral (the Shepherd seeks his lost sheep), or medical (the sick are healed by the great Physician), or domestic (a waiting Father forgives his prodigal son). Most are drawn from common human life (the soiled ones are cleansed, the poor enriched, the foolish made wise). In the broad organic inspiration of the biblical authors, a wealth of imagery was pressed into service to describe what God was doing in Christ. Out of all these images and descriptions, especially three were developed into full-blown "theories" on the atonement. The most dramatic is what is called the *Christus Victor* theory. Here the emphasis is on the great biblical account of Christ's triumphant victory over the devil and all the powers of evil. This theory was developed in the Greek East, and has always had a huge popular appeal. Much of the best-selling book *The Exorcist* depends for its drama on *Christus Victor* themes.

Liberal theology, which finds the *Christus Victor* motif repellent because of its alleged "mythological" trappings, has turned especially to a second account of the work of Christ. This theory derives from Abelard (1079-1142) and stresses the fact that Christ is our *example*. There are no "transactions" going on behind the scene at the cross—surely nothing so crude as a "ransom to the devil." Rather, in Christ God offers an example of suffering love so that we may be humbled by this profound spectacle, seek to imitate it, and thus turn from our selfish ways.

But in Reformed theology, the predominating idea has been that of "vicarious *satisfaction*" or "penal substitution." This is a legal theory. Here, the beginning question, as with other theories, is Anselm's. Anselm (1033-1109) wrote a most influential book on atonement. Its title is the question *Cur Deus Homo?* (Why did God become man?). Medieval Christians were fascinated with this question. Some especially able thinkers have wondered endlessly whether Christ would have come even if we had not fallen. Duns Scotus (1265?-1308) and the Scottists said He would have. Thomas Aquinas (1225-1274) and the Thomists said He would not. John Calvin (1509-1564) and the Calvinists said we must not ask such questions. But given the fall as an historical fact, Calvin and the Reformed tradition has mainly said that Christ came to satisfy God's justice and thus mercifully to bear the punishment of our sins. Thus the first sentence of Article XX is typically Reformed.

Where does this idea come from? It comes ultimately from the Bible, as do both of the other theories. That Christ is our example is a biblical idea (John 13:15; I Pet. 2:21). Again, that Christ appeared to "destroy the works of the devil" and victoriously to triumph over the "powers" is a biblical teaching (I John 3:8; Col. 2:15). Likewise, the favorite Reformed description of Christ's work as vicarious satisfaction and penal substitution (both of which will be explained in a moment) can claim as sources a number of Romans passages (3:21-26; 5:18-21; 8:1-4,32) besides such famous texts as Isaiah 53:5,6 (which lies behind I Peter 2:23-25, and is quoted in Article XXI). In other words, the legal themes of satisfied justice and punishment for wrongdoing are genuinely biblical.

These legal themes were picked out of all the other biblical themes and developed by Anselm. His main idea is "vicarious satisfaction." Man,

THE VERNON BOERMAN FAMILY
11·13·78

said Anselm, has infinitely offended God's honor by his sin, and thus owes an infinite satisfaction. He has to pay back with interest the honor he has stolen. Yet he cannot do so. He is too weak and sinful. In fact, his debt keeps mounting (remember Answer 13 of the Catechism). So, in Christ, God Himself becomes man. Because He is man, He is able to satisfy in the same human nature in which the disobedience was first committed (Article XX of the Confession). And, because He is wholly divine, the offering of His sinless life has infinite worth. Thus Christ earns surplus merits which may be credited or "imputed" to our account. In this way, God's honor and justice are satisfied "vicariously" (i.e., by another).

Calvin, who had legal training, liked Anselm's description of Christ's work. In fact, he added the additional legal language of retributive justice. He and other Reformed theologians talked not only of satisfaction, but particularly of punishment; not only of Christ's death, but also of His passion. Christ's substitutionary work is thus *penal*. He takes our penalty, our stripes. He stands in at our execution.

Look at Articles XX and XXI for these themes. The first sentence of XX has the heart of both. There is "punishment." There is "passion and death." It is noted that these are "most bitter."

The article points out that we who were literally guilty of hell have gotten undeserved mercy, while God's Son has gotten undeserved death.

Article XXI goes on in the same way. De Bres, like Calvin, is deeply moved by the fact that the Son of God *suffers*. The scene in Gethsemane and the cry of dereliction from the cross ("My God, my God . . . .") are summoned as powerful examples of His passion, of His feeling "terrible punishment" in both body and soul. From all this, but especially from Christ's wounds, de Bres takes particular "consolation."

This is a clear and heartfelt statement of Christ's work as penal substitution. Our Lord's passion and death are punishments for sin—but not His sin. He "has suffered all this for the remission of *our* sins."

Now we are able to see something very important. The previous chapter, on incarnation, might have let us think that the church in the fourth century was interested only in who Christ *is* and not in what He *did*. And, admittedly, the statement of the Chalcedonian Council does seem to support such a view. But the historical fact is that the great champions of Christological orthodoxy were mightily concerned with what Christ did. Athanasius, for example, fought Arius because he thought Arius' halfway god could not save us! Christ had to be *very God* to save us.

We can see that in the Anselmian and Reformed view of the atonement, Christ had to be very man too. We sinned; we must pay. So we do in the *man* Jesus Christ. "*Very God* and *very man*" says Article XIX. "To appease His wrath by His satisfaction," and "to purge away our sins," adds Article XXI. Here the doctrines of the person and work of Christ come together. As Article XXI concludes, even the *name* of this person means Savior, "because He would *save his people from their sins.*"

Sacrifice and Appeasement

There is, however, some other atonement language in Article XXI. We have already seen the characteristically Reformed focus on passion and death as penal substitution. This is, we said, *a* genuine biblical theme, and (literally) a crucial one. Paul, for instance, does not care about "lofty words or wisdom" or anything of that sort. He cares only to know "Jesus Christ and him crucified" (I Cor. 2:1,2).

But Article XXI says something new. It mixes in *sacrifice* and *priesthood* descriptions of Christ's work with those others we have already discussed. The ideas of sacrifice for sin and of the roles of priests and victims, were profoundly in the mind and tradition of every Jewish writer of the New Testament. Especially the book of Hebrews makes use of priesthood and sacrifice ideas to say how God was at work in Christ. It is from there that Article XXI derives the mysterious claim that Christ is "a High Priest after the order of Melchizedek" (Heb. 5:6,10; 6:20; chapter 7). Nobody knows for sure how we are to understand this strange figure, Melchizedek, who appears briefly in Genesis 14:17-20 and Psalm 110:4. Scholars even disagree about how the author of Hebrews understands him. Is he considered an archangel? An actual "king of Salem" (Gen. 14:18)? Christ Himself incarnate? But the point is, however Melchizedek is understood, that he belongs to an order of priesthood superior to the common run of Aaronic priests. He is both king and priest, and he (or at least his office) is everlasting. Thus he is a type of Christ.

That is what the Confession makes of Melchizedek. But what Article XXI is trying to say with all of this priesthood imagery is that Christ stunningly combines and transforms the Old Testament institutions of priest and sacrifice. Here is Christ the priest, carrying His own altar through the streets of Jerusalem, along the Via Dolorosa, and up to Golgotha. Once again a beloved Son is offered on a hill. But this time it is not Isaac, the son of Abraham. It is Jesus Christ, the Son of God. And this time the cutting iron is not stayed, but blood is shed. This time the sacrifice is *the Priest Himself*—"the Lamb of God, who takes away the sin of the world" (John 1:29). The Priest Himself mounts the altar to offer up His life in atonement for sin. This, according to Paul, was "a fragrant offering and sacrifice to God" (Eph. 5:2).

Why *fragrant*? Can God be pleased by the suffering of His only begotten Son? Does this killing and this blood-letting propitiate an angry God? Does it "appease His wrath" (Article XXI)? We remember from the account of the flood in Genesis 8 that when all of the flooding was over, Noah "built an altar to the Lord . . . and offered burnt offerings on the altar. And when the Lord smelled the pleasing odor, the Lord said in his heart, 'I will never again curse the ground because of man . . .'" (Gen. 8:20,21). Does the Lord need to smell burning flesh before He will turn from wrath to mercy? Are not the "pagan" and biblical ideas of atonement then distressingly alike?

They are not. Already in the Old Testament it becomes increasingly clear that God's attitude toward sin offerings is not to be confused with the change from anger to pleasure in a hungry man who relishes the savory food steaming under his nostrils. In the Psalms and great prophets we discover that what God really wants for His people is repentance, genuine thanksgiving, and a life of justice toward the poor. It is not the formal sacrifice which pleases God, but "a broken and contrite *heart*" (Ps. 51:17). It is not the squadrons and relays of priests with all their hustle, busyness, and blood—it is not this which delights God. After all, He is not some hungry, pagan deity: "'If I were hungry, I would not tell you; for the world and all that is in it is mine'" (Ps. 50:12). He does not care to "eat the flesh of bulls or drink the blood of goats." What He wants is a "sacrifice of thanksgiving" (Ps. 50:13,14). What He wants is for justice to "roll down like waters, and righteousness like an everflowing stream" (Amos 5:24).

In other words, we are never to think of God as merely famished for roasted lamb and thirsty for spilled blood. What truly satisfies Him is rather the right turn of the heart in His children. Remarkably, He Himself graciously provides the sign of repentance and the means of atonement—already in the old sacrificial system of Israel (Lev. 17:11). In fact, we can now see why the classic Old Testament illustration of this grace became so hugely important to the New Testament writers.

This illustration is found, as we know, in the story of Abraham and Isaac (Gen. 22:1-14) to which we have already referred above. Isaac trudges along beside his tortured father until he finally asks the sudden, inevitable question: "But where is the lamb for a burnt offering?"

Every word of Abraham's reply is heavy with significance for all the Christian ages: "God will provide himself the lamb for a burnt offering, my son."

"God will provide himself!" "The lamb!" "My son!"

As it turns out, it is not the immediate seed of Abraham who is sacrificed. It is, after all, not Abraham's son, but his faith, that God wants. Yet, as all Christians celebrate every time they have communion, the seed of Abraham, the lamb of God, "my son," *was* slain for us.

This self-offering was "to appease His [God's] wrath," says Article XXI. But we know now that God was not thus *converted* by Christ. It is not as if God changed from being hostile to being kind. For this whole plan of atonement depends from the foundation of the world on God's gracious in-itiative. Profoundly within the mysterious counsel of the holy Trinity, the Father and Son agree that in the fullness of time, the Son shall make His journey into the far country.

Conclusion

So we must never minimize the mercy of God or His steadfast love. But neither may we forget His justice. In fact, in our own cultural climate, the latter is probably the greater danger. Our age is self-indulgent, and widely hospitable more to the liberal heresy than to the pagan one. The much-quoted words of the dying Heinrich Heine ("God will forgive me; that is his business") do not sound as blasphemously presumptuous to many people as they should.

People forget that God hates sin, and that even His love therefore has an edge on it. God's love is sharp, forever keen to cut away the growths of sin which block our access to Him. The cutting hurts. But all of it is "for us" (Article XX) and "in our behalf" (XXI). God wants His children. As we have seen, He will stop at nothing to get them back.

GENE PROCTOR
12-14-78

CHAPTER 19
Justification and Faith

Belgic Confession, Articles XXII and XXIII

Introduction

Deeper than most other human hungers is the hunger for happiness. A child who tries to escape a spanking by wailing, "But I want to be *happy!*", is talking very human language. Everybody wants to be happy. The question, as Augustine said more than once, is who or what can make us happy.

Psychologists say that a basic ingredient in happiness is acceptance. A person needs to be—and to feel—accepted. Otherwise he suffers. One wise minister used to point out how cruelly children reject each other simply by assigning nicknames. Call a ten year old "monkey-face," or "fats," or something worse, and he may spend much of his life trying to overcome this early humiliation. He has not been properly accepted, and his name says so.

The craving for acceptance never stops. Teenagers are often consumed by it. Even those of us for whom high school is only a dim memory remember how it was: Clothes were picked for their impression on others. Even sloppy clothes were carefully chosen for their choice sloppiness. There was much standing in front of mirrors, and a certain amount of combing of individual hairs. Being seen in the right places, clinging to friends, cultivated carelessness in school, the right slang (do you call a good thing "mellow," or "cool," or "far out," or "dandy," or "peachy-keen"?)—all of this was calculated to gain acceptance from others and thus from ourselves.

We chuckle over it now, but not without a wince. There was, after all, both pain and slavery in it. We were never really *free*. We could not easily relax, open up to others, freely praise another person, laugh at ourselves, or humbly befriend someone who was unpopular. Many of us tried too hard for social salvation. We did it with fear and trembling. We built a prison out of pride and insecurity—pride outside and quaking within—and had to live in it.

Many adults spend practically their whole lives in such prisons. Their need for acceptance is old and deep, and they keep on trying to satisfy it. Some attempt to get rich, or famous, or learned. Some get drunk. A few get sick—on the unconscious theory that it is better to be a somebody sick than a nobody well. A number of single people throw themselves into marriages or housekeeping arrangements more tragically lonesome than anything they endured before. In America's mid-seventies, the "me-decade," thousands of confused secularists tried to find themselves, accept themselves, and generally get in touch with themselves by means of packaged "human potential" and "self-realization" schemes. Esalen, Arica, Silva Mind Control, Psychosynthesis, Guided Fantasy, E.S.T., Inner Cooking, Underwater Primal Scream—and seven or eight thousand other expensive indoor sports—all enriched the sleazy "facilitators" who peddled them and fooled unhappy people into thinking they could save themselves.

Occasionally the lack of acceptance can have even darker results. Occasionally we get a look into the wretched lives of those desperate nobodies who are determined to make a splash even if they have to do it violently. Lee Harvey Oswald, James Earl Ray, Arthur Bremer, David Berkowitz (New York's "Son of Sam") were all brooding, lonesome, dismally unaccepted figures who came at last to the idea that there was only one way they would never be forgotten. So they got guns.

Deep in the Christian gospel is a word of *acceptance.* That word is "justification." God accepts us because of Christ's atonement—an act spring-

ing from God's profoundly gracious desire to receive and welcome back His estranged children.
We, in turn, must accept this acceptance by
means of a given instrument. That instrument is
faith. Justification and faith are a pair. Here lies
the acceptance, and even the self-acceptance, we
crave. De Bres sees keenly how self-acceptance is
linked to our justification. Faith, he says, involves a "humbling" of ourselves before God, in
which there is a realistic "acknowledging our-

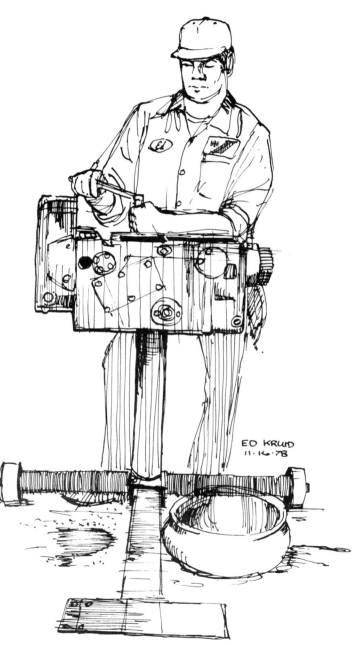

ED KRUID
11·16·78

selves to be such as we really are, without
presuming to trust in any thing in ourselves . . ."
(Art. XXIII). The Confession frankly adds that in
justification lies "the blessedness of man." The
promised Savior of Article XVII, who "would
make [man] blessed," has done His work.

Justification

Let us stop for a moment to see where we are in
the overall scheme of the Confession. As we
learned in chapter 9, the Belgic Confession has a
broad trinitarian frame. It first deals with God
(with revelation, Trinity, providence, creation).
Then it deals with Christ (with man's fall and
need of a Savior, election, incarnation, atonement, justification, intercession). Finally it deals
with the Holy Spirit (with the Christian life of
sanctification, church, sacraments, relation to
government, and last things).

In chapter 17 we considered the incarnation,
which has to do with the person of Christ. We are
now concerned, however, with Christ's work.
Thus, in chapter 18 we reflected on Christ's gracious and courageous atonement. What we now
want to know is how this work benefits us. The
Heidelberg Catechism asks pointedly, "What
good does it do you, however, to believe all this?"
(Question 59). So we ask: How does the atonement affect us? How do its benefits get to us? The
answer, in Articles XXII and XXIII, is that the
great effect of the atonement is our *justification*.
This benefit gets to us through *faith*.

Justification is acceptance. We had been guilty,
and our guilt had alienated us from God. But (to
use the legal, Reformed language) Christ satisfied
God's justice by taking our penalty. God's response was twofold: He both forgave our sins and
also transferred (or "imputed") Christ's righteousness to us. Now He accepts us for Christ's
sake.

Let us get our terms and concepts straight. The
first part of justification, just mentioned, is
variously described as the forgiveness (XV), or
purging (XXI), or remission (XXI, XXIII), or
covering (XXIII) of our sin. These descriptions,
though differently shaded, come to about the
same thing. The second part of justification is
positive. Something bad (sin's guilt) has been
done away; now something good is put in its
place. Thus the "merits," "holy works,"
"righteousness," "obedience," or "benefits" of
Christ are imputed to us so that they "become
ours" (XXII, XXIII). These two parts together
make up what we could call—again with only
slightly different nuances— justification (XXII),
or salvation (XXII, XXIII), or reconciliation

(XXI), or deliverance (XV, XVI), or even election (XVI).

In the Reformed understanding justification is a single, legal act of God's. It is not a continuing process of some kind, as was taught at the Roman Catholic Council of Trent. Reformed theologians also believe, of course, that by a gradual process believers are increasingly rid of sin. But they call that process *sanctification* (see chapter 20) and distinguish it as a later process from the initial, once-for-all act of God which justifies.

In justification sin does not suddenly disappear. It remains. But guilt does disappear. We are forgiven. And though we are not actually or "properly" righteous (that is, without sin), we are *declared* righteous. We are seen as, regarded as, accepted as righteous. We are credited with Christ-righteousness just as if we really deserved to go scot-free. The Heidelberg Catechism puts it very clearly:

God grants and credits to me
the perfect satisfaction, righteousness, and
    holiness of Christ,
  as if I had never sinned nor been a sinner,
  as if I had been as perfectly obedient
    as Christ was obedient for me.

This powerful answer (60), with its memorable pair of *as if* clauses, concludes: "All I need to do is to accept this gift of God with a believing heart."

Faith

All I need to do is to accept my acceptance. Justification is by faith. Or, is it *through* faith?

It is the latter, and the difference is important. Why? Because "by" suggests that faith itself justifies us. Yet it does not. God justifies, by His grace. Faith is only the given channel through which we receive this benefit. De Bres is remarkably eager to make this clear. After paraphrasing Paul in Romans 3:27,28 ("we are justified by faith alone"), he hastens to add: "However, to speak more clearly, we do not mean that faith itself justifies us, for it is only an instrument with which we embrace Christ our righteousness." Faith is "only an instrument." That is why it is better to say that we are justified "through" faith than "by" faith. "For by grace you have been saved through faith" (Eph. 2:8).

People sometimes get this wrong. They imagine that faith is the sort of good work which God admires, and then rewards with salvation. So they bear down, grit their teeth, and try to crank out an acceptable level of belief. They think that after all this work and sweat to produce a shaky belief, God will surely be pleased and gratified.

It is a mistake. Faith is not some do-it-yourself attempt to believe what is unbelievable. It is rather, as Calvin said, a certain kind of *knowledge*, an unshakable inner persuasion of the divine grace toward us. This is not merely "doubtful opinion." Nor is it only intellectual conviction. Calvin insisted that the whole person is involved in faith. There is even a feeling or experiencing of the goodness and sweetness of God. Altogether, besides the beliefs that certain persons (such as Christ) exist and that certain events (such as Christ's resurrection) have occured, faith includes a personal, trusting *attachment* to the Christ whose benefits we receive.

Union with Christ

Now we can see why Article XXII uses attachment language. Faith is an instrument. But one of the things it is an instrument *for* is attachment to Christ—what theologians call "union with Christ." This phrase covers all those strange New Testament claims that believers are "in Christ," that Christ is "in us," or that we do certain things "with Christ."

In this union, as de Bres has it, faith plays two closely related roles. First, when we get it, faith possesses Jesus Christ and "appropriates Him." We get mysteriously close to Christ through faith—so close that, as de Bres dares to say twice, we "embrace" Him. In this bonding, or union, the benefits of Christ—notably justification in its two parts—flow to us. But secondly, "faith is an instrument that keeps us in communion with Him." This is a *continuing* union.

So far we may nod, or nod off, piously. We have heard such talk before. But what concretely does this "embracing" or "appropriating" or "communion" with Christ amount to? How does it work?

Perhaps we cannot say with certainty. It is no accident that union with Christ is sometimes called "mystical union." Calvin said we cannot so much analyze as experience it. Still, we know something about it. We know, for example, that we must not take it too narrowly. For in the New Testament (and in Calvin) union with Christ is as broad or large a description of our relation to Him as we have. It includes, but is never limited to, such things as personal piety and the attempt to "follow in His steps."

The incarnation and atonement are graciously carried out, Paul says, to make *all* things new (Col. 1:20). God was in Christ reconciling the *world* to Himself (II Cor. 5:19). There is an unimaginably broad, cosmic sweep to the work of Christ. In Articles XXII and XXIII, of course, the Confession limits itself pretty much to justification. But what Christ did had much wider results too. Thus, in later articles, we will see some of the vaster implications of Christ's work and our union with Him "in all His benefits": Sanctification, or new life (XXIV); the church, "dispersed over the whole world," which everyone is "in duty bound to join" (XXVII, XXVIII); church government and sacraments which God uses to strengthen faith and to confirm justification and sanctification (XXIX-XXXV); the state's reordered role in promoting the kingdom of God (XXXVI); finally, the cosmic judgment associated with the last days and the second coming of Christ (XXXVII)—all these things derive in some way from the cross and resurrection, and all are implications of union with Christ.

In *All Things Made New*, Lewis Smedes emphasizes this broad, deeply biblical perspective. Union with Christ is not merely a sentimental "walking in the garden" with Jesus (where the dew is still on the roses). It is not merely an attempt to "do what Jesus did" morally. Nor are we by love so personally swallowed up into Christ that we and God become "eine Kuche" (one cake), as Luther said in one of his many unguarded moments. Union with Christ is rather that vast communion with Christ in which all that we are and do is part of His new creation. By the cross and resurrection, God has created a whole new cosmic situation, routing the "powers" (Col. 2:15) and beginning the renewal of all creation by His elected agents. Smedes sums it up:

> The phrase "in Christ" is an epigram for the total reality of the new community under Christ's lordship, a community called by His voice, ruled by His Spirit, and forming the embryo of a total new race and a whole new creation united and renewed by Him.

In this vast context we have to hear de Bres' talk about communion with Christ. He is following Calvin, and will be followed by all those stalwart Reformed thinkers who see the divine intent of re-creation in arts, sciences, government, economics, education—in the whole range of created life. This field of calling for God's redeemed community is as broad and wide as the world.

Christ Alone and Faith Alone

So faith embraces Christ "in all His benefits." And it embraces nothing else. Both articles are firm against the Roman Catholic position (affirmed at the Council of Trent, January, 1547) that in justification, faith must be completed by obedience. For Trent, it is not Christ alone who justifies, but Christ and the believer together. It is not through faith alone that justification is received, but through faith as completed by voluntary obedience.

Lutheran and Reformed thinkers deny this. In fact, justification through faith *alone* is (in Calvin's phrase) "the hinge of the Reformation." Faith is the only instrument we need. It moreover attaches us to Christ alone. Here the Reformation attempted to grow a hedge between Christ and the hosts of auxiliary saviors. We all tend to be polytheists, trusting in "Christ *and* . . . ." We trust Christ and saints, Christ and the American Way, Christ and religion, Christ and social security, Christ and "a little bit o' luck." Against all medieval and modern polytheism, the Confession asserts that faith seeks "nothing more besides Him [Christ]." Else He is only "half a Savior."

Now Catholics have always been suspicious of this Lutheran and Reformed way of understanding justification and faith. They have thought that it leads to laxity and moral inertia. But the Reformed *do* have a place for good works, as we saw in our study of the Catechism's third section. It is just that we regard faithful obedience as a *result* of justification instead of as an ingredient in it. The Reformation was very much afraid of any idea that our salvation depends partly on us. For then we are tempted either to false confidence ("I can make it on my own") or else to the sort of black despair ("I'll never make it") which tormented the early Luther.

The Holy Spirit's Work

Article XXII begins with a mention of the third person of the Trinity. As the Confession moves into the application of the work of Christ to believers, more and more the Holy Spirit will come into view. Here in XXII the Spirit "kindles in our hearts" an upright faith. Since Pentecost, the Spirit has often been associated with light, or illumination; with fire, sparking, kindling, igniting. The point here is that the faith which accepts God's acceptance and which binds us into union with Christ is not of our own making. It is a gift. It comes from the outside. Grace is a flame downward which makes faith flare up. In this our cold hearts are strangely warmed. We who had been bored or rebellious now find ourselves mysteriously attracted to the things of the faith. They seem believable. The preaching of the Word, as on Pentecost, begins to *take*. We begin to know for the first time the sense of being rooted, secured, and deeply accepted by God and the com-

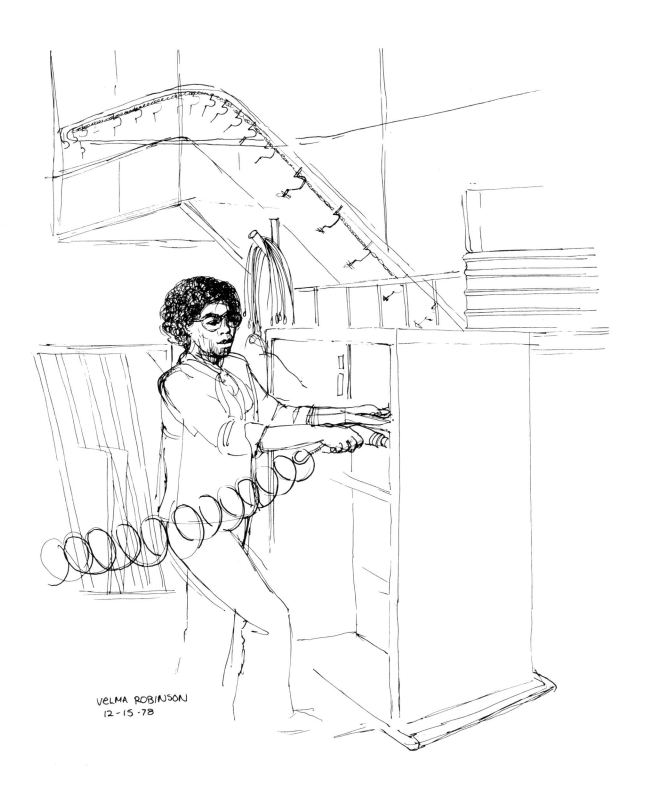

VELMA ROBINSON
12-15-78

munity of believers. Christian faith has been kindled, and as we look back, we confess with de Bres that we did not do the kindling. Even in dark or dingy moments we know what union with Christ means. It means that nothing "in all creation, will be able to separate us from the love of God in Christ Jesus our Lord" (Rom. 8:39).

But once again we must be sure to take the long and broad view. The faith which unites us with Christ must flower with obedience in every area of our lives. Faith is meant to issue in those good works which seek to transform society in the midst of all of its old brokenness and sadness. The sanctification to which we now proceed must be as deep and wide as human life itself. To mention just one example, it was John Calvin who said that a most important test of our faith is how we treat the poor! For God "sends us the poor as His receivers" (Sermon on Deut. 15:11-13).

Conclusion

The Confession ends its treatment of justification and faith with the sort of warmth and personal assurance which reminds one of the Heidelberg Catechism. With another striking reference to the "trembling" of Adam and his desperate attempt to fix up, hitch up, and cover up after his sin, de Bres assures us that since the second Adam has come, we may now have "confidence" in approaching God. The basis of this confidence, as in the Catechism, is that we are not our own. We do not come to God claiming any merit in ourselves. We come in humility, accepting ourselves "as we really are" because we have been accepted by God. The "terror" of a trembling Adam or a guilty Luther; the "dread" which afflicts such anxious humorists as Woody Allen ("Death wouldn't be so bad if you didn't have to be there"); the alienated "fear" of God which is struck deep into the sensitive soul—from all these things we are liberated through faith. If only this liberation could be gotten while we are teenagers, enthralled with the need for acceptance! If only it could be gotten to those desperate souls whose sweaty hands finally resort to violence! If only it could remain with all of us!

For, of course, all of us, no matter how Protestant we are, keep slipping back into the trap of "relying on ourselves." That is why de Bres ends Article XXIII with a warning. It still applies. Even today, many people brought up in the Christian church are inexplicably ignorant of justification through faith alone. Somehow they have missed the point of hundreds of sermons. If you ask such people (on a "Kennedy method" evangelism visit, or on some other occasion) why God should let them into His heaven, they are still entirely likely to say something like this: "Well, I've always *tried* to live a good life."

"I've always tried." There is a touching humility here (no claim to total success). But there is also the same dismal old idea of self-salvation which nearly wrecked the church in the Middle Ages and which keeps infecting the lives and worship of Protestants today. Somehow many of us cannot be satisfied with Christ alone and faith alone. Thus a number of Catholics still turn to saints. Some Protestants turn to success gospels and self-help religions. More than a few seek comfort in their assorted legalisms. They attend both Sunday services, give up cigars, read clear through the book of Leviticus, and are kind to granny and the kittens.

These things may be admirable. But they cannot save us. And "if we should appear before God, relying on ourselves or on any other creature, though ever so little, we should, alas! be consumed."

CHAPTER 20
Sanctification

Belgic Confession, Articles XXIV and XXV

Introduction

Many people who smoke cigarettes try to quit. Most try often. They say with Mark Twain: It's easy to stop smoking—I've done it a hundred times. But they know it isn't easy to stop smoking for good. Like alcohol or other drugs, cigarette smoking can hook a person. It becomes part of his life-style. He has regular times and seasons for lighting up. After a breakfast of pancakes and coffee is one good time. After an exam is another. With liquor, with friends, after dinner, at intermission, a person smokes. He *associates* smoking with these circumstances. His habit is deeply rooted into his life.

He knows he ought to stop. He believes the reports of danger to his health. He wants to clear the air inside him. Moreover, especially if he is a Christian, he may be aware that smoking has become much too important to him. That becomes distressingly clear whenever he tries to quit. He makes many false stops. Each time he fails. The very thought of a smokeless life fills him with anxiety and self-pity. He will be deprived! Nothing will be any fun anymore! Dinners, visits, victories, and defeats will all become flat and tasteless. Parties will drag. Tension will remain unrelieved. A gray future stretches miserably ahead.

But he trusts those who urge him to give up smoking. Trembling and unsure, he believes those who say all is not lost. After prayer and perseverance, with much sweat and determination, he succeeds. He gets over the hump and throws away his Camels forever. He may still have nightmares of succumbing and wake up feeling guilty. But in reality he has got a new life and life-style. He likes it. He tries, sometimes too hard, to convert others.

What about his old fears of a drab and joyless future? In a wonderful way, just the opposite turns out to be true. Food tastes good. (It may taste so good that the convert temporarily becomes a heavyweight.) Things smell better. Even the ex-smoker does. His sports and endurance improve. He is likely to feel stronger and more capable in general. He is free.

His liberation is, of course, a little allegory, a homely parallel to that great conversion Christians call "salvation." *Salvation* derives from a Latin word which means "health." Sinners become healthy again—not just after they quit smoking, but generally and everlastingly.

Articles XIV and XV taught us that the fallout from Adam's sin was a human "hereditary disease" of guilt and pollution. We are legally to blame; we are also fouled or tainted. Salvation restores us to health in both cases. Last chapter we saw how justification removes our *guilt*. We are accepted as blameless for Christ's sake. This chapter deals with the cure for *pollution*. It is called "sanctification" and has to do with holiness. Sanctification is the work of the *Spiritus Sanctus*, the *Holy* Spirit, and lasts a lifetime. Its goal is nothing less than perfection.

Articles XXIV and XXV say three main things about sanctification. They will be familiar to us from our study of Part III of the Heidelberg Catechism. They say, first, that true faith naturally flowers into good works; secondly, that these works are both stimulated and rewarded by the grace of God; thirdly, that the standard for this goodness is the law or will of God.

Faith and Good Works

Article XXIV begins by linking justification and sanctification. The link is faith. "This true faith" which has accepted God's acceptance now further "excites man to the practice of those works which God has commanded in His Word." Ursinus speaks at this point of gratitude. De Bres talks about love. There is in the redeemed life a "love of God" and "faith working through love" (Gal. 5:6). We have been declared righteous by God even though we are sinners. That is justification. Now we are gradually to become *actually* more righteous. That is sanctification. The latter follows hard after the former.

What does the faith-love combination achieve? Two main things. There is both a freeing "from the bondage of sin" and also a "new life." They go on together. As our smoker is gradually unhooked, he begins to enjoy new breath and health. As a conceited person is liberated from his need for applause, his openness to others and new happiness begin.

But a caution: Liberation and sanctification in the Bible are vaster than we might think. We sometimes think of freedom from sin and holiness (*sanctification* means "the process of becoming holy") only narrowly in connection with personal vices and individual faults. That is a mistake.

Surely sanctification and liberation are personal. But they are also corporate. An oppressed Israel, a whole nation, is liberated "out of the house of bondage" to become "a holy nation" (Ex. 19:6; 20:2). Part of the sanctifying of this nation includes the divine insistence on social justice. Thus the Lord who "executes justice for the oppressed" also "sets the prisoner free" (Ps. 146:7). Sanctification within a Christian community may indeed cause some people to give up oppression as well as smoking, to be freed from racism as well as pornography. The passionately Reformed Scots Confession of 1560 mentions "oppression" and "cruel tyranny" as sins from which the sinner must be sanctified in order to show his faith. Both his own bondage to power and his victims' bondage to him may be broken by the power of God.

Then new life begins. It too is both personal and corporate. We remember that the whole context for de Bres' discussion of sanctification is "communion with Him [Christ] in all His benefits" (Article XXII). New life is a benefit. And we do not get it in splendid isolation from others.

MARLYN VISSER FAMILY
11·16·78

After all, one of the main images in the Bible for what we call "regeneration" is rebirth. We must be "born again" (John 3:3). Sometimes this phrase becomes the hallmark of those who use it exclusively for "personal" salvation by "my personal Savior," but it need not refer only to that. If it seems to us that birth is a pretty private affair (except, of course, if one thinks of twins or more), we might also consider the fact that the world did not start when we were born. Each of us was born into a preexistent world and culture and family. Other people knew and did things long before we arrived. We only joined them. Similarly, when a person is born again, he is not a pioneer in the faith. He becomes a member of a prior community. So when the Confession speaks of "a new man" and "a new life," it means the kind of newness which the other members of the church will recognize. They have seen this wonderful thing happen before.

The new life is marked by the flowering of good works. All the Reformed leaders were sensitive to the Roman Catholic charge that the Reformation made Christianity too easy. Indeed, there were some radicals in the Reformation who, at least for a time, condoned moral laxity and lawlessness. That is why de Bres is so careful here to deny that justifying faith "makes men remiss in a pious and holy life." Just the opposite is true, he says. It is only when you are free both from pride and anxiety, both from "self-love" and "fear of damnation" that you can do any good at all. Only when your salvation has already been graciously secured are you free not only *from* sin but also *for* good deeds to others. The Confession puts it as strongly as possible: "It is impossible that this holy faith can be unfruitful in man."

The imagery is, of course, from the Bible and from husbandry. Faith is "a good root," in contrast to the bad root of original sin (in Article XV), and produces good works like the fruit of a tree (cf. Matt. 12:33, John 15:5). The idea is that faith now *naturally* (by second nature!) produces the fruit of righteousness (Rom. 1:17). There is an instinctive, inevitable, organic connection between faith and works. The secure, justified person naturally goes out of himself to serve God and others. He is no longer obsessed with his own salvation or paralyzed by his own ego-needs. He is rooted, stable, like a good "tree planted by streams of water" (Ps. 1:3). He knows nothing can ever separate him from the love of God. Therefore he dares to risk himself and to extend himself for God and neighbor. He dares to extend himself for his own family. Bullinger of Zurich frankly called the home duties of parents "in

God's sight holy and truly good works" (Second Helvetic Confession, chap. 29). A Christian does not extend himself bitterly.

As C. S. Lewis says, there are some people who "'live for others,' but always in a discontented, grumbling way—always wondering why the others do not notice it more and always making a martyr of [themselves]." Such people are "a far greater pest" than if they had stayed selfish. They are a bit like the laborers in the vineyard (Matt. 20:1-16) or the elder brother in the parable of the prodigal son (Luke 15:25-32). They do not yet have enough of the new life to prize it.

Grace and Sanctification

Justification is completely an act of God's. We play no role in it except to receive it as an accomplished fact. But in sanctification we do play a continuing role. We are called upon to exercise faith, to do good works, and to live for God's glory. God operates in sanctification. But so, in our own way, do we. Faith is not only "wrought in man by the hearing of the Word of God and the operation of the Holy Spirit," but it also causes "him to live a new life." Reformed theologians have always been willing to talk cautiously of cooperation in sanctification. God works salvation *in* us; we work it *out* (Phil. 2:12,13).

Still, de Bres wants to shut the door against pride and the perverse idea that God owes us a reward for goodness. He observes that in an important sense good works are God's gift to us—not ours to Him: "We are indebted to God for the good works we do, and not He to us."

Why? Because it is God who stimulates us to lead the new life. From election on through atonement and justification, God is at work. Faith, too, is kindled by His Spirit. And for the birth, growth, and final glory of the Christian life we are indebted to Him. That is why a faithful Christian might say about his good deeds or his preservation from moral collapse: "Thank God, I was able to help," or "There, but for the grace of God, go I." Saints know that even the best of us is not immune to temptation and that even the strongest of us may lapse into gross sin. It is most distressing, but not really surprising in this twisted world, that a kindly person is found to be an embezzler or a respected person is discovered in the wrong bed. Sanctification needs God's continuing work. Else we stagnate, or even go back to our old ways. It also needs His stimulus. Sins of omission, after all, are at least as hard to overcome as the other kind.

But, by grace, we make progress. Certain old habits begin to lose their grip on us and certain

ALICE & RICHARD VELDMAN
11-13-78

gracious new ones take their place. What does all of this transformation get us? Nothing—by itself. The Reformation was deeply concerned to guard against any suggestion that we have a claim on God because of what we do or are. Even the person who is far advanced in saintliness is still tainted by sin. There is no perfection in this life. That must wait. So "we do not deny that God rewards good works, but it is through His grace that He crowns His gifts." Our works have no merit on their own.

The Law of God

In Article XXV de Bres makes a point similar to the one made by Ursinus in Part III of the Catechism. The good works which mark our sanctifi-cation are not just any deeds that appeal to us, but those which are in conformity with God's will, with what "God has commanded in His Word" (XXIV). Of course, we do not live under the Old Testament ceremonial law. We do not follow the minute rules for cleansing, atonement, and observance of holy places and days. For Christians all of this apparatus has been dismantled since the coming of Christ: ". . . he entered once for all into the Holy Place, taking not the blood of goats and calves but his own blood, thus securing an eternal redemption" (Heb. 9:12). The ceremonies were mere "shadows" waiting for the light, mere "figures" or silhouettes, waiting for the flesh-and-blood reality.

Yet, as the Confession says, "we still use the testimonies taken out of the law and the prophets." We do not abandon the Old Testament as some early Christian heretics did. We need it to help "regulate our life in all honorableness." We need *reformed* good works. This is where the distinctively Reformed "third use of the law" comes in (chap. 8).

Notice, however, that de Bres mentions not only the law but also the prophets. We still read Amos, Micah, and all the others for our sanctification. Indeed, we learn much of its communal dimension from the great social justice teaching of these prophets. To pursue justice, to heed the cry of the poor, to fight oppression and liberate the down-trodden is to give evidence of new life!

Most Reformed churches have recognized this. Calvin was deeply concerned with economic justice and the questions surrounding such things as usury. The Scots Confession, as we have seen, has a very political ring to its treatment of sanctification. In the nineteenth century, the great Reformed movement in the Netherlands, associated with the name of Abraham Kuyper, followed in this tradition. Kuyper and the Kuyperians have always seen the transformation of culture in all of its parts as a main thrust of the redeemed community and a true sign of sanctification. This vision has had a most enlightening influence on Dutch Reformed Christianity, keeping it from understanding faith and life too narrowly, guarding against the heretical notion that Christ came only to change a few of our personal vices and bad habits.

In this line of thinking, there is acknowledgment that the *church* must be sanctified (Eph. 5:26). A whole church grows in grace and in the knowledge of our Lord. There is a communal willingness to submit oneself to the will of the Lord. That is why various synods have spoken about the will of God in such areas as education, corporate responsibility, racism, and war. These social ethics statements are intended to help our sanctification—so that faith may be supplemented with virtue, and virtue with knowledge (II Pet. 1:5).

The aim of all this is the enhancing of God's name. We are to reflect creditably upon our Redeemer. We are "to regulate our life . . . to the glory of God."

Conclusion

The Confession's treatment of the redeemed life is admittedly not quite as rich as that of the Catechism. It seems a bit bloodless by comparison. But we should remember that there is more to come. Where the Catechism has little to say about church and government (both ecclesiastical and secular), the Confession will have much to say. So we take the best from both documents!

Perhaps the most memorable of contemporary Christian reflections on sanctification is that of C. S. Lewis, to whom we have referred above. Lewis remarks that so few of us know what we are in for when we become converted. In one way, the process of giving ourselves over to new management is easy. We had been trying to lead double lives, trying "to remain what we call 'ourselves,' to keep personal happiness as our great aim in life, and yet at the same time be 'good.' " It will not work. It is too hard. We must be transformed:

> It may be hard for an egg to turn into a bird: it would be a jolly sight harder for it to learn to fly while remaining an egg. We are like eggs at present. And you cannot go on indefinitely being just an ordinary, decent egg. We must be hatched or go bad. (*Mere Christianity*)

The transformation, while easier than trying to live with an impossible compromise between God and the world, is not without its struggle. The Christian images (the dying of the old, the birth of the new) suggest that mortification, labor, and labor pains will be necessary. In sanctification, as in childbirth, there is no going back. We must "go the whole route," sit for the whole treatment, let God have His way with us. In a parable from George MacDonald, Lewis likens the process of sanctification to the remodeling of a house:

> Imagine yourself as a living house. God comes in to rebuild that house. At first, perhaps, you can understand what he is doing. He is getting the drains right and stopping the leaks in the roof and so on: you knew that those jobs needed doing and so you are not surprised. But presently he starts knocking the house about in a way that hurts abominably and does not seem to make sense. What on earth is he up to? The explanation is that he is building quite a different house from the one you thought of —throwing out a new wing here, putting on an extra floor there, running up towers, making courtyards. You thought you were going to be made into a decent little cottage: but he is building a palace. He intends to come and live in it himself. (*Mere Christianity*)

CHAPTER 21
Intercession

Belgic Confession, Article XXVI

Introduction

It is sometimes said that a tax revolt, or some other sign of citizen unrest, puts "the fear of God" into politicians. No doubt that is one of the few times they know such fear. The fear of God is no longer a major part of popular piety. In the modern era and in democratic cultures it is thought unseemly to bow or scrape before a superior or to hold him in awe. You do not acknowledge your "betters" with a lowered head, or a sidestep, or a doffing of your tattered cap, because you have no betters. Everybody is equal before the law. From this principle the culture has gone on to a general approval of equalizing, leveling, and homogenizing. Even the President of the United States carries his own luggage. Many people like that.

Indeed, democratic tendencies are to be generally applauded. Class and status divisions gain no backing from the Bible, and have caused untold human suffering. But part of the residue from the democratizing of Western culture is religiously regrettable—even disastrous. People have tried to include God in the leveling process. They have little fear of God or His wrath. They do not think God punishes sin—at least not severely. They have in general lost much of the ancient sense of mystery and awe in His presence. People have tried to cut a transcendent God down to size.

They do this in many ways, some of them unconscious. They pray with a casual or familiar tone of voice. They refer, if they are like the manager of the major league baseball team in Los Angeles, to "the great Dodger in the sky." They adopt Jesus as a pop-idol and put Him on the cover of *Time*. When they begin worship services, they do not say solemnly "Our help is in the name of the Lord." They grin and say "Good morning!" or even "Hi!" Those who are far advanced in familiarity compose songs with such prayers for titles as "Drop-kick me, Jesus, through the goal posts of life." For many of them God is a chum.

Article XXVI of the Confession will not make much sense to such people. They will not see what the fuss is all about. For anyone who believes that he can easily go right to the top, the notion of an intercessor will seem quaint and alien. An intercessor is a person who acts, or especially who pleads, on behalf of another. He is a go-between. And the Confession was written for a time when ordinary Christians who wished to approach God desperately sensed the need for such a person. In fact, the Reformation faced the problem of trying to cut back or limit the number of intercessors.

The medieval Roman Church, it must be said, did not help the situation. As P. Y. De Jong has observed, the church managed to portray even Jesus Christ as so unapproachable a figure that "the very name of the Savior filled men's hearts with fear" (*The Church's Witness to the World, II*). The pious Christians of the Middle Ages dreaded God. Their tendency was just the opposite of the modern Christians. Instead of familiarity or boredom with God and the idea of God, medieval Christians felt terror and smallness in God's presence. And they could not turn for comfort to Christ. Christ Himself was thought to be exalted above the hope and consolation of ordinary believers.

So they did the only thing left. They turned to saints. They prayed for help to those who had been sinners like themselves, but were not perfected. They joined with others to gather and venerate the relics of the saints. In worship, they begged the souls of the dead for protection, guidance, and for intercession with Christ. It did not take long for cults and legends to gather around the memory of a saint. Each believer could choose a hero or favorite and could devote his/her attention and prayer to such a creature.

The Reformers tried to cut the nerve of saint worship. One Reformed confession said tersely, "God alone is to be invoked through the mediation of Christ alone." For trembling, wary sixteenth century Christians this alternative was frightening. It was too bold! Thus, we see in the likes of Article XXVI an attempt to encourage and reassure hesitant Christians. God knows they are sinners and unworthy. But because of "the worthiness of the Lord Jesus Christ," they may dare to pray to God through Him: "For there is no creature, either in heaven or on earth, who loves us more than Jesus Christ."

Let us look more closely.

The Medieval Situation

The Reformation may in many ways be regarded as a simplifying process. The Bible alone is to be our authority—not the Bible and tradition. Grace alone saves us—not grace completed by obedience. Salvation is to be received through faith alone—not through faith and works. And, in this article, God is to be approached through Christ alone—not by way of Christ and the saints. Everywhere the Reformers scraped off some of the crust which had developed over the ages.

What was the origin of belief in the intercession of saints? That is very hard to say. The New Testament says nothing about the prayers of believers in heaven for believers on earth. But it was not long before the early church began to express an interest in the help of those who had died "in the Lord." First, it was especially martyrs who were mentioned as possible intercessors. Later, as the split in the church between ordinary and "wholly consecrated" believers widened, virgins, hermits, and all heroes of the faith became cult figures thought to have intercessory power. By the Middle Ages, the growth of interest in and appeal to saints was largely unchecked.

The theology behind all of this seems partly right and partly wrong to Protestants. What seems wrong is found in the connection between saint-invocation and the Roman penitential and merit system. Saints were thought to have accumulated extra merits by their heroism—merits which their younger brothers and sisters might draw upon. This belief, of course, ties saint-intercession into the whole Roman conception of how salvation is accomplished and received. On

this Protestants and Catholics still devoutly disagree. Listen to a contemporary Catholic:

> In the 16th century the heads of the Protestant reform rose in violent revolt against the Catholic doctrine concerning the intercession of the Saints and their invocation. If these attacks were occasioned also by the exaggerations and abuses existing in this sector, it must be said that the true motive of these attacks is found in the Protestant concepts of the Incarnation, Redemption, justification, merit, and the Church, insofar as they are opposed to Catholic teaching. To counteract the wrong interpretations of the Protestants, the Council of Trent . . . solemnly reaffirmed Catholic doctrine . . . .
>
> (P. Molinari, *The Catholic Encyclopedia*, vol.12)

Protestants, of course, think their interpretations are right and not wrong. But one feature of belief in saint intercession seems acceptable—even laudable—to Protestants. Part of the root of the doctrine of the intercession of "dead" saints is the belief in the intercession of living ones. Protestants believe just as firmly as Catholics do in the need of those who are "members one of another" to pray for each other. "Please pray for me" is a request made across the universal church. It is based on the conviction that believers are in Christ together, and is stimulated by the numerous examples of the intercessions by Christ and the biblical saints. Christ's high priestly prayer is one long intercession (John 17). And St. Paul hardly wrote a letter without mentioning to his churches that he was praying for them, and without asking for their prayers for him in return.

So far, so good. The living pray for the living. But Catholics extend this idea. If the saints on earth pray for other believers, why suppose that they stop when received into heaven? In the Middle Ages, as we have already seen, common believers especially welcomed the belief in saint intercession because of their dread of God. The more buffers or layers between them and God, the better. Especially Mary, "Mother of God," became a favorite buffer. "Mary, Mother of God, pray for us" was (and is) on the lips of millions of ordinary people. Soon the Hebrews' "cloud of witnesses" became a crowd of witnesses. There were patron saints, saints for holy days (now holidays), city saints, country saints, and even occupational saints. Thus carpenters could approach St. Joseph, hunters Hubert the Hunter, physicians St.

Luke, and so on. Eugene Osterhaven tells more:

> Sufferers from toothache pleaded with St. Appolonia for relief, for she had had all her teeth extracted rather than deny Christ. St. Florian guarded against fire, St. Nicholas in time of shipwreck, St. Crispin all cobblers, and St. Anthony those who drove mules. St. Ulrich heard the prayers of those whose places were infested with rats . . . .   (*Our Confession of Faith*)

The Reformation wanted to sweep all of this away. True, the Catholic counter-reformation showed real sensitivity to the dangers and abuses in this area, but the theology which nurtured saint intercession remained. Indeed, as we have seen above, it remains today. Among more liberal Catholics, the practice of praying to Christ or God via the saints may be diminishing—perhaps along with a general belief in the supernatural. Among older Catholics, and in such traditionally Catholic countries as Spain and Italy, the practice continues. It is specifically endorsed by Vatican II (1962 to 1965) as an implication of the solidarity of the church. Sensitive to Protestant charges that devotion to saints interferes with union with Christ, Vatican II is quick to assert the contrary:

> Because some have imagined that the veneration and invocation of the saints, as practiced by Catholics, necessarily interferes with the relationship which the Christian should have to Christ, the Council here points out that a properly ordered devotion to the saints should cement more closely the believer's relation to Christ.

With respect to Mary, "glorious, ever-Virgin," and "Queen of all":

> The maternal duty of Mary toward men in no way obscures or diminishes the unique meditation of Christ, but rather shows its power.
> (*The Documents of Vatican II*)

Christ Our Only Intercessor

Reformed believers disagree. De Bres, and Calvin before him, found the medieval proliferation of saints to be uncomfortably redolent of paganism. It seemed to them that a bevy, a host, a panoply of creatures was getting in between Christ and the believer. For the Reformed in the sixteenth century, any intervention of that kind had the tang and flavor of idolatry. They did not hesitate to say so—often in colorful language.

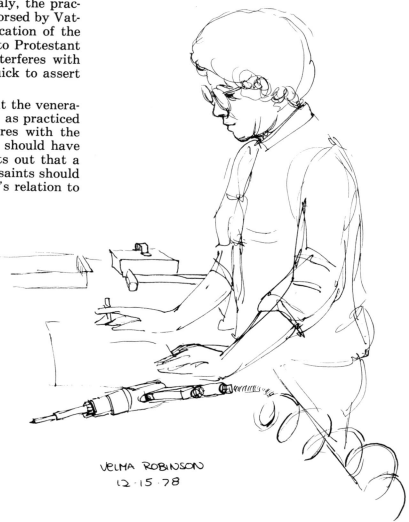

VELMA ROBINSON
12·15·78

So Article XXVI, the longest article in the Confession, insists on Christ alone as Intercessor. Much of the article is a series of biblical quotations. Passages from Hebrews on the high-priesthood of Christ (cf. Art. XXI) are amply cited. Jesus' own self-description as "the way" is quoted. With all of this passage work, the Confession aims to reassure hesitant and fearful believers. In effect it says: "The Bible itself, Christ Himself, tells you that you may approach God through Him who died for you. You do not need to work your way up through layers of departed saints. In fact, you must not do this."

The article begins with a reaffirmation of the incarnation. In Jesus Christ divine and human natures are united. As we know, the Bible teaches that Christ represents God to us. He speaks (John 12:49,50) and acts (John 14:31) on the Father's behalf. But the Confession emphasizes the other side of the biblical picture; namely, that Christ also represents us to God. He speaks (Rom. 8:34, Heb. 7:25) and acts (Heb. 6:20) on our behalf. Weaving together testimonies from John, Hebrews, and Paul, the Confession uses several biblical terms to characterize this representative role of Christ.

Christ is our "access" (Rom. 5:2; Eph. 2:18, 3:12). He is a way through. This sort of road imagery is familiar to anyone who has traveled or bought secluded property. In either case one is interested in access routes. But here the access is a person. One goes to God *via*, by way of, Christ. "Access to the divine Majesty...would otherwise be barred against us," but now we have in high places a way through. We have a highway to God.

Mediator (I Tim. 2:5, Heb. 8:6) is a general term for someone who stands between two sides and, as suggested above, represents the one to the other. He tries to bring them together. He is a negotiator, even an arbitrator.

Advocate is a narrower term for someone who pleads the cause of another. The biblical word (*paraclete*) is more usually associated with the Holy Spirit than with Christ. But both the Holy Spirit (John 14:16, Rom. 8:26) and Christ (I John 2:1) are called paracletes.

For us this is a most mysterious idea. How do Christ and the Holy Spirit plead our cause before the Father? What did Paul mean when he described the Spirit's intercession as "sighs too deep for words" (Rom. 8:26)? In some deep way beyond our comprehension such intercession overcomes the dark testimony of him (Satan) who is our "adversary" (I Pet. 5:8) and "accuser" (Rev. 12:10).

Christ's intercession gives us consolation and peace (John 14:27), "the peace of God which passes all understanding" (Phil. 4:7). This is, indeed, the way de Bres explains it. He emphasizes his "consolation" theme here in several ways. Jesus Christ can intercede for us because He is "the righteous." Nobody "loves us more than Jesus Christ." Therefore He "ought in no wise to affright us by His majesty." He understands us and our needs. If we imagine that the gap between heaven and earth is so great that God cannot speak our language, or understand our unhappiness, or sympathize with our suffering and weakness, we have to look again—and look at Christ. We do not have to deal with a God who is infinitely removed. The same God who made the heavens and the earth has been represented among us. The high way has swung low. The Lord has become a servant. A member of the holy Trinity has been, and still is, one of us. He has felt the tug of our temptations, known the sad feelings of griminess and defeat in a prostitute, the bitter hopelessness of a leper, the patient, suffering love of a father who waits for a disgraceful son to come home. He has lost friends, lost popularity, lost life itself. From all of this, we are to take consolation: "For in that he himself hath suffered being tempted, he is able to succor them that are tempted." We are to forsake all others and cling to Him, "since it has pleased God to give us His own Son as an Advocate."

That is the point of this article. The gap between wretched creatures and a holy God could only be bridged through some Way who was both. So it has. Of course, believers are still sinners. They still need mercy and grace and help. That is why they must never come to God casually or familiarly. Yet we are now allowed a measure of sanctified *boldness* in our approach to God: "Let us therefore draw near with boldness unto the throne of grace, that we may receive mercy, and may find grace to help us in time of need."

Conclusion

An article which exhorts Christians to approach God with more boldness seems a bit superfluous in the modern atmosphere. People today may need not more, but less, boldness in their approach. The article is a little like a fire hose offered in a flood.

Yet there is here both a warning and a reminder which still seem apt—even for Protestants. The warning is that believers must never trust another creature to do for them what only Christ can do. Dependence on others, particularly if the others are Christian heroes, can easily begin in respect and end up in something like worship. The danger of belief in saint intercession is idolatry. And the misery, even the murders and mass suicide, which may result from such idolatry has been impressively relevant in various Western cult movements in recent years. The danger is always that we may be distracted from Christ—that we may become gradually more fascinated with someone or something else. No Protestant buffer—no formal worship, or man-made creed, or legalist or utopian program—may ever plead our worth before God. The result of such substitutions is always idolatry and disaster.

In Acts there is a memorable episode in which Paul and Barnabas stand before the citizens of Lystra. The stunned locals are convinced that Zeus and Hermes have made another landing, and they are ready to kiss the dirt at the missionaries' feet. A horrified Paul and Barnabas lift these groveling human beings from the dust and say something for all the ages. In every age of hero worship and creature idolatry, the word is fresh: "Men, why are you doing this? We also are men, of like nature with you, and bring you good news, that you should turn from these vain things to a living God. . . ." (Acts 14:15). De Bres has a passage like this in mind when he says that the saints themselves "steadfastly rejected" all tendencies to elevate them into demi-gods.

Besides the warning, there is a reminder to be gleaned from reflection on this material. The reminder leads us into chapter 22.

It is this: Part of what the medieval church, and Roman Catholicism today, has been looking for in the intercession of the saints is valuable. They have been after a sense of mystical solidarity in the church. They wanted to foster the idea that we are not in Christ alone, that there is a great communion of the members of His body with Him and with each other, and that those who have died in Him are still members of His body. All of that is a necessary reminder.

As a matter of fact, for all we know, the departed saints *do* intercede for us. Maybe St. Paul still pleads for the saints who are *now* in Corinth. Maybe St. C. S. Lewis advocates for Oxford dons. Possibly St. Abraham (Kuyper) prays for the needs of the Dutch Reformed.

We do not know. We have no biblical warrant for being very confident of the matter either way. So we stick to the biblical principle that Christ and the Spirit intercede for us, and proceed as if they do it alone. But it would be a great error to minimize the communion of the saints. We must never lapse into the intolerable individualism which neglects this communion. Let the Catholic practice—ranging, as it does, beyond biblical warrant—at least remind us that those who die in the Lord are *still* in the Lord as we are.

At the end of Article XXVI is a last word. We are to approach God (if we may say it reverently) "through channels." These are not many but one. So we pray "in Jesus' name," and "for Jesus' sake," and "through Jesus Christ, our Lord." This is an acknowledgment that He who prayed for Peter, for children, and for all His disciples, prays for us still.

Tonya Boluma
2ND GRADE
ORANGE CITY CHRISTIAN
11·16·78

CHAPTER 22
Church

Belgic Confession, Articles XXVII-XXIX

Introduction

Over ninety percent of American adults claim to believe in God. Most of them also think Christ is God's Son. But only about forty-five percent of them belong to a church. Many read the Bible, pray, and regard their belief as important. Some think the country needs nothing so much as a return to powerful, moral religion. A number of these unchurched believers identify themselves as "Protestants" or "Catholics" even though they are not members of any Protestant or Catholic church. Perhaps that tortured and self-denying Russian, Leo Tolstoy, speaks for some of them:

> The churches are arrogance, violence, usurpation, rigidity, death; Christianity is humility, penitence, submissiveness, progress, life.
>
> *(The Kingdom of God Is Within You)*

What accounts for this free-floating Christianity? Why do so many self-professed Christians see the inside of a church only when one is being demolished? In 1977, J. Russell Hale published a small book which studies the motives of the churchless and attempts to group them accordingly. After months of interviews, Hale concluded that only a tiny number of the unchurched are "True Unbelievers" (atheists and agnostics). Easily the largest number of them are what Hale calls "Publicans." These are people who complain that the church is full of hypocrites and Pharisees. They cannot stand to see other sinners look or act pious.

But there are others. The "Burned-Out" used to belong to churches and do church work, but came to resent the constant drain on their time and energy. The "Locked-Out" felt unwanted— some because of their life-style, and some merely because they were the "wrong" color. The "Anti-Institutionalists" regard Christianity as free and open but "organized religion" as stifling and oppressive. The "Nomads" move a lot. One of this highly mobile group explains: "We've discovered that to prevent the pain of saying good-bye, we don't say hello anymore."

Hale names seven other categories of unchurched. Altogether, his study offers fascinating evidence of what some evangelists and home missionaries have known for years: In many cases the greatest barrier to evangelism is not Christ, but the church. People are fed up or put off or scandalized not by Christ, but by Christ's body. For them the church is not a saving ark, or a refreshing wayside inn; it is not a healing community, a herald of good news, or a noble, suffering servant in society. The church to them is a joke, or an impertinence. It is an obstacle to Christian belief and life.

People have surprisingly strong views on the church. So does Guido de Bres. In Article XXVIII of the Confession, he dares to say that outside the church there is no salvation. What does he mean by this? How do Reformed people see the church? How do you tell the true church from false ones?

These are questions raised and answered by Articles XXVII-XXIX. Some of the answers seem, at least at first, puzzling. We have to remember that this whole Confession is written in the heat of ecclesiastical persecution and reform; thus, issues are sometimes stated with less nuance or shading then we might expect.

Let us proceed by articles.

Article XXVII—One Holy Catholic Church

People talk loosely about "the church." The church ought to speak and act on social issues. The church "has left nothing untouched by its depravity'' (Nietzsche). "You cannot have God for your Father unless you have the church for your Mother" (Cyprian). What do people mean by "the church"?

In chapter 5 we saw that every Reformed Christian is a member of five groups, large to small. He is a Christian, a Protestant Christian, a Reformed Protestant Christian, a member of a Reformed Protestant Christian *denomination*, and a member of one of its local congregations. Which of these groups do we mean when we speak about "the church"? Well, we might mean any of them. It depends on the context of our discussion.

Which group does de Bres mean in Article XXVII? He means the first. He means to talk about Christians: "one catholic or universal Church, which is a holy congregation of true Christian believers." The church is a certain group of people. It is the company of those who are saved. It is the assembly of all those who are in Christ. Although de Bres does not say it, he would surely have agreed with Calvin that the church is the number of the elect. For he adds that "this Church has been from the beginning of the world, and will be to the end thereof." Thus, in XXVII, he has the broadest possible view of the church. It is the set of true believers—and not just those living in 1661.

This raises a question. Was someone like Abraham a "true Christian believer"? Wasn't he rather a true Jewish believer?

Reformed theologians have always regarded the Old Testament saints as saved by Christ, or in Christ, even though Christ had not yet been born. In that respect these saints were "Christian" believers. According to Calvin, for example, Adam and Abel believed in Christ. Their knowledge of Him was merely less clear than that of, say, Paul. All believers of the old covenant "had and knew Christ as Mediator, through whom they were joined to God and were to share in his promises" (*Institutes* II, x, 2). How did they know Him? Under the law, in the old ceremonies, by prophecies, through shadows or figures or types (cf. Art. XXV).

Thus it was a small step to call Old Testament believers members of "the church." All the Reformed confessions do it: The church is gathered "out of the entire human race, from the beginning of the world to its end" (Heidelberg Catechism, Answer 54). There is "the same Church for the old and the new people" (Second Helvetic Confession, chapter 17). Article XXVII, as we have seen, takes the same line. Its supporting reason is very interesting. From some of the "royal psalms" and from Luke 1:32 and 33, de Bres infers that Christ is an "eternal King." Therefore He can never have been without subjects—not even in Old Testament times!

The article mentions a number of traditional attributes of the church. The church is one, holy, and catholic. These attributes come from the Apostles' Creed ("I believe a holy catholic Church") and the Nicene Creed ("one holy catholic and apostolic Church"). The *oneness* or unity of the church was an especially sore issue during the Reformation. Obviously, the church had been much more visibly unified before Luther's break in 1517 than after it. By 1561, when the Confession was written, the breaking (or branching) had gone much farther. There were now Catholics, Lutherans, Reformed, Anabaptists, and others. All of this was, of course, scandalous in the eyes of faithful Catholics. They were quick to call the Reformers schismatics. The Reformers, in turn, wanted to say that the church had always been one and was still one—in some respect. They had to say this and believe it on account of Ephesians 4:3,4 and other passages. There is one true church, united by one faith, and oriented to one Lord. Calvin observed that "there could not be two or three churches unless Christ be torn asunder—which cannot happen" (*Institutes* IV, i, 2). Thus, to preserve scriptural and creedal testimony, Luther and Calvin did a scholarly thing. They made a distinction between a *visible* and *invisible* church. The visible church includes all who make a Christian profession, even some whose profession is false. The invisible church is truly one body even though it "is not confined...to a certain place or to certain persons, but is spread and dispersed over the whole world" (Art. XXVII).

This one church is said to be *holy*. By "holy" Reformed thinkers meant two things. They meant first that true believers are always *ekklesia* (the Greek word for *church*). They are always "called out" or separated, or set apart—not for self-congratulation, but for work and mission:

But you are a chosen race, a royal priesthood, a holy nation, God's own people, that you may declare the wonderful deeds of him who called you out of darkness into his marvelous light.
(I Pet. 2:9)

They meant, secondly, that this *ekklesia* is gradually made holier by the same Christ who "gave himself up for her, that he might sanctify her" (Eph. 5:25,26). Sincere believers are also sincere sinners. They need to be sanctified.

De Bres adds a poignant observation on the

church's universality. The *catholic* (or universal) church does not always appear as large as it is, or as strong. There are periods and places in which the number of committed believers seems disheartingly small. So de Bres refers to that fascinating passage in I Kings where a self-pitying Elijah complains that of all the faithful, "I, even I only, am left." Elijah had never bothered to get in touch with "seven thousand men, who had not bowed their knees to Baal"! The congregation of committed ones will sometimes seem to be diminished; it will seem harassed, ignored, threatened, or scorned into insignificance. The church will seem puny: "in the eyes of men...reduced to nothing." But believers are to take the long and universal view. As Theodore Beza said: "Sire, it belongs in truth to the church of God in whose name I speak, to endure blows and not to inflict them. But it will also please your majesty to remember that the church is an anvil that has worn out many hammers" (Henry Baird, *Theodore Beza*).

Article XXVII is clear in its concept of the church. The church is a "congregation of true Christian believers." Article XXVIII begins with the same concept: "This holy congregation is an assembly of those who are saved." But the reader may begin to feel uneasy. A shift in meaning is taking place. The first clue is that de Bres thinks it necessary to add about this company of the saved that,"Outside of it there is no salvation." This was a famous old phrase of the medieval Roman Church: *extra ecclesiam nulla salus*. But there *ecclesia* meant the visible, organized, Roman Catholic Church. Outside of *it* there is no salvation.

Of course de Bres does not mean that. It looks as if he means the invisible church. On first glance, he seems only to say that outside the "assemblage of those who are saved" there is no salvation. And that is a clear but not very startling thing to say. It is like saying, "Outside of Chinese people, there are no Chinese." That is true, of course, but it is not news.

But de Bres goes on with other statements which suggest that he is shifting over to a different concept of the church. No person may "withdraw himself" from the church. All persons are "in duty bound to join it." All must submit "to the doctrine and discipline thereof." How is any of this possible so far as the assembly of those who are saved is concerned? In the Reformed view no member of the saved *can* withdraw his membership. If he is once saved, he

MARGARET LITTLE
12·14·78

THERESIA MULDER
11·16·78

always is. That is the point of the doctrine of the perseverance of the saints. Moreover, in the Reformed view no person can *join* himself to the company of the saved either. God does the joining. That is the point of the doctrine of salvation by grace alone.

So what is going on here? Apparently, something like this: De Bres begins in Article XXVII with a notion of the assembly of all true Christian believers of all times and places. That is the invisible church. But then he subtly shifts to a notion of the church as the assembly of those who have "the marks of Christians" and among whom there are "marks by which the true Church is known" (Art. XXIX). Article XXVIII is the transition. It too starts with "the assemblage of those who are saved" but gradually, and without announcement, passes over to the assembly of those who have right "doctrine and discipline," who edify each other with their talents, who, in general, bow "under the yoke of Jesus Christ."

This (visible) assembly includes some unbelievers. It was this assembly that Augustine referred to when he said "many sheep are without and many wolves are within." And Article XXIX acknowledges at least the wolves within. They are the "hypocrites" who are "mixed in the church with the good, yet are not of the church." This recognition of chaff among the wheat (to change the image) was necessary to account for the simple fact of apostasy. Some people who sat for preaching, partook of sacraments, submitted to discipline, and displayed many marks of faith later fell away. In an important sense they had been members of the church. Before they stumbled, nobody could have challenged their uprightness. But it later became clear that in another sense they had never really been members of the church at all. They had apparently not been members of the "the assemblage of the saved."

Now Article XXVIII blends together the ideas of invisible and visible churches. What de Bres wants to do is to urge the seriousness of joining the visible church. That is the only one we *can* join. He wants to point out how queer, how wrong, how perverse is the attempt to be a Christian by oneself. It is like trying to be a spouse by yourself. It is like trying to play tennis by yourself. It is like trying to be a glowing coal separated from the rest of the embers. Your little light will go out.

More than that, de Bres wants to urge the seriousness of joining the *true* visible church. Among all those who make a Christian profession, in the whole visible church, only some organizations or manifestations or "denominations" of it deserve to be called part of "the true church."

Article XXIX—The True Church

Which are they? Where do you find, or how do you identify, the true church?

In one of its best-known sections, the Confession says that you must look for certain "marks." You test the various organizations or groups by certain criteria. You ask certain pertinent questions.

About the assembly as a whole, you want to know three things: You want to know if "the pure doctrine of the gospel is preached," if there is "pure administration of the sacraments as instituted by Christ," and if "church discipline is exercised in punishing of sin." That is, does the assembly govern itself according to the Word of God and the lordship of Christ?

De Bres is here looking out of the corner of his eye at "sects" and at "the false Church." It is not entirely clear which groups he had in mind when he used the term "sects." Possibly he just meant to refer to false churches. Or perhaps de Bres meant especially the radicals and members of the Reformation's left wing. If he did mean the latter (in XXXVI he will "detest the Anabaptists and other seditious people"), he would have been thinking of such false doctrines as Docetism, such impure administration of the sacraments as the refusal to baptize infants, and such lack of discipline as the failure to curb lawlessness and occasional fanaticism.

But when "the false Church" is mentioned, we may be sure that de Bres means the Roman Catholic Church. It is Roman abuses that the end of XXIX has in view. Tradition and her ordinances are elevated above the preaching of the Word of God. Both sacraments (baptism and Lord's Supper) are misinterpreted, five extra sacraments are added to the original two, and the cup is taken from the laity. Instead of disciplining herself to get rid of her "errors, covetousness, and idolatry," she persecutes those who have sought to rebuke her for these things.

But Article XXIX suggests that the seeker must ask not only about the assembly as a whole. He or she must also ask about the attributes of individual members. Do they show real faith? Avoid sin? Love God and neighbor? Stay single-minded? Mortify their old nature?

To counter the impression that he is suggesting perfection as a test of faithfulness, de Bres hastens to add that there are "great infirmities" even in true members of the true church. But what is characteristic of true believers is that they refuse to rest with their infirmities. They hate them and keep on fighting them. They do so by appealing to Christ alone for refuge and help.

The Confession concludes Article XXIX by stating that true and false churches "are easily known and distinguished from each other."

Conclusion

This last sentence of Article XXIX raises only one of a number of controversies which have always surrounded this material. Is it easy today to tell the true church from a false one?

That depends. In some cases it is easy. Churches who abandon their belief in God or Christ, or who deny all miracles, are obviously false. But how about those Baptists who differ from the Reformed faith on the matter of infant baptism? How about the Lutherans who hold a different position on the relation of Christ's two natures? What about many Roman Catholics who trust in Christ alone for their salvation—no matter what some of their theologians may be interpreted to say? Surely it is contrary to all humility and wisdom to suggest that none of these Christians are saved, that all these groupings are false churches, and that all judgments of relative faithfulness are "easy."

Did Guido de Bres think the Reformed church was the only true one? One gets that impression. Some of the statements in XXVIII and XXIX sound absolute. But it is actually unlikely that he thought so. Both he and Calvin regarded certain other groups of Christians, especially Zwinglians and Lutherans, as true visible manifestations of the one holy catholic church. So should we. Calvin himself made a distinction between major and minor theological differences. It is one thing to differ over the precise relation of our Lord to the elements with which we celebrate His supper; it is another to differ over the question whether our Lord still lives.

Possibly the major conclusion we draw from this material is that de Bres and the Confession take the visible church with enormous seriousness. Certainly it is possible to be one of God's children without having much to do with the assembly of Christian believers. There are special cases: infants die; unchurched people have deathbed conversions; in His grace, God may have "other sheep." Thus the Westminster Confession shades its statement about the visible church to say that it is through its ministry that people are "ordinarily" saved. We have to allow for the freedom of God.

But the duty of ordinary Christians is also plain. We must bend our efforts and wills to strengthen the ministry of our local churches. By these assemblies of forgiven sinners the very work of Christ, in a hurt and confused world, is carried on. We are trying to do a grotesque and sinful thing when we live alone or hold aloof. We are depriving others of the edification and support they need. We are comforting God's rivals in the world. We are acting "contrary to the ordinance of God." God may have His way with those who are infants, or ignorant, or late in believing. But we do not dare to presume on such grace for ourselves. We have been exposed to the needs of our local church. We have lost our innocence. For us the call of the gospel includes a summons to join publicly and visibly with others in doing the work of the Lord.

CHAPTER 23
Church Order

Belgic Confession, Articles XXX-XXXII

Introduction—Order

Order fascinates Calvinists. They like their ardor liberally sprinkled with order. Sometimes their penchant for order is strenuously enforced. One unruly soul in seventeenth century Scotland was arrested for smiling on the sabbath. An outspoken heretic was burned at the stake in Geneva. Anabaptists were persecuted, sometimes killed, by other Protestants, including Calvinists.

Calvinists inherited their zeal for order from the medieval world in which political force was commonly used to guarantee good order in church and state. Regrettably, Calvinists did not learn from the atrocities perpetrated on them, and they turned the same atrocities on others. They could have—should have—known better.

Still, while we admit the shame of those dark days, we may recognize the insight whose excesses we deplore. The insight is that God is a God of order. He brings cosmos out of chaos, governs His world in regular ways, and issues orders for the redeemed life. God is a kind of King or Lord. Thus He is not merely to be contemplated, but especially to be *obeyed*. To know God is to serve Him. To love God is to seek to please Him. To live the sanctified life is constantly to reform according to His will.

Clearly all of this applies to the life of God's people together. It applies to the church. We have just seen how much the Confession makes of the church. This church is like a body. It is a living, pulsating organism. But, as we now learn, in Articles XXX-XXXII, this body has spine and structure. It is *organized*. It is governed. It is both comforted and disciplined. It is deliberately shaped in certain ways and bent to certain tasks.

It has a church order. For Calvinists, I Corinthians 14:40 has always been a big test: "All things should be done decently and in *order*."

Why do Reformed people value church order so much? For one thing, they think it is a gift from Him who heads the church. Church government is not our *ad hoc* invention. In Ephesians 4, it is *Christ* who gives the gift of office so that all the saints may be edified. The Reformed idea is that Christ wills His church to be policed—that is, to have "polity" (XXX) or policy. The visible, institutional church is His instrument for calling disorderly persons to order and for outfitting them to serve others.

For another thing, Calvinists think faith and order influence each other. Take a church's concept of sin as an example. You can tell what sins truly offend a given church by noting which ones it aggressively pursues. What sort of offense (if any) starts the engines of discipline? Does a church regard fornication, for example, as a sin more in need of confession than pride, racism, or greed? Again, what is a church's general, confessional estimate of human nature? Well, look at its church order. Calvinists do not dare entrust church government either to totalitarian hierarchies, on the one hand, or to the whims of the masses, on the other. As opposed to both Catholics and left-wing radicals, the Reformed believers of the sixteenth century settled in between. They set up representative government in which the assembly of believers elects as representatives of Christ those in whom it recognizes the official gifts. Why? Because this procedure seemed to them to be "according to the Word of God."

All Reformed church order depends on two principles. The first is that Christ alone is head of His church. The other is that, at least in major outline, all church government must be done according to the Word of God.

Let us proceed, once again, by articles.

Article XXX—Church Government and Offices

Article XXX is linked with Article XXIX by the phrase "this true Church." But there is also another link. While XXIX lists the marks of the true church, XXX goes on to say how the church must be organized so that the marks may actually be present.

The article is about the necessity of office. If there is going to be pure preaching and administration of sacraments, if there is going to be faithful discipline, then somebody will have to *do* these things. There "*must* be ministers or pastors...elders and deacons" to do this work. As Calvin said, "Some form of organization is necessary in all human society" not only for dividing up the work, but also for general "peace" and "concord" (*Institutes* IV, x, 30).

Which form? We need to go "by that spiritual polity which our Lord has taught us in His Word." Here the Confession follows the general Reformed conviction that our Lord has instituted at least the principles and offices of church government. De Bres obviously does not mean that we can find a detailed church order in the gospel words of Jesus. He means that in Ephesians 4:11 and 12, I Corinthains 4:1 and 2, and other passages, we are given God's basic "spiritual polity."

This polity provides for helpful officers. *Ministers* are attendants or servants in the New Testament. But they are not merely busy-persons, or "conveners," or stewards for church suppers. They are supposed to be "servants of Christ and stewards of the mysteries of God" (I Cor. 4:1). The Confession regularly calls them "ministers of God's Word." They serve Christ and, by preaching the Word, they serve the church.

Pastors are literally shepherds. In the Bible the church is often pictured as a flock in a pastoral setting. Pastors imitate "the great shepherd of the sheep" (Heb. 13:20). Thus they "restrain" those who err and "comfort" those who are distressed. In dark days, as de Bres would soon discover, pastors sometimes even lay down their lives for their sheep.

The Confession lists preaching the Word and administering the sacraments as the two main duties of ministers or pastors. The Reformation, as James Nichols says, was the greatest revival of preaching in church history. Calvin called preachers "the mouth of God." The Zurich Reformer, Heinrich Bullinger, declared that what a preacher said could be called the Word of God.

One idea here lies behind the whole Reformed concept of office. It is an idea of representation. The minister is God's spokesman, deputy, delegate, or ambassador (II Cor. 5:20). He represents God. He speaks on God's behalf. He uses his own words, as any delegate might, but he is not preaching his own word. Thoughtful people have been intrigued by this "high view" of preaching for years. Some think, indeed, that it is too high. They regard it as "papist"—a nearly idolatrous elevation of human words similar to the Roman Catholic elevation of bread and wine in the Lord's Supper.

Besides preaching, pastors or ministers also administer the sacraments. Do the Scriptures limit this work to these special officebearers? Not clearly. The limiting is less a matter of clear biblical direction than of historical custom. The concern was to make thoughtful provision for preserving order in the use of sacraments and for coupling their use with the minister's preaching.

An *elder* is a "presbyter" in the New Testament (hence the "presbyterian" form of church government). There are no sharp distinctions in New Testament usage among such terms as "bishop," "presbyter," "pastor," and "minister." Still, by the time Paul wrote to Timothy, a difference was beginning to emerge between those presbyters who have preaching and pastoring gifts, on the one hand, and those who have more general supervisory gifts, on the other (I Tim. 5:17). The former sort are now ordained to the ministry of the Word and sacraments and the latter sort to the office of elder.

Deacons are ordained to office following the historical example of Acts 6:1-6. But the passage most often cited in connection with the diaconate is the terrible parable of the sheep and the goats (Matt. 25:31-46). Here the evidence of our belonging in the kingdom of heaven is said to be the lifting of a cup to someone's thirst or the bringing of cheer to someone's discouragement. None of us are excused from such lifting and cheering (because none of us are excused from the general ministry of Christians). But some of us with obvious gifts are particularly set apart to represent Christ and His body in doing this merciful work as efficiently as possible.

Together these three sorts of officers form a *council*. De Bres' word is actually *senat*—a government word favored by Calvin. The senators or council members are supposed to blend authority and service in their approach to the rest of the assembly. In so doing they follow a wonderful New Testament pattern from the life and work of Christ Himself. He who is Lord of the world also humbly condescends to take upon Himself the

BILL GREVENGOED
AND HIS JUNIOR HIGH
BASKETBALL TEAM
ROSELAND CHRISTIAN
11·13·78

form of a servant. In Reformed practice, the problem has often been that elders were thought to be the rulers and deacons the servants. Deacons, in this view, are reduced to second-string or apprentice elders. Yet in the New Testament *all* office is *diakonia*, or service. So ministers and elders serve. And deacons work with Christ's delegated power and authority. In fact, in many small Reformed churches the duties of deacons are scarcely distinguished from those of elders. And in all churches, as members of the council, deacons become trustees of the church's property, join in the nomination and discipline of council members, participate in the call and care of pastors, and provide for the church's public worship. As more than one observer has said, it is a Reformed conviction that all office is at bottom one and indivisible. All officers serve in their ruling and rule in their serving.

The article goes on to mention some of the typical work of the council. The most general is the preservation of "true religion." Additionally, there is the propagation of "true doctrine everywhere." This provision undoubtedly reflects the Reformed interest in catechetical instruction more than it does a missionary zeal. As John Leith says in his *Introduction to the Reformed Tradition*, Calvin and de Bres could hardly have imagined our contemporary situation in which the church dwells as a minority among a majority of secularists and non-members. Still, we can easily read and use the phrase today with missionary interest.

The punishment and restraint of "transgressors" refers, of course, to discipline, the third mark of the church. "Punishment and restraint" admittedly looks a bit narrow to us today as we absorb the broader ideas of Calvin. It was

Calvin's idea that discipline should not only reaffirm God's glory and protect the church from corruption, but also that it should help to heal and restore those who have fallen into sin. Discipline thus aims to reclaim. Moreover, as J. H. Kromminga has pointed out, discipline in the sense of guidance or teaching is something the whole assembly does! Paul says to the Romans, "you are capable of keeping *one another* on the right road" (Rom. 15:14, Phillips).

So we might want to flesh out what de Bres says. However, we do not want to fall into that modern indifference which refuses to discipline at all. The church is hindered, scandalized, and rendered feeble by those who do not take the Christian life and mission seriously. It may even be that those unchurched persons who now regard the church as a joke would sober up if they saw a disciplined, caring community which knew its task and was determined to do it.

In any event, says de Bres, the church must discipline by "spiritual means." You do not baptize at the point of a sword or fine-tune a heretic's trinitarian doctrine over a fire. You rather use *persuasion*. You reason and witness from the Bible. In every case you count on the work of the Holy Spirit.

The relief of "the poor and distressed" is an especially gracious and satisfying work of the church, usually carried out particularly by deacons. Once again, Calvin set an example for the rest of the tradition. He was intensely interested in such things as unemployment, hygiene, and usury. He regarded politics as a most high calling. What we think of as "spiritual concerns" included for Calvin matters of plumbing, banking, and housing. So for us. Perhaps our question today concerns the role the diaconate should play in a largely middle-class church and in an expanding welfare state.

In general, says de Bres in summary, these offices and tasks should combine so that "everything will be carried on in the Church with good order and decency." He adds that faithful "men" must be chosen. Actually, *he* does not add that. The English translator does. De Bres' word is *personnages* which means "persons." And persons, as at least half of us know, come in two kinds.

Article XXXI—Ministers, Elders, and Deacons

Here three additional things are said about church order. The first is that church officers must be chosen "by a lawful election by the Church." Why? What is the background? Again, the historical background is both Roman Catholicism on the right and Anabaptism, or radicalism, on the left. Medieval Catholicism had been badly weakened by widespread abuse of offices. One such abuse was an arrangement in which well-heeled clergymen held several offices—even several kinds of offices—simultaneously. These plums were called "benefices" and could be had for a price. No congregation ever elected its "benefactor." Congregations simply endured them.

On the radical side, ministers were often just wandering preachers who gathered followers. These self-starters were not elected either.

Steering between such alternatives, the Confession urges that no hopeful person "intrude himself by improper means." With this piquant phrase de Bres means to rule out local power plays and nepotisms. You do not "run for" office. People who feel in their heart that they are called to office must wait for an outer call of the church to confirm their inner call.

The second thing Article XXXI says is that all ministers have equal standing. They have *parity*. No minister is "under" another as in episcopal or hierarchical systems. Ministers have equal "power" and "authority" wherever they are.

Finally, Article XXXI emphasizes the need for esteeming and cooperating with the church's officers. Unfortunately, in his haste de Bres forgot to mention deacons. Or else he was somehow thinking of ministers and elders as estimable in a way that deacons are not. Yet our esteem and peaceful cooperation surely extends to *all* officers of the church. Note that we esteem them "for their work's sake." They do not stand higher in God's sight than we. They are not holier, more valuable, or better privileged than we. It is not even the case that the ministers among them do "full-time Christian service" while the rest of us have to be content with part-time. Rather, in the general strategy of the church's ministry, these people do particular ministries for which Christ has gifted them.

That work is to be prized. A deacon, for example, who relishes the careful fitting of the church's resources to a person's special need is doing something which all of us admire.

Article XXXII—Order and Discipline

Reformed students of polity (Reformed politicians) have always recognized the fact that New Testament guidelines are broad and flexible enough to allow for local and denominational adjustments. A general organizational structure is suggested in the Bible, but not a detailed plan for every local situation. Thus Calvin, for instance, regarded school teachers as a fourth sort of officer. Seventeenth century Dutch churches, as Howard Hageman reminds us, had the office of *Krankenbezoeker* (visitor of the sick). Calvin proposed that whatever practices are not necessary to salvation may be "variously accommodated to the customs of each nation and age" (*Institutes* IV, x, 30). So churches now set up prison visitation programs, call layworkers in evangelism, settle on times and seasons for worship and celebration of sacraments, institute a staff ministry, con-

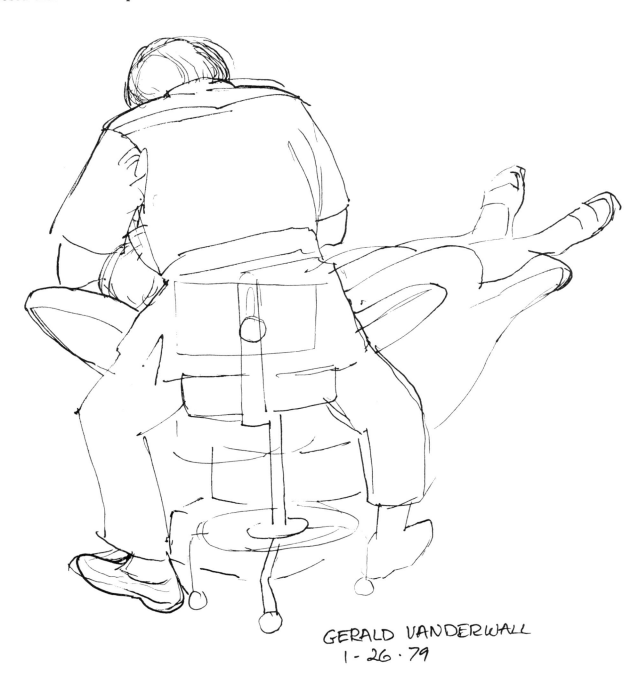

GERALD VANDERWALL
1-26-79

duct church schools, and appoint well-educated musicians to keep some fittingness and order in the church's use of music. Some churches fly a national flag in their sanctuaries. Others find this practice dangerously suggestive of civil religion. Some churches include "special music" in their liturgy. Others wish a more integrated liturgy with no diversionary pauses. The problem is always one of deciding what is a non-essential matter and what is truly a matter of principle.

Along this line de Bres offers three checks on our human "ordinances." The first is that we must not "depart from those things which Christ, our only Master, has instituted." No doubt, once again de Bres means not only those directives found in the gospel words of Jesus, but rather all biblical guidelines for those who are in Christ. For example, one such guideline is the recognition of the priesthood of all believers; no church will want to grant its pastor a final vote, or veto power, over other believers.

The second check on our human ordinances is that they must not "compel the conscience" of believers. Calvin's famous example is that of kneeling at public worship. Calvin regarded it as commendable but not obligatory. You do not force believers to their knees. Still, if a church wants to install kneeling benches, it is doing well. It is allowing for the freedom of those who wish to follow their Lord in kneeling at prayer. Indeed, it is lamentable that only a few Reformed churches allow their members this freedom.

The last test of human ordinances is whether they tend to nourish concord and obedience. Concord has to do with harmony or unity. Does some local innovation build up or tear down? Does it foster growth in grace, or does it set the church back? These are central questions. But they are not the only ones. Some churches cultivate a kind of sleepy and superficial unity in which nobody dares to confront anybody else. This is no advance. For besides unity there is obedience to consider. In Nazi Germany, in segregated cities, and in South Africa, believers have sometimes had to suffer temporary disunity for the sake of obedience to Christ. They had to settle for peace "as much as possible" (XXXI).

Conclusion

Calvinists love order. Expectably, Articles XXX-XXXII contain much order language: "governed," "punished," "restrained," "power," "authority," "rulers," "ordinances." This kind of talk has earned Calvinists a reputation for being obsessed with law and order.

Indeed, we must make two acknowledgments. The first is that it is easy to forget, in the middle of all the Reformed power language of XXX-XXXII, that the New Testament notion of office is that of *diakonia*. *Diakonia* means "service" and must be blended along with authority into whatever concept of office we promote. Secondly, it is quite true that many Calvinists have tended in general to see law and order as the basis for freedom rather than freedom as the basis for law and order. As someone once put it, there never was much room in Calvin's Geneva for the serious oddball.

Still, with respect to the first acknowledgment it must be said that Calvin had seen enough medieval straitjackets to love freedom dearly. His chapter in the *Institutes* on Christian liberty is widely regarded as one of his most inspired pieces. Moreover, where church order is concerned, Calvin and his followers regularly warned against hierarchical tendencies and the multiplication of "law upon law, precept upon precept." That is why de Bres pointedly rules out human ordinances which bind the conscience. The only thing which finally compels our obedience is the Word of God.

With respect to the second acknowledgment it must be said that not all Calvinists rank order over freedom. Calvin himself, as we shall see in chapter 25, allowed for political revolution in certain cases as a means to regain order. Here freedom from the old disorder came first. And, for that reason, today in South America Reformed freedom fighters gladly claim Calvin as their father.

Perhaps, then, the Reformed tradition broadly follows the biblical paradox that we are most free when we are slaves of God.

CHAPTER 24
Sacraments

Belgic Confession, Articles XXXIII-XXXV

Introduction

Practically nothing in the Reformation period was more blood-warming than the issue of sacraments. First it was Protestants against Catholics. Protestants regarded Catholic doctrine and practice of sacraments as they did most other Catholic doctrine and practice. They found it fatty and gristled with human tradition. So Protestants trimmed the number of sacraments from seven to two, rejected the "magic" dimension in both of them, and joined the sacraments to the preaching of the Word.

Perhaps for Protestants one particular Catholic sacrament, the mass, most vividly symbolized all that had gone wrong with the church. The church had become a house around an altar on which the "sacrifice of the Mass" occurred, E. A. Dowey writes, a place "in which the body of the Victim was retained day and night" (*A Commentary on the Confessions of 1967*). To Protestants the shadowy movements and hoarse whispers of the priestly power-dispensers suggested mummery and hocus-pocus. The idea that a captive Lord was sacrificed again and again seemed dreadful and loathsome. The whole scene provoked even the mildest commentators to use strong language. This, said the third edition of the Heidelberg Catechism, was a "condemnable idolatry" (Answer 80).

But after 1517, Protestants still quarreled over the sacraments. Now the dispute was intramural—Protestants against Protestants. Zwingli, Luther, and Calvin could not agree on Christ's presence in the Lord's Supper. None of them could go along with the Anabaptists, who rejected infant baptism. And all of them spent considerable breath in sacramental argument.

Why? Many Christians today, after all, find sacraments merely a pleasant and genteel embellishment. It is hard for most of us to imagine the religious atmosphere of the sixteenth century when all of the current differences were first stated and sharpened. Sacraments were holy things attended with awesome power, beauty, and significance. For a reformed Catholic to *hold* bread and, for the first time, to be granted a drink from the holy cup was a deeply humbling and gratifying experience. Sacraments were not only theologically, but also experientially, at the heart of the Christian religion. For by them grimy persons were washed, and weak, hungry persons richly fed.

The Confession offers a straight Reformed statement on the sacraments. Much of the language and many of the concepts are familiar to Reformed people. But two things ought to be kept in mind by way of general perspective. One is that in this chapter we are still talking about the church and the marks of the true church. Sacraments are church rites. There are no private baptisms at kitchen sinks or individual celebrations of communion (indeed, this last idea is self-contradictory). Sacraments are God's gifts for God's people. They have meaning only where the church gathers.

Secondly, our broad perspective on union with Christ (chapter 19) must be always at the back of our minds here. Faith attaches us to Christ *in* His redemptive and historical significance. Union with Christ and His benefits implies not only my membership in His new community in history, but also my willingness to undertake the work of that community. Sacraments, we notice in these articles, are meant both to secure our union with Christ and to strengthen us to do His work in the world.

For a final time, let us take three articles in order.

BEULAH BANDSTRA
11·15·78

Article XXXIII—Sacraments

The word *sacrament* does not appear in the Bible. It comes from a Latin word (*sacramentum*) which means "that which obliges or binds." A *sacramentum* in Roman society was a kind of binder. For example, two parties in a civil suit would bind themselves to litigation with a financial pledge of their seriousness. The winner would take all. The earnest money, or binder, was a *sacramentum*. Or, a soldier would bind himself to the military with an oath of allegiance, with a solemn sacrament. Obviously a term with such binding, pledging, signifying, and sealing overtones was readily usable by Latin-speaking Christians who wished to talk about those things which bind us to Christ and signify God's grace to us.

At first these Christians used the term widely for many such things—exorcism, the gesture or sign of the cross, the death of Christ, even the general works of the Creator. Calvin still speaks of the rainbow after the flood and Gideon's fleece as sacraments in a broad sense. They are simple signs of God's grace. But gradually *sacrament* was reserved for those church rites in which people participate and in which, or by which, God *communicates* grace. In all these an outer, visible action or thing was thought to be a sign of an inner, invisible grace.

Medieval theologians disagreed about the number of such sacraments. One theologian, for example, counted thirty of them. But by the fifteenth century the church had settled on seven: baptism, confirmation, eucharist, penance, priestly consecration, marriage, and extreme unction. Controlling the spigots of the grace containers, the church also controlled the spiritual lives of believers from cradle to grave.

We have already noted that the Reformers cut back the number of sacraments from seven to two. De Bres likes to reflect this sacramental economy by saying that "we are satisfied" (XXXIII) or "rest satisfied" (XXXV) with what Christ and the apostles have instituted. Moreover, he detests the error of the Anabaptists (those who "baptize again") because they "are not content" with the baptism they already received as infants.

Besides expressing his contentment, de Bres says three other things about sacraments. Perhaps the most general is that they are "visible signs and seals of an inward and invisible thing." A sign points to or suggests something else which may not be immediately obvious. A sign is an *indicator*. In sacraments, the signs are the "elements" (water, bread, wine) plus the ceremonial actions which accompany their use. Baptism, for example, includes the use of water to sprinkle or immerse a person. The water and the sprinkling or immersing point most immediately to ordinary washing and, from there, to an internal "washing, cleansing, and purging our souls of all filth" (XXXIV). That is one "inward and invisible thing" which baptism signifies.

A seal is very close to a sign. *Seal* and *sign* have the same Latin root. Kings and other dignitaries used to have "signet" rings or "sign" rings which bore their figure. With these rings they could seal—authenticate or certify—a document. Nowadays we simply "sign" a document. Or, in some cases, we must get a notary public to confirm it with his seal. So a seal is something which assures, or confirms, or attests something else.

What is the "inward and invisible thing" which the sacraments seal? It is the same thing that they signify or "sign." The washing with water and the partaking of bread and wine seal or confirm God's "promises," as de Bres has it. These are many: justification through faith (Rom. 4:11), forgiveness of sins (Matt. 26:28), and God's covenant of grace (Gen. 17:11). More generally, sacraments seal or confirm union with Christ ("For Jesus Christ is the true object presented by them") or, simply, salvation.

Secondly, sacraments are effective only "by the power of the Holy Spirit." Calvin never tired of saying that the Holy Spirit is our binder to Christ. Sacraments have no inherent or magical power. Catholics, on the other hand, thought that, so long as the recipient did not block it, a sacrament would "take" in anybody. The idea was that sacraments *contain* grace, that grace somehow "resides in" them. Of course this notion gave the church enormous power. Priests could dispense God's favors *ex opere operato*—"by the work (the sacrament) worked," or "by the act performed." Protestants objected. Sacraments, they argued, are not containers of grace but *means* of grace freely used by the Holy Spirit in connection with the faith of the recipient. Indeed, they strengthen that faith.

That is the third point. Sacraments not only point to God's "good will and grace" toward us and seal His promises, but also "nourish and strengthen our faith." They are gracious aids on "account of our weakness and infirmities." In that respect sacraments resemble the written Word of God. That too, as we recall from chapter 10, was "a special care" because of our fallenness. The Word comes through the ear to blind and self-deceived persons who can no longer see God in creation. Now the sacraments are added to appeal to the other senses. They are tangible, visible—even consumable signs and seals of what the Word says. God has linked our faith to His Word. His Word tells us that He is gracious and kind, that He loves us and wishes to save us. The sacraments *show* this. The Word tells and the sacraments show. They are (if we may say so reverently) God's "show and tell" for sinners. Instead of merely hearing about it, we are now given to "*taste* and *see* that the Lord is good" (Ps. 34:8).

The idea is that God wants to make Himself unmistakable to us. He wants to get through to us by all means. Our fallenness keeps us from seeing Him plainly in nature. Thus, He "makes Himself more clearly and fully known to us by His holy and divine Word" (Art. II). Now, we discover, He goes farther yet. He joins the sacraments to the Word "the better to present to our senses both that which He declares to us by His Word and that which He works inwardly in our hearts."

So sacraments not only show us what the Word tells: namely, that God is gracious. They also bind us to Him more firmly. They "strengthen our faith." It is as if a tired and grimy child were told by his father that they would soon be home and that a shower, clean clothes, and a fine meal were waiting. The child may believe his father. He may take him at his word. But along the way the father helps strengthen that belief. He stops here and there to let his son rest. He offers the boy small amounts of food and drink and moist towel-lettes for cleaning up a bit. There is not yet a full shower or a full meal. They are not yet *home*. In the wilderness you do as well as you can. But the future delights have been powerfully suggested, and the father has made himself thoroughly believable in his promises; the son has been refreshed to go on.

Article XXXIV—Holy Baptism

The key to Article XXXIV, and to the whole Reformed understanding of baptism, is the idea of covenant. Covenant links old and new sac-raments (circumcision and baptism), old and new Israel, even old and new people (adults and children) within a context of grace.

The first link is forged at once. De Bres stands in an old tradition of those who see the letting of *blood* as the important thing in circumcision. Cir-cumcision is thus regarded as a bloody sacrifice, a bloody cutting away or stripping off of flesh as a symbol of cutting away the guilt and pollution of sin. In the baffling story of Exodus 4:24-26 such cutting seems to propitiate an angry God. Hence circumcision is part of the old ceremonial scheme of "propitiation or satisfaction for sin" which Christ ended by courageously sacrificing His own blood.

But how is any of this like baptism? Baptism, after all, involves not blood, but water. The con-nection between these two sacraments is made most clearly by Paul in Colossians 2:11-13. The controlling idea is that Christ's sacrificial death was a kind of large circumcision, a putting off or giving up of the whole "body of flesh." But He was also made alive again. And the connection is that our own baptism is a dying and rising par-ticipation in these dying and rising events of Christ. "Putting off the old man" and "putting on us the new man," as de Bres says, is one of the main things of which baptism is a sign. Baptism, in other words, is a sign of union with Christ and the events of Christ: "We were buried therefore with him by baptism into death, so that as Christ was raised from the dead by the glory of the Father, we too might walk in newness of life" (Rom. 6:4).

The main image for this newness is washing (Tit. 3:5). We have been buried, but we come up quite clean. That is because we have been buried in water. Here, in a striking juxtaposition of sprinkling and immersion imagery, de Bres talks about the "sprinkling of the precious blood of the Son of God; who is our Red Sea, through which we must pass"! A blood Red Sea, the blood of cir-

GERT BOER
11·17·78

cumcision, the sprinkled blood of the Passover lamb, the shed blood of Christ the Lamb, and the water of baptism all flow together here. In the old ceremonial law water washes and blood purifies. Now these are mingled in baptism. To Him "who came by water and blood, Jesus Christ" de Bres now adds the names of Father and Holy Spirit, combining the baptismal formula with the bap-tismal gifts:

> ...as water washes away the filth of the body...so does the blood of Christ by the power of the Holy Spirit...cleanse [the soul] from its sins, and regenerate us from children of wrath unto children of God.

We are still baptized into the covenant, but now we are baptized into the covenant church. There is still a sense of being separated, or called out, but the separation is now from "strange reli-gions," not from Gentile nations. So what circum-cision was to the old Israel, baptism is to the new Israel. In either case, de Bres emphasizes, the promises are the same. Washing, renewal, fa-therly comfort, and all the rest are comprehended

116

under the general promise of God "that He will forever be our gracious God and Father."

Two pointed claims are added, the first against Catholics and the second against Anabaptists. The first is that baptism is good for life; it does not "avail us only at the time when the water is poured upon us." Catholics believe that baptism only takes care of original sin, and that the sacrament of penance is needed to absolve *actual* sins. Not so, says the Confession. Baptism attests God's forgiveness of sins "through the whole course of our life."

The other claim, against "the error of the Anabaptists," is utterly typical of the Reformed way of seeing baptism. Baptism is primarily a sign not of human faith, but of God's covenant grace. That is why, like circumcision, baptism ought to be applied to children. For they are members of the covenant church too. "Infants as well as adults are in God's covenant *and are his people*" (Heidelberg Catechism, Answer 74, italics added). In fact, as E. A. Dowey puts it, "the baptism of a helpless child was [to Reformed believers] the most dramatic and precious symbol of God's freely given grace" (*A Commentary on the Confessions of 1967*). Of course, there must sometime be a response in faith. But that may come later. The baptism of infants signals God's love for us even when we cannot love Him back.

Article XXXV—The Lord's Supper

In Israel slaves could eat the Passover only after they had been circumcised (Ex. 12:44). In the New Testament Jesus instituted the holy supper long after He had been baptized by John. The church has always kept this order—first baptism, then the supper. The holy supper, de Bres says, is for the nourishing of those who have already been "incorporated into [Christ's] Church."

It is moreover for those who have already been "regenerated." Infants are baptized long before they display faith. But the Lord's Supper is served to build muscular faith among those who already believe. Here, as we have seen, Reformed leaders clearly distanced themselves from Rome. Against all *ex opere operato* ideas, the Reformed insisted that sacraments yield their treasure only "by faith, in the Spirit," or "by the Spirit, through faith." Hence when unbelievers eat and drink, they do not receive "the truth" of the sacrament. They receive condemnation instead.

What goes on in the Lord's Supper? We engage, once again, in a deeply symbolical act. Just as water suggests washing, so food suggests the process of nurturing. Thus, for symbolizing the fostering of faith nothing seems apter than bread and wine. That is what de Bres' analogy of "twofold life" is about. After birth everybody's life is supported by nourishment—typically from a mother's breast. When we are born again we are nursed again. Calvin says the church is a mother "to give us birth" and "nourish us at her breast." The new life is begun or "effected" by the preaching of the gospel; after that it is sustained by the life-supporting gifts of Christ. Thus the communion elements do not merely symbolize the strengthening of faith. For the person who has any faith at all, these elements actually make faith stronger. The faith which may be slipping or wobbling is secured and stabilized.

But this leads us to the central question of the Reformation debates. How, exactly, is Christ present in the Lord's Supper? De Bres says that what actually strengthens us is not the sheer physical elements of bread and wine. Those support only physical life. What builds faith is union with the "living bread," the "true body and blood of Christ," the "proper and natural body and the proper blood of Christ." How does this work?

Neither de Bres nor Calvin could say. They believed heartily that the supper both points to and thickens union with Christ, but they could not explain it. Here Reformed believers characteristically confess humility and talk about mystery. The "manner" of this union "surpasses our understanding," says de Bres. Still, this much is clear: Reformed leaders tried to avoid both fleshly realism on the Catholic-Lutheran side and mere pyschological remembering through symbolism on the Zwinglian side.

Catholics and Lutherans seem excessively fastened to the physical elements. Calvin was always urging his Lutheran friends to look away from them, lift up their hearts to heaven. *That* is where Christ's body and blood are! But the position associated (not quite fairly) with Zwingli seemed to err in the opposite way. The Zwinglians thought of the elements as symbols useful for helping us look back to and remember Christ's death. There was little *present* focus in their sacrament. Lugubrious hymns and a mournful or funeral atmosphere fit well with the Zwinglian position.

Reformed thinkers took a position between these two extremes. They said that in the supper we actually do receive the real body and blood of Christ—now. Of course we do not crassly suppose that we chew flesh with our teeth or swallow blood. We receive these gifts "in our souls" and "by faith (which is the hand and mouth of our soul)." That is, we are joined to Christ in all His benefits.

That is the main idea in the supper—union with Christ. We do not bodily merge with Him. Nor, perhaps, are we mystically swallowed up by Christ's personality. Yet union goes far beyond mere remembering. It has to do with much more than my personal feelings when I take in the bread and wine. Union with Christ, as we saw in an earlier chapter, has to do with being a member of the redeemed community in history, being "in" Christ's whole new cosmic order. And for our work in this community and our role in this new order the supper is both symbol and strength. The Israelites were nourished by "supernatural" food and drink (I Cor. 10:3,4) on their way from Egypt to Canaan, that is, from liberation to final rest. So are we.

Conclusion

This last line of thought suggests two final observations: One is that all sacraments, as the Introduction mentions, are community gifts, covenant gifts. To be united with Christ is to be baptized into His body, into His new community in history. That is the reason for asking the *congregation* to make a solemn pledge when an infant is baptized. And to partake of our Lord's Supper is to be bonded more firmly to His other children. Spokes are closest together at the hub. There is no isolated communion. We *all* partake of the one bread. No one of us at communion should think only "Christ died for me." One rather should reflect on the fact that Christ's gifts are for the saints—for my grandfather, and my aunt, and my mother, and my fearful, hopeless neighbor. And—for me. For me *too*.

Secondly, the right focus of sacraments is not just backward, but also forward. In baptism we are marked and graciously set in a nourishing matrix. But we must grow up and out in faith and obedience. We must lead baptized lives. What is more, we have promised to look out for the baptized children of others. Some of these children are not the same color as we are and have had a different sort of history. Yet, as Richard Mouw observes, if we baptize a child and promise to love him, care for him, and encourage him, we at once involve the church in politics. For whites to adopt and love a black child, for example, is to "look at the world from his point of view, to make his hopes and fears our very own." It means protesting on his behalf if he should be maltreated; it means suffering as he suffers when racist jokes are told; it means the use of discipline *as a guarding of the sacraments* if the word *nigger* should be heard among us! Because it involves the community and looks ahead to life in community of these little ones, baptism is an intensely activist and political sacrament.

So with the Lord's Supper. Its focus is not only backward to Christ's death. Insofar as we do look back, we recall our Lord's whole career—including His triumphant resurrection. "Do this as a memorial of *me*," He said. And the Lord whom we adore and for whose redemptive acts we give thanks is alive. So we look to the present and future. The Israelites celebrated the Passover with their shoes on (Ex. 12:11). They had to be ready to move out into the wilderness. There was to be no delicious lingering over a meal. They were to be on their feet, faces set toward the future, staff in hand for the journey ahead. So with us. Our Passover Lamb has been sacrificed. Now we look forward. The Lord's Supper is no time for lingering at the cross and arriving late at the tomb. Rather, as de Bres says, this sacrament must spur us on, fire us up, move us out. We are to be *"moved* by the use of this holy sacrament to a fervent love towards God and our neighbor." The gifts of God are given to the people of God not to inspire weepy feelings but to rouse us for action. We have been refreshed; now we must go on.

CHAPTER 25
Civil Government

Belgic Confession, Article XXXVI

Introduction

Should public schools allow prayer and Bible reading? Must Christians respond without question whenever their governments call them to war? Do Christian opponents of abortion on demand seek to impose a *religious* view of life on a secular nation? Should the state's treasury support every legitimate sort of education—including Christian education? May Christians try to get stores to close on the Lord's Day and porno theaters to close permanently? In what way and on what grounds? Is it a dangerous symbolism for Christian churches to fly a national flag in their sanctuaries?

These and similar questions test one's general understanding of the relation of church and state. It is on that relation and on the nature of civil government that Article XXXVI speaks. It speaks in a way that seems very up-to-date because of our very modern concern with the sorts of questions which the church and state issue raises. But it seems dated because it speaks from a perspective that nearly everybody, including Reformed believers, now rejects. That perspective is *sacralism*. A sacral society, as L. Verduin says, "is a society held together by a religion to which all members of that society are committed." In a sacral society, the state naturally favors the one religion. Like most everyone in the sixteenth century, except the Anabaptists, both Calvin and de Bres thought the state *ought* to be the church's strong arm, discouraging its heretics by the sword and officially promoting orthodox doctrine. But because of the healthy influence of the Anabaptists (who were following a small, but old, tradition of Christians who rejected sacralism), and because of the subsequent rise of modern democracy, practically no Reformed people now take the position from which XXXVI was written. That is why the article appears in historically mutilated form. It has submitted to surgery but, unfortunately, the surgeons did not quite get all the dead parts. They did cut away the part about the state's duty to "remove and prevent all idolatry and false worship." But they overlooked the last paragraph which offers several intolerant and inaccurate reasons for our own duty to "detest" certain other Christians.

Let us examine the issues in this fascinating and troublesome article: first, the origin and purpose of government, secondly, the duties of citizens with respect to government; finally, the attack on Anabaptists.

Origin and Purpose of Government

Article XXXVI begins where all biblical views of the state begin—with God. In Romans 13, the classical place to look for the Christian idea of the state, Paul says that the governing authorities have been "instituted by God" (vs. 1). He says twice that such authorities are God's servants. The words he uses, as is sometimes pointed out, are instructive. Magistrates are "deacons" in the Greek of verse 4 and "liturgetes" in the Greek of verse 6. The idea is that God employs human beings to speak and act on His behalf. He uses deputies, ministers, servants. He uses magistrates. Therefore, says Paul, "he who resists the authorities resists what God has appointed."

De Bres follows Paul. It is not we but "our gracious God" who has appointed kings. Nobody in the sixteenth century could have dreamed of the humanist social contract theories, for example, which arose in eighteenth century France. Even the Anabaptists, who were routinely said to "reject the higher powers and magistrates," insisted that the state is "of God." People in the

ALICE VELDMAN
11·13·78

sixteenth century were generally devout where the state is concerned. Did not Paul say that obedience to governing authorities was a matter not of practical strategy but of "conscience"? (vs.5).

The state, then, is a divine institution. It is an instrument of God's general sovereignty, as Abraham Kuyper liked to say. It has its own sovereignty, derived from God, in its own sphere. What does the state do in its sphere? For one thing, it restrains "the dissoluteness of men." The state holds a leash or raises a curb. It restrains wildness and lawlessness for the sake of "good order and decency." Because of human fallenness, because there are marauders, swindlers, and disorderly persons, God has arranged for state "punishment of evil-doers and . . . protection of them that do well."

How? By investing the magistracy with the sword. Some medieval popes claimed that God had actually equipped the *church* with two swords. One is the Word of God (Heb. 4:12). The other is the police power of the state. Catholics liked to think of the state as under church control. The Reformers tried to reserve more independence for the state. But both groups simply assumed that the sword of the state should back up the work of the church. If somebody was delinquent in doctrine or in life, if somebody was reckless or lazy in the things of the faith, the magistrate's sword would bar his/her way or prick him/her into action.

Nowadays, of course, we see the matter quite differently. We keep the two swords much farther apart. We have a high wall of separation between church and state. Thus, we do not expect an FBI agent to pack a pocket Bible for the reproof of counterfeiters. We do not want meter maids to quote I Corinthians 7:29a on our parking tickets. Nor do we hand over a liberal theology professor to some strong-armed detective, to the end that he might be labored with and get his doctrine adjusted. We want our theologians to get right doctrine voluntarily. In general, because of the Anabaptist and democratic influences already mentioned, we simply assume that the state should be impartial among all religions and that the church should be content with the Word of God and moral persuasion to make its way in the world.

But de Bres still has the older view. Part of what he says we hold too. God has ordained a hierarchy of "kings, princes, and magistrates" (we would say "presidents, governors, and mayors," or the like) to punish evildoers and protect them that do well. So far, so good. Thieves are to be punished; householders protected. Killers are to be punished; innocent citizens protected. Molesters are to be punished; children protected. That is part of "the welfare of the civil state."

But de Bres goes much further; he includes heretics among evildoers and orthodox believers among them that do well. He believes the state's police power should reach into the church. Thus, in the originial version of XXXVI we read this:

> Their office is not only to have regard unto and watch for the welfare of the civil state, but also that they protect the sacred ministry, and thus may remove and prevent all idolatry and false worship, that the kingdom of antichrist may be thus destroyed and the kingdom of Christ promoted.

Here the Confession plainly reflects its time. Since the fourth century, when Constantine Christianized the Roman Empire for political reasons (he had a vision of the cross and of the words "In this sign you shall *conquer*"), the church regarded the state as its ally and aid. The Reformers kept this Constantinian notion. Calvin did not personally burn Servetus over a slow fire of green wood; the civil magistrates performed this service (Calvin urged beheading). The Dutch Reformed in Groningen did not themselves run local Anabaptists out of town; they tried (not always with total success) to get the local police to do it.

In sixteenth century Protestantism, only the Anabaptists—the "radicals," the "left-wingers," the "Stepchildren of the Reformers"—rejected Constantinianism and the sacral society. They thought of the church as an assembly of true believers, not as the mass of people who merely happened to live in a certain region. They thought the church ought to be disciplined only by the Word of God and excommunication, not by the police as well. For these "seditious" ideas they were cruelly persecuted by Catholics, Lutherans, and Reformed alike. To all these, anybody who protested the sacral hookup of church and state was a subverter of justice, a dangerous anarchist, a denier of "higher powers and magistrates."

It was not until a century or two later that Anabaptist ideas really took hold. Many Christians, including Reformed Christians, began to take stands against the forcible eradication of idolatry and promotion of Christianity by the state. Thus, in our century, synods of the Christian Reformed Church said in 1910 and 1938 that use of the sword in the church was unbiblical and was an abridgment of religious freedom. Hence, the use of the sword to trim Article XXXVI.

The trimming left us with a modest testimony to the state's duty to "protect the sacred ministry." Most Christians agree with the First Amendment of the U. S. Constitution, that the state must not *establish* a particular religion as dominant (as was done in the old sacral system). Nor must it interfere with, or allow the interference with, the free exercise of any particular religion. In the 1960s there was a classic example of how these principles work. A Christian Reformed Church in Grand Rapids, Michigan, held its evening worship at the same time as, and near to, the games of a semi-professional football team. The Reformed people of that church did not try to get Sunday football canceled as a violation of the fourth commandment. But they did try to get the city government to outlaw the shooting of cannons after touchdowns—on the grounds that it interfered with their freedom to worship in peace. They won.

Citizens' Duties

The most general duty of citizens to their magistrates is to "subject" themselves. Nobody rules him or herself. Everybody is born a subject of some state. To bow the head before a mere human would be intolerable, said Kuyper. But when we bend ourselves in subjection to a person who rules by God's leave, we become taller.

De Bres lists four dimensions of this general subjection to magistrates. First, we are to "pay tribute." We pay taxes. Why? Obviously because the state needs money to do its work. Here it is important to remember that Calvin (whom de Bres generally follows) held a very positive idea of the state's work. The state does not merely restrain sin. It does do that, but it also does much more. It also promotes social justice. It is not only a bridle on sin, but also a spur to good, as Calvin put it. Some political analysts have called Calvin's own view of the state's role a kind of

YOUNG ADULTS, INWOOD CRC
11·16·78

socialism. However, it is at least clear that the "depravity of man" in the Reformed view is such that greed must sometimes be curbed and redistribution of resources promoted. The state protects my having and holding of property and my gaining of assets—but may also limit these things for the sake of justice. As Calvin saw it, because God has made us social creatures, our individual rights may never override our social duties. Perhaps we can read this Calvinist idea into de Bres' claim that God has ordained the state so that "decency" may prevail among us.

Secondly, we are to "show due honor and respect" to governing authorities. This is an implication of the fact that the magistrate represents God. Calvin did not shrink from using exalted language about governors. We are to "reverence them as God's ministers and vicegerants." Their judgment seat is "the throne of the living God." Their mouth is "an instrument of divine truth." They may properly be called "gods." In fact, as Calvin extravagantly concludes, "no one ought to doubt that civil authority is...the most sacred and by far the most honorable of all callings in the whole life of mortal man" (*Institutes* IV, xx, 4).

This from a man who criticizes "the flatterers of princes"!

Still, extravagance aside, Calvin and de Bres are on solid biblical ground when they counsel the honoring of rulers. In the same passage (I Pet. 2:17) in which we are told to "honor all men" we are also told to "honor the emperor." *God* rules through this person. A magistrate who is greedy, lazy, and stupid still has divine power and majesty. For Calvinists, no officer of the law is a "pig." Calvinists do not object to standing up for presidents or to addressing judges as "your honor." They hope for a worthy officer for so high an office, but in any case, look past the person to the divine ordination of his function.

Thirdly, we are "to obey them in all things which are not repugnant to the Word of God." Here is a rule—with its famous exception from Acts 5:29—on which Christians have never been able to agree. In modern times Christians have screamed at each other over the question of obedience to a government that engages in dubious and undeclared war. Pastors have participated in plots to assassinate Hitler. Priests have gone to jail for encouraging draft resistance. Civil rights

122

workers have refused to be bound by racist laws. Netherlanders have tried in every way to undermine and subvert Nazi rule. Christian Scientists have refused mandatory medical treatment for their children.

The question of civil disobedience has long engaged the minds of thoughtful Reformed Christians. For Calvin, obedience is primary. You do not disobey a law whimsically or lightly. You do not disobey merely because you disagree with a law or find it inconvenient. Even when rulers are unjust and tyrannical, said Calvin, our main posture is one of patience and prayer. Doubtless God is punishing us for our sin.

Yet, there are limits. No citizen may ever obey a ruler who tells him to do what is wrong or forbids him to do what, under God, is his duty. Calvin would have none of the idea, sometimes advanced by Christians today, that our business is to obey government unquestioningly and let the *governors* worry about the morality of it. Not at all. That is to surrender one's God-given conscience to another. In fact, says Calvin, there are times when "in his goodness" God raised up revolutionaries! God gets tyrants off our backs by allowing "lesser magistrates" to revolt and lead the rest of us in revolt. In a rare passage of impassioned revolutionary mood, Calvin claims that when earthly princes "rise up against God" we ought to "spit on their heads" rather than obey them.

Finally, to change the mood, we are to pray for magistrates. In I Timothy there is an urging that prayers be made "for kings and all who are in high places." De Bres passes the injunction along. Thus, many congregational prayers in Reformed churches today include prayer for government executives, legislators, and judges. This is a way of recognizing both their status as God's deputies and the difficulty and ambiguity of their work.

Attack on the Anabaptists

In his penetrating book, *The Reformers and Their Stepchildren*, Leonard Verduin fully documents what many Reformed people have suspected for a long time. They have suspected that the last paragraph of Article XXXVI is neither charitable nor accurate.

For one thing, it claims that we *detest* certain other Christians. Yet, as we know from the teaching of our Lord, detesting other persons—even enemies—is gross sin. We may hate what people do or say. But we may not hate any people.

For another thing, the paragraph accuses Anabaptists of things which most of them never did and of one thing which is scarcely to be detested. There was indeed a lunatic fringe of Anabaptist-like persons in the Netherlands and elsewhere (those involved in the Munster incident, for example). But these were at least as great an embarrassment to the majority of Stepchildren as they were to anyone else. The majority of people did not "reject the higher powers and magistrates." Their Schleitheim Confession of 1527 specifically says that "the sword is an ordinance of God." It is, however, to be used "outside the perfection of Christ"; i.e. the church. Fair enough. That is what we think today. Moreover the Stepchildren can hardly be called "seditious." Sedition is an act of inciting people to rebellion against the state. Anabaptists were opposed to acts of rebellion—surely to violent ones. The "fault" of the Anabaptists was that they rejected the sacral setup. They regarded the alliance of church and state as an evil. They wanted no part of a system in which the church calls upon the state to use swords in hacking away heresy. Nor did they want to take office and rule. Nor, because they were pacifists, did they want to fight wars.

The result was inevitable. Because they did not found a state-supported church in any area, Anabaptists had to live in areas officially Catholic, Lutheran, or Reformed. In these areas they were regarded as enemies of both church and state. Because they rejected the sword in matters of faith, they were accused of rejecting the sword in general. So other Christians made life miserable for them. Some were drowned ("You believe in adult immersion? Then get your fill of it!"). Some were cut or burned. Most were banned, harassed, and pursued. The sixteenth century persecution of Anabaptists is one of the saddest and most regrettable chapters in the story of Protestantism.

One of the things which Article XXXVI charges against the Anabaptists is that they "introduce a community of goods." But, as Verduin shows, very few Anabaptist groups practiced common ownership. And, obviously, the ones who did (the Hutterites, for example) did it freely among themselves, in their own religious group. Most groups simply provided generously by diaconal arrangement for the care of the poor and needy among them. That is scarcely anything detestable. Why would a Reformed Confession regard a community of goods, in either a tight or loose sense, as objectionable? Surely de Bres knew about Acts 2:44,45. Surely Calvin himself promoted social welfare and an active diaconate in Geneva. "Community of goods!" as an *accusation* does not seem to make much sense at all. Indeed, as many commentators have said, if Christians in the nineteenth century had practiced it more, Marxism could not have appealed so effectively to the Christian poor.

Conclusion

Three brief observations may be made: First, Reformed people have come to adopt the main part of what Anabaptists were advocating in the sixteenth century. We stand closer to them on church/state relations than to Calvin and de Bres. We do not think government ought to support a particular religion. If we lived in a largely orthodox Jewish community, we would be annoyed if the community tried to pass Saturday-closing-laws for stores: Similarly, Reformed Christians who want stores closed on Sunday properly appeal to reasons other than the fourth commandment's prohibition of Sabbath work. In general, we tend to support legislation based on the second table of the law (commandments 6-10) rather than that based on the first. For changing society with respect to the first table, we rely on preaching of the Word and on individual and group witnessing.

Secondly, a number of Reformed thinkers have urged that we follow the Anabaptists in conceiving of the state as religiously *impartial*—but not neutral—in a pluralist society. The state must not try somehow to be *neutral*, these thinkers say. That is, the state must not try to insulate itself from all religious and irreligious concerns. Rather, so far as it can, it should seek to give all religions and irreligions equal sway. It is in this context of impartiality that we should see the debate over state funds for Christian education. Can the state be impartial while unnecessarily requiring some of its citizens to pay extra for the practice of their religion?

Finally, the debates over church/state relations are not merely academic. We have seen in modern history examples on both the political right and left of the muzzling of the church by the state. In Nazi Germany, an order went out to the churches in 1934. Preachers were not to comment on political and social affairs. They were to confine themselves to "the preaching of the pure gospel." Many did. Here they conceded, as the Barmen Declaration has it, that there are "areas of our life in which we would not belong to Jesus Christ, but to other lords." In communist countries, speaking out as a Christian is still hazardous to your health. Communist governments continue a regular campaign by force and propaganda against the growth and independence of the church. In Poland, for example, the most popular television programs all seem to be shown on Sunday morning!

States can easily become monsters. Churches and church people can easily be bent to conform to state wishes. It can all begin in small and seemingly harmless ways—requiring the pledge of state allegiance instead of the Apostles' Creed in Christian schools, regarding patriotism as the first fruit of the Spirit, charging treason against anyone who questions the government. But the results in our own era have shown us the twisted face of the totalitarian state and the astonished face of the church that is no longer free.

124

CHAPTER 26
The Last Judgment

Belgic Confession, Article XXXVII

Introduction

We come, at last, to the end. Not only the Confession, but also all history drives toward a climax in which our Lord returns to make all things permanently new.

The study of this climax is called *eschatology*, or doctrine of "the last things." Eschatology is disquieting. Here, as someone put it, the gap between Christians and the world yawns widest. Confession of the last things is among the most "supernatural" of all our confessions. It deals, after all, with angels, recovery of bodies dead for centuries, and heaven and hell. Even many Christians find the whole subject somehow embarrassing. They know it sounds fantastic to unbelievers; they find it quite bewildering themselves. So some Christians restrict their interest to current secular questions about the "other side" of death ("What happens to me when I die?"). Others keep learned silence, or maintain a studied ignorance of all things eschatological. But some, notably those called "premillenarians," readily apply obscure Old Testament prophecies to complex current events with a confidence which baffles everybody but themselves.

So there is either determined silence or controversy. Mainline churches tend toward the former. Fundamentalist and sectarian groups tend toward the latter. Often what is at stake is the question of how one reads the Bible. How much of the biblical language about the last things is to be taken literally? What about the Son of Man "coming on the clouds of heaven"? What about the shouts and the sound of the trumpet? Or, to stay with musical instruments, how about the heavenly harps of Revelation 15? What do we make of "streets of gold" in heaven and both outer *darkness* and a lake of *fire* in hell? Are these

images? Just images? Are some of the descriptions of last things to be understood literally and some not? How do we know?

But beyond the question of understanding biblical language, there is another question. In discussion of the end we face the issue of the everlasting punishment of the wicked in hell. That this is a delicate and troubled issue is shown by the deafening silence of pulpits and theological books. Do we dare talk calmly and with assurance about everlasting punishment for others—no worse in their sins than we? Do we dare picture the last judgment as Michelangelo did?

> . . . who is not familiar . . . with Michelangelo's famous painting of the last judgment on the wall of the Sistine chapel? The central figure is Christ, the irate judge who with a gesture of repudiation turns to the damned who are lying at his feet, their faces twisted with despair. The martyrs who surround Christ encourage him to revenge them. But Mary, seated at the right hand of Christ, turns with horror away from this scene.
>
> (H. Berkhof, *Well-Founded Hope*)

It must be admitted that Christians have traditionally been too glib about the temperature of hell and the trappings of heaven. Some have even smacked their lips over the prospect of other human beings' everlasting torture. What is needed in this whole area is a kind of faithful shyness, a willingness to follow Scripture with humility. There are secrets here and great surprises, as our Lord's parable of the sheep and the goats (Matt. 25) makes clear. Care, compassion, and restraint are called for in our discussion of final things. We now see through a glass darkly. Our talk must reflect the dimness of our vision.

But in our eagerness to avoid some traditional errors, we must not fall into modern ones. Some liberal Christians talk matter-of-factly about universal salvation, as if there were no biblical evidence on the other side at all. Others allow embarrassment to rob them of the Christian's deepest and most magnificent hope. One day the poor who cry to God *will* be vindicated. One day those of us who endure cerebral palsy will have splendid new bodies. One day those of us who have struggled miserably with depression shall be clear and bright again. One day the whole cosmos, the whole created world—with all of its corruptions, injustices, and fears—shall be restored. Finally, the God who has been masked to so many for so long shall come without disguise. The glory of His purposes and the rightness of His ways will be unmistakable to all. We must look forward to such things. "If for this life only we have hoped in Christ, we are of all men most to be pitied" (I Cor. 15:19).

Let us gather the material of Article XXXVII around the four eschatological confessions of the Apostles' Creed:

> From thence he shall come
> To judge the living and the dead.
> I believe the resurrection of the body;
> And the life everlasting.

From Thence He Shall Come...

De Bres starts his last article, as always, with "We believe." But this time it is "*Finally*, we believe." We believe that "when the time...is come" then "our Lord Jesus Christ will come."

Two preliminary remarks: First, "the second coming" is short for all those last events which fundamentalists and sectarians find so fascinating and mainliners or liberals so embarrassing. In the first case we sometimes see what Calvin called "subtle and extravagant speculation...an inordinate desire of knowing more than is right." In the latter case we sometimes see subtle agnosticism, an inordinate desire of knowing nothing at all. Thus, it is not unusual to hear general talk of the coming of the kingdom—with no mention of the coming of the King.

Secondly, it seems a bit strange to refer to a *second* coming. It sounds as if our Lord is now absent. The fact is that He is very much with us—"to the close of the age" (Matt. 28:20). He is present both by His Spirit and in His body, the church.

But what Article XXXVII wants to emphasize, of course, is that this new or last coming, this final parousia (or "presence"), is different. Our Lord is not now with us physically. In the second coming He will come "corporally." He will come

with a *body*—just as He ascended. This suggests that heaven may be understood as a place, since bodies occupy space. But wariness and care is in order. Christ's resurrected body (assuming it is the same one in which He ascended and will reappear) had strange qualities in the post-resurrection appearances. It seemed to be able to appear and disappear unusually. So we must not be dogmatic about heaven as a place.

Another difference between Christ's presence now and then is that then it will be apparent to the senses. He is to come back "visibly." The New Testament often uses the word *revelation* in this connection. There will be a disclosure, an unveiling, a visual revelation of Christ (Luke 17:30, I Pet. 1:13, etc.).

Part of the "great glory and majesty" associated with this return is that it is in the company of others. It will not (we may say seriously) be a solo appearance, although it is a public appearance. Here we will *see* some of the communal context with which we have all along associated union with Christ. The hosts of heaven, only slightly represented at His ascension, will be back in force (II Thess. 1:7). The sons of God, the church, the armies of heaven are all part of this great disclosure (Rom. 8:19, I Thess. 4:17, Rev. 19:14). Christ returns as the center of a community.

Just as the Bible does, the Confession seeks to cut off speculation about the *time* of His return. It is simply "when the time...is come," or "[when] the number of the elect [is] complete." But this time is "unknown to all creatures." Indeed, those of us given to making confident predictions, or to computing with pocket calculators, or to confident reading of the "signs of the time" are reminded in the Scriptures that the precise time is none of our business! We are to watch and be alert.

We are to do one more thing. We are to "repent, for the kingdom of God is at hand." In one of the great passages in contemporary Christian literature, C. S. Lewis states the urgency of it unforgettably:

> God is going to invade, all right: but what is the good of saying you are on his side then, when you see the whole natural universe melting away like a dream and something else—something it never entered your head to conceive—comes crashing in; something so beautiful to some of us and so terrible to others that none of us will have any choice left? For this time it will be God without disguise; something so overwhelming that it will strike either

126

irresistible love or irresistible horror into every creature. It will be too late then to choose your side. (*Mere Christianity*)

To Judge the Living and the Dead

The last judgment is the purpose of the second coming. It is called a *last* judgment because there are others. God is always using ways and means for reestablishing His order. Through His acts in this life He "executes judgment, putting down one and lifting up another" (Ps. 75:7). In fact, all through their lives people are judged by whether or not they live in Christ. Then, when they die, they are privately judged by their residence either with or apart from God. It is only at the end that there is *final* judgment.

Isn't it superfluous? Hasn't it already been decided who is ready to be with Christ?

Yes, it has already been decided. The other judgments are individual and private. The last judgment is corporate and public. Its main goal is the glorifying and vindication of Him who "declares Himself Judge of the living and the dead." Some will be living; some will have been dead for centuries. All will be summoned and hosted by Christ. Then every knee shall bow—gladly or reluctantly.

Everybody, says the Confession, will have to "give account." All "secrets and hypocrisy" shall be revealed, "laid open before all." This is a most puzzling and fearful prospect. What do we make of it? How could it work? Are we to imagine, as E. A. Dowey asks, that "billions of people from countless millennia of life on the planet" will individually be examined and exposed in front of all the others? The righteous who have enjoyed bliss for ages will have to reenter the life of sin at least mentally? They too will be publicly reminded of stray thoughts, harsh words, and unkind deeds?

It is all very mysterious. The relevant biblical passages (I Cor. 4:5, Rom. 2:16, Rev. 20:12,13) are not very specific. But we may at least make three observations: First, however it works, believers are included in it. What the Confession says about "all men" seems confirmed by Revelation 20:12,13.

Second, this judgment is strangely oriented not to our trust in Christ, but to our *works*. We are judged according to what we "have *done* in this world." Here we see a very biblical theme (see, for example, Matt. 25 and the epistle of James) coming to bear on a sensitive place in our relationship with God and others. Works matter. Works

JEANNE ENGELHARD
1-25-79

count. According to Matthew 25, moreover, the goats are not so much those who did what was wrong as those who failed to do what was right,

> as if to make us fairly sure that the heaviest charge against each of us turns not upon the things he has done but on those he never did—perhaps never dreamed of doing.
>
> (C. S. Lewis, *Reflections on the Psalms*)

Faith is judged by its fruits. There is an ultimate seriousness about life and the use of its gifts and opportunities even for the redeemed.

Why? After all, they are already saved with a salvation which cannot be lost. Perhaps a clue lies in the strong hints which the Bible gives that there may be *degrees* of bliss and horror in the final state. That is the third observation. Relatively "innocent" heathen will find things more tolerable than those who have been knowingly exposed to God's mighty works (Matt. 11:22). Some believers, on the other hand, will "suffer loss" on the day of judgment, though they themselves will be saved, "but only as through fire" (I Cor. 3:15). The focus in either case is works.

I Believe in the Resurrection of the Body

The resurrection of the body, which precedes the last judgment, is a very distinctively Christian emphasis. Lots of pagan religions believe in the continued existence of the soul. Greek philosophers such as Plato firmly believed that the soul was immortal and could not be destroyed.

The Christian confession is rather that the soul's continued existence after death is a work of God. It is not an inalienable right. But it is very real. And it is without a body. There can be no doubt that in Reformed confessions the separability of soul and body is assumed. Persons are not the same things as their bodies. A body dies or "sleeps" (cemeteries are literally "sleeping places"). But persons do not. Certain Reformational believers claimed that at death a believer falls into "psychopannychia," or soul-sleep. Calvin and the Reformed always denied it. Calvin regarded it as an implication of our union with Christ that when we die we are *consciously* with Him.

Yet not even Calvin believed, like the Greeks, in merely disposable bodies. True, souls can live without bodies. Yet bodies are still very important in God's scheme. Bodiless existence for believers after death is temporary, provisional, incomplete. It is a yearning existence (Rev. 6:9). Calvin affirms that there is already an "enjoyment of promised glory." Yet there is not total fulfillment. For fulfillment we need bodies. Till

then we are in a state of waiting and wanting. "All things are held in suspense until Christ the Redeemer appear" (*Institutes* III, xxv, 6). There may be an echo of this in the Confession's acknowledgment that only after the last judgment do the righteous find "full deliverance" as "perfected."

The thought of billions of decomposed bodies being resurrected is staggering: "all the dead shall be raised out of the earth, and their souls joined and united with their proper bodies in which they formerly lived." Calvin claimed this was "a thing difficult to be believed," and supposed that the difficulty partly accounted for the fact that ancient philosophers accepted only the immortality of the soul.

Perhaps it is difficult for some. Yet, as Calvin adds, there is help: "the Scripture supplies us with two assistances." One is the plain fact, frankly to be confessed, that God is omnipotent. We who are creatures have small minds and poverty-stricken imaginations. But God, with whom all things are possible, is the unimaginably potent Creator and the inconceivably resourceful Recreator. No doubt He can rearrange His creation in the requisite ways so that we get our bodies back.

The Confession says that these will be our "proper" bodies. It is not referring to seemliness or gentility (bodies dressed up right and proper as suits the occasion). It means our *own* bodies—the same ones "in which [we] formerly lived." The thinking behind this is that we have had in history an example of the resurrection of the body. Our Lord was the firstfruits of the general harvest of bodies. And His body was the same one He had before: It had the wounds He had received, for example, and was recognizably His. Yet it also had some new properties. We have already mentioned His ease of appearance and disappearance. But also, though He could be recognized, He could be recognized only with *difficulty*, only when people's "eyes were opened" (Luke 24:31).

But are we entitled to draw inferences about our own resurrection bodies from the case of our Lord? We are. It is the second *biblical* assistance of which Calvin talks. The Lord, says Paul explicitly, "will change our lowly body to be like his glorious body" (Phil. 3:21). Here is the uniquely and graciously Christian assurance. Secularists offer no hope to those sons and daughters of God who have had to put up with bodies twisted by paralysis or deformed at birth or vulnerable to every infection. They have been dealt a bad hand by fate, and that is all there is to it. But Christians see far beyond that. They see bodies of power, beauty, and freedom. To the poor of spirit and body whom God blesses, C. S. Lewis once said, "[God] knows what a wretched machine you are trying to drive. Keep on. Do what you can. One day . . . he will give you a new one."

And the Life Everlasting

The life everlasting comes in two kinds. One of them is not good. God's "terrible vengeance" shall be executed on the wicked. They too shall "become immortal." But their existence is really nothing but a constant death. They "shall be tormented in the eternal fire which is prepared for the devil and his angels."

Here is perhaps the most terrible doctrine of orthodox Christianity. Usually those who oppose it are thought to be soft on sin and insufficiently informed of its seriousness. But that is not necessarily so. Thoughtful Christians in every age have wondered and agonized over this doctrine. Their wonderings are familiar to us. Many of us have had them too. Why must the wicked be punished *forever*—if that is what is implied by an "eternal" fire? Why not only enough to induce repentance? Or else, why aren't they painlessly annihilated? In any event, how does any one of us dare talk presumptuously about "the wicked," as if they were somehow a different animal from ourselves? After all, part of the confession of salvation by grace alone is that any saved person richly deserves whatever punishment anybody else receives.

A couple of comments: First, the doctrine of punishment in the life to come is scriptural. Strikingly, some of the strongest language about it is on the lips of our Lord (e.g. Matt. 25;41; 13:42). Any discussion of the dark side of everlasting life must squarely face this fact. Secondly, it is undeniable that according to the Bible sin is an evil which grievously offends the holiness of God and deserves retribution. We ourselves get a feeling for it when the Nazi atrocities "come home" to us or when we consider the fact that most human misdeeds, including many human crimes, are never found out—let alone punished. Do we suppose that the bombers of black churches and the murderers of little girls shall never have to face up to what they have done? When we become genuinely angry and indignant over sin—including our own—the idea of retributive justice in the life to come seems terribly believable. But, thirdly, we need to approach this subject with great caution and humility. According to Matthew 7:21 and 22 it is religious people—people most likely to be discussing the afterlife—who may be stunned by the slam of that everlasting door and the terri-

ble words "I never knew you." This, together with the surprises in Matthew 25, ought to prevent any casual self-assurance about the life to come. It is one thing to have a humble, trusting "assurance of salvation." It is another to simply *assume* that those who have to pay personally for their sins will have other names than ours.

Hendrikus Berkhof, a Dutch Reformed theologian with impeccable credentials for taking sin, evil, and the supernatural seriously, points out that the biblical word on the finality of punishment is of two kinds. One kind includes the texts we have already mentioned—sayings of Jesus, and other passages which point to "torment for ever and ever," or "the punishment of eternal

BILL BOORSMA
1-26-79

destruction." These texts, says Berkhof, "are not to be reasoned away."

But neither are some others—ones, for example, in which the word "all" appears: "For as in Adam all die, so also in Christ shall all be made alive"; "God desires all men to be saved"; "God who is the Savior of all men, especially those who believe"; "Jesus Christ . . . is the expiation for our sins, and not for ours only but also for the sins of the whole world."

Now no liberal theologian made these sayings up. They are in the *Bible*. They must be faced just as biblically and just as squarely as those on the other side. And here, it must be admitted, we have sometimes resorted to exegetical maneuvers of dubious validity—understanding "all men" for example as "not all men, but all *kinds* of men." We have used the everlasting punishment texts to adjust our interpretation of the universal texts while universalists have done it just the other way around.

Berkhof concludes with a "hope" that God's rejection of unbelievers has its limits and that

> hell means a purification . . . I know that to many this sounds strange and heretical. But the attitude of these "many" is often strange and cruel; they would immediately warn their nonbelieving neighbor when his house was on fire, but they believe at the same time that he is rejected forever and they seem to be easily reconciled to this fact. Or do they perhaps not really believe it? I think so and I hope so. How could we as a Christian minority live in a de-Christianized world if it were not for the fact that we may believe that God in his mercy knows what to do with all this lack of willingness and power to believe? But at the same time we shudder to think of the deep crisis and purification through which everything has to go first. To be elected to believe already now becomes a matter of both grateful wonder and high calling. (*Well-Founded Hope*)

Berkhof goes farther than Reformed people have traditionally dared to go. Yet he offers a healthy rebuke to any of us who talks with a smile or a yawn about the everlasting punishment of other human beings. And he reminds us—even when we stick to the traditional view—that we had better remember that the same Scriptures which provide us with strong statements about the seriousness of sin and the reality of divine punishment also speak in wondrous, aching ways about God's *all*. Let us, at least, be slow to let that *all* somehow dwindle to *some* among whom, interestingly, we do not fail to find *us*. G. C.

LION WEDDING
9 30 78

Berkouwer rightly approves the attitude of H. Vogel: "If there is hope from God even for me, how much more so for others!"

The other kind of "life everlasting" is marked by "glory and honor." The faithful are received, welcomed, acknowledged. Their *names* are confessed. In some final, magnificent way the faithful get inside the presence and splendor of God. Glory—that "glory as never entered into the heart of man to conceive"—is a rich and weighty thing beyond the stretch of our minds. C. S. Lewis suggests that we think first of fame or good report:

> To please God...to be a real ingredient in the divine happiness...to be loved by God, not merely pitied, but delighted in as an artist delights in his work or a father in a son—it seems impossible, a weight or burden of glory which our thoughts can hardly sustain. But so it is.   (*The Weight of Glory*)

But there is more. The biblical associations with glory are so often ones of shining, of light, of luminosity. It is not that, one day, we shall merely *see* glory. In some unspeakable way we shall ourselves be glorious. At present we see the glory of a landscape in a way which makes us yearn to "pass into it, to receive it into ourselves, to bathe in it, to become part of it:

> At present we are on the outside of the world, the wrong side of the door. We discern the freshness and purity of morning, but they do not make *us* fresh and pure. We cannot mingle with the splendours we see. But all the leaves of the New Testament are rustling with the rumor that it will not always be so. Some day, God willing, we shall get *in*.
> (*The Weight of Glory*)

Conclusion

We have only touched in this chapter on a host of fascinating questions. One cannot miss, for example, the note of urgency and poignancy in the writing of Guido de Bres, so soon to be martyred for the Reformed faith and to possess the glory of which he writes.

Neither can one miss a tragic irony. In his cruel circumstances, de Bres writes of the "cause, which is now condemned by many judges and magistrates as heretical" which will one day "be known to be the cause of the Son of God." Undoubtedly he partly has the Reformed cause in mind. In that day, says de Bres, "their innocence shall be known to all, and they shall *see* the terrible vengeance which God shall execute on the wicked, who most cruelly persecuted, tormented, and oppressed them in this world."

Here de Bres falls victim to the ancient temptation of the persecuted to comfort each other with the prospect of a turnabout, of the opportunity to view the suffering of those who now cause suffering in others. What a thing to see! If a child who has been beaten up by a neighborhood bully can just be given the chance to *watch* his older brother minister retribution to the bully, his comfort is complete.

We are "allergic" to this kind of seeing and watching language, as someone has said. It smacks too much of gloating and of a pleasure in the death of the wicked which is foreign to God and the godly. But the tragic irony is, of course, that while the Reformed were being persecuted by the Catholics, the Anabaptists were being persecuted by (among others) the Reformed. These are the people de Bres himself detested. They too were "condemned by many judges and magistrates as heretical." Their literature in this period contains some of the same profound belief that God will one day vindicate them against the Reformed and others who have "most cruelly persecuted, tormented and oppressed them in this world." The whole picture of Christians calling on God to punish other Christians while they watch is, to say the least, not a pleasant one.

But, then, so few of us have ever been willing, as de Bres was, to offer our backs to stripes, our tongues to knives, and our whole bodies to the fire for the sake of the gospel. It is easy to use measured language when you are safe.

CHAPTER 27
Introduction to the Canons

Introduction

The Canons of Dort have gotten a bad reputation among certain people. Many non-Reformed readers regard them as a classic case of Calvinism gone wild. Even some Reformed people would like to see these Canons muzzled. Theologians complain that the Canons' treatment of reprobation is unbiblical, abstract, and generally to be discouraged. Others spread the idea that the Canons so enlarge divine sovereignty as to crowd out human responsibility altogether. Do the Canons not claim, after all, that God causes unbelief in the reprobate—and then blames and damns them for what He has caused?

We shall see. In the chapters which conclude this course, let us take a fresh look at the Canons. There may be some small surprises. Are there internal "tensions," or even outright contradictions in the Canons? Do they take a different and harsher position on election than does the Belgic Confession? Are the Canons merely Dutch Reformed theological weapons for blasting Arminians or are there some warm, practical, pastoral dimensions to them as well?

We may note at the outset that the Canons have a far greater international reputation than many Reformed people realize. Of course they are of substantial theological interest as a distinctively Calvinist doctrinal statement and as an anti-Arminian polemic. But beyond that, there are wide historical-cultural waves spreading out from the Synod of Dort. The Synod was a gathering of some first-class minds, and was called, influenced, and discussed by political heavyweights. Because of the central role which the Netherlands played in seventeenth century European affairs, the issues surrounding the Synod gained international circulation and status. This was especially evident in England. So luminous a figure as John Milton, for example, refers in his *Areopagitica* (a famous speech in defense of freedom of the press) to "the acute and distinct Arminius [who] was perverted merely by the perusing of a nameless discourse written at Delft, which at first he took in hand to confute." One standard commentator, Samuel Miller, claims that "the convocation and proceedings of the Synod of Dort may be considered as among the most interesting events of the seventeenth century."

In this chapter, let us look briefly at the background to Dort, the Synod itself, and the general shape of the Canons it leveled against the Arminians.

Background to Dort

The Netherlands in the mid-sixteenth century was dominated by Spain and Spanish Catholicism. But as the century wore on, such courageous and colorful figures as William of Orange led the Netherlanders in a mighty effort to get Spain out of their lives. In this fight for independence, Reformed Netherlanders, who constituted, perhaps, only a tenth of the population, played a major role. They had learned from Calvin that God, in His goodness, sometimes "raises up open avengers from among his servants, and arms them with his command to punish the wicked government and deliver his people" (*Institutes* IV, xx, 30). The Dutch had some skillful avengers, and most of them seemed to be Reformed. The result of the Reformed leadership in the struggle for political independence was that the Reformed Church was declared the official state church of the Netherlands in the 1570s.

The Reformed paid a large price for their privileged position—as churches yoked with states always do. State and local governments assumed an enormous role in determining the policy, and even the doctrine, of the church. This became painfully clear in the doctrinal controversy which gradually emerged in the Netherlands around 1590 and climaxed at Dordrecht in 1618-1619.

The central figure in it was one of the church's ablest thinkers, James Harmenszoon (or Arminius, in Latin). In 1582 the magistrates of Amsterdam sent this keen twenty-two year old at public expense to study theology with Theodore Beza, Calvin's successor at Geneva. After several years of study and travel, Arminius returned to the Netherlands in the fall of 1587, was examined by Classis Amsterdam in 1588, and began fifteen years of ministry in the Old Church of Amsterdam. Even his theological opponents concede that Arminius was an unusually gifted, kindly, and attentive pastor.

But he was also accused of straying outside the lines of the Calvinist orthodoxy favored in the Netherlands. Probably Arminius had struggled with Beza's stark way of stating the doctrine of predestination already as a student in Geneva. But in Amsterdam in the early 1590s, two events embroiled Arminius in the controversy which still bears his name. The first was the incident to which Milton refers in the quotation above. Arminius had been asked by two different parties, the ministers of Delft and his own consistory, to defend Beza's brand of predestination against certain humanist attacks. But the more he studied the issues, the more convinced Arminius became that he could not in good conscience defend Beza. In fact, he could not defend any statement of predestination which employed causal concepts. That is, Arminius became convinced that the doctrine of predestination when stated with causal concepts (God *causes* the elect to believe or, even, *causes* the reprobate to disbelieve) was unbiblical. The second event was Arminius' study of and preaching on Romans. Several of his sermons on Romans 7 and Romans 9 excited the suspicions of Reformed people in Amsterdam. Arminius seemed to them to place too much emphasis on human freedom in the process of repentance and belief.

Affairs in Amsterdam were settled enough to allow Arminius to continue his ministry. In fact, by the time he left Amsterdam in 1602, both his consistory and classis praised him without qualification.

The occasion for leaving was Arminius' appointment to a theological professorship at Leyden. Several voices were raised in protest because of the Amsterdam controversies, but the appointment was made and Arminius began to

teach in 1603. He was soon engaged in public theological debate on predestination with his colleague Gomarus. Gomarus was a follower of Beza and developed great hostility toward the views of Arminius. Their debates were extremely technical and subtle, centering around the question of the logical order of God's eternal decrees.

Relations between Gomarists and Arminians deteriorated after 1605 to the point of widespread hatred and caricature. It is a mark of the rancor involved that when Arminius weakened and died

JEANNE ENGELHARD
1-25-79

in 1609, "his affliction was seen by some as an apt fulfillment of Zechariah 11:17 and 14:12. The first passage reads:

> Woe to my worthless shepherd,
>   who deserts the flock!
> May the sword smite his arm
>   and his right eye!
> Let his arm be wholly withered,
>   his right eye utterly blinded.

(Carl Bangs, *Arminius*)

The controversy did not die with Arminius. In fact, it gained new life. It must be remembered that the issues were now joined not between Calvin and Arminius, nor between Calvinists and Arminius, but between Calvinists and Arminians. Some of the Calvinists in this fray were of the "high" type, followers of Beza and Gomarus. Their form of Calvinism was especially rigorous—some would say rigid. Meanwhile, some of the followers of Arminius also hardened and simplified their teacher's subtly shaded and nuanced positions.

In 1610, forty followers of Arminius, led by Hans Uytenbogaert, met at Gouda. These Arminians, all of whom were ministers, wished to solicit the favor and protection of the States General of the Netherlands. They had been in grave danger of being deposed from office by consistories which regarded Arminius's teaching as heretical. Thus the forty ministers drafted a "Remonstrance," a "pleading protest" against the attacks of their opponents. The Remonstrance is shaped according to the accusations which it attempts to answer, and appears in five articles. This structure is followed throughout the following controversy, including Dort, and persists to this day among those who refer to "five points of Calvinism" (often remembered according to the acronym TULIP). The Remonstrants claimed the following: (1) that God has decreed to save those "who by the grace of the Holy Spirit shall believe," and "to leave the incorrigible and unbelieving in sin"; (2) that Christ died "for all men and for every man, so that he merited . . . forgiveness of sins for all . . . yet so that no one actually enjoys this forgiveness of sins except the believer"; (3) "that no man does not have saving faith of himself nor by the power of his own free will"; (4) that the grace of God must commence, progress, and complete any good in man "so that all good works . . . must be ascribed to the grace of God in Christ. But with respect to the mode of this grace, it is not irresistible, since it is written concerning many that they resisted the Holy Spirit"; (5) that those who are "incorporated into

Jesus Christ" are abundantly assisted in their struggle to persevere by the power of Christ and His Spirit, but "whether they can through negligence fall away . . . must first be more carefully determined from the Holy Scriptures."

The Calvinists replied that *they* were the ones who were always misunderstood and misrepresented. Accordingly, when the States General called for a Remonstrative-Calvinist conference at the Hague in 1611, the Calvinists issued a counter remonstrance against the Arminians. The conference was inconclusive.

Meanwhile ordinary people everywhere had been taking sides. To a degree few of us would now understand common people argued, split hairs and families, and entertained hostile thoughts about their neighbors over the issue of the logical order of God's decrees and the freedom of the human will. Of course it is simplistic to suppose that most of the Netherlanders were passionate theologians. Actually their interest in the Calvinist-Arminian questions was bound up with a whole complex of religious, military, political, economic, and social issues. The Netherlands was a loose confederation of provinces in which the province of Holland was in many ways predominant. Always relationships with Spain and Spanish Catholicism—both of which the Dutch hated—were in the background of the Calvinist-Arminian controversy. Thus Prince Maurice of Holland led a party of people who wanted to continue to fight Spain in the early years of the 1600s and Jan van Oldenbarnevelt, the grand pensioner of Holland, led those who wanted peace with Spain. Theological issues were attached to one party or the other. Maurice, who "did not know whether predestination is blue or green" favored the Calvinists while Oldenbarnevelt had always supported the Remonstrants. Thus:

> There would be a war party, militaristic, staunchly Calvinistic and anti-Catholic, predestinarian, centralist, politically even royalist, and ecclesiastically presbyterian. There would be a peace party, trademinded, theologically tolerant, republican, and Erastian [roughly, Constantinian]. The first would support the war and fight Arminianism; the second would support a truce and fight Calvinism.

(Carl Bangs, *Arminius*)

Because of the civil unrest and danger of civil war, the States General finally agreed to call a national synod to resolve at least the theological issues. For this the Calvinists had been hoping and petitioning for years. But because it took the civil government to call a synod, and because the

134

civil government was inclined to tolerate Arminians, it took a long while for the Calvinists to get their way.

It is worth noting that other nations were looking on with interest. Indeed James I, King of England and patron of the King James Bible, although "a man of very small mind and of still less moral or religious principle" according to one Reformed commentator, had admonished the States General to summon a national synod and restore peace to the Netherlandish churches.

The Synod of Dort

The Synod of Dort was called by the civil government, held at its expense, and opened with a prayer in which the government was lavishly praised "for walking in the footsteps of your illustrious predecessors, Constantine, Theodosius...."

Anthony Hoekema has described some of the pertinent features of the Synod. It met in 154 sessions from November 13, 1618 to May 28, 1619 in a sort of National Guard armory in Dordrecht, a town fairly close to Rotterdam. Besides calling delegates from the Netherlands, the Synod also invited foreign delegates from Great Britain, Germany, and Switzerland. The delegation included Calvinists only—eighty-four of them, of whom about a quarter were foreign. Thirteen Remonstrants were summoned to appear within two weeks. Though much of the controversy of previous years had concerned the doctrinal soundness of positions on both sides as measured by the Heidelberg Catechism and the Belgic Confession, it was determined by this Synod that decisions

were to be made by appeal to Scripture alone. Thus each member of the body swore an oath that

> during the course of the proceedings of this Synod, which will examine and decide, not only the five points, and all the differences resulting from them, but also any other doctrine, I will use no human writing, but only the word of God, which is an infallible rule of faith.

Both before and after the Remonstrants were present at Dort, the Synod conducted other business than the consideration of the five points. For example, it adopted an authoritative Latin text of the Belgic Confession, devised a formula of subscription for Reformed ministers (still signed by CRC officebearers), and made decisions on catechism preaching, Bible translation, missions, and church order. If this seems to be a full agenda, recall that the delegates had 154 sessions. If that seems to be a large number of sessions, remember that a national synod had not met for about thirty years and would not meet again for

NICK BRANDERHORST
11·14·78

another two hundred. The Synod of Dort had to make the most of its opportunity.

When the Arminians arrived, six weeks of procedural and theological skirmishing began. It ended when the president of the Synod, Johannes Bogerman of Friesland, lost his temper on January 14, 1619. Exasperated by what he and many others regarded as duplicity, ambiguity, and stalling tactics on the part of the Remonstrants, Bogerman finally exploded:

> Go as you came. You began with lies and you end with them. You are full of fraud and double-dealing. You are not worthy that the synod should treat with further. Depart! Leave! You began with a lie, with a lie you ended! Go!

> (S. Kistemaker,
> *Crisis in the Reformed Churches*)

They went. After they were gone, the Synod unanimously condemned the five Arminian articles. Arminians who refused to accept the Canons which the Synod adopted were exiled from the Netherlands and their property confiscated —both by government power. Meanwhile Oldenbarnevelt, who had championed the Arminian cause, was beheaded.

It is very difficult to make a fair historical assessment of the Synod's proceedings. Arminian sympathizers at once referred bitterly to "The Triumph of the Reformed Devil over his Synod, Gathered at Dordrecht." Modern theological historians such as John T. McNeill speak of Oldenbarnevelt's execution as "an execrable deed" based on "a trumped-up charge." Reformed accounts tend to describe the situation differently. But even standard Reformed commentators admit that politics played a large role at Dort and that the church/state alliance which allowed exile of the Remonstrants and confiscation of their property was regrettable, to say the least.

What was at issue at Dort? There were really a number of issues. Predestination was one important issue, but was linked theologically to a number of others having to do with sin, free will, atonement, and the mode of God's saving grace. In other words, there was a complex, a bundle of doctrines which tend to go together. In the chapters which follow, we shall examine them individually, always bearing in mind their mutual relation. Perhaps Philip Schaff is right when he says that overall the controversy at Dort

> involves the problem of the ages, which again and again has baffled the ken of theologians and philosophers, and will do so to the end of time: the relation of divine sovereignty and human responsibility.

> (*Creeds of Christendom I*)

Structure of the Canons

A fast glance at the Canons reveals the hot polemical circumstances which surround their birth. "Canons" are standards or criteria. In this case, they are criteria for measuring Reformed soundness on the issues disputed between the Calvinists and Remonstrants. Both the structure and some of the language of the Canons are polemical.

The document contains five Canons, each of which has a number of positive articles and a set of negative paragraphs. The latter, the "Rejection of Errors," are again divided into a statement of heretical Remonstrant teaching ("those who teach . . .") and an appropriate Reformed rejoinder—nearly always from Scripture. The third and fourth Canons are combined under one heading. The order follows that of the discussions since the Remonstrance of 1910. The Canons end with a "Conclusion" which attempts to ward off certain possible misunderstandings of sensitive issues in the body of the document.

Conclusion

Though the issues are technical and the language often provocative, it would be a mistake to conclude the document is intended for theologians. It is not. It is intended for members of Reformed churches, and contains a notable sensitivity to the pastoral dimensions of the issues it treats. Take Canons I, Article 16, for example. Those who are making a real attempt at "filial obedience" are counseled "not to be alarmed at the mention of reprobation, nor to rank themselves among the reprobate, but diligently to persevere in the use of means, and with ardent desires devoutly and humbly to wait for a season of richer grace."

The Canons of Dort, then, have far more than historical interest. The document is not just a period piece. We shall discover, in fact, that there is a mighty effort in these Canons to safeguard the freedom and grace of God, and to distinguish the Christian religion from all self-help schemes.

CHAPTER 28
Divine Election and Reprobation

Canons of Dort, First Head of Doctrine

Introduction

People respond to the gospel differently. Some people who hear or read about a waiting father who runs out to embrace his prodigal son experience a shiver of joy and recognition. They hear of mercy for sinners and, like John Wesley, find their hearts "strangely warmed." They view their own sin with new clarity and sorrow. They feel humility before the God who has loved them through all of their boredom and rebelliousness. They discover a mysterious inner conviction that the things of the faith are true. They begin to care what the church is doing. The Word of God *speaks* to them. People notice a sense of security in them even when they are hurt, betrayed, or sick. They have pinned their hopes on nothing in this world, and yet their commitment to worldly justice has increased. They have "good momentum." They are the sort of people of whom Jesus said, "To him who has will more be given" (Mark 4:25). Through it all, these people have an uncanny sense of being tugged at, or drawn from beyond themselves. Like some beginning jogger, they have felt ridiculous at times. More than once they have been tempted to give up. Yet, mysteriously, they keep on.

But other people who hear the gospel have a different response. The father who takes back a wasted son seems to them a fool. The account of mercy for sinners leaves them cold. Indeed, they find the very word "sinner" offensive and keenly resent any implication that it might apply to such as they are. They see the church as a group of sissies, flower boys, and hypocrites. They decide that prayer is talking to oneself. The Bible seems to them fantastic. These people have pinned their hopes on making it in this world because it is the only world they think there is. They do not care to

discover whether and where God might speak. Like a person with no ear for a tune, they find the Christian faith boring, offensive, or ridiculous. They have "bad momentum." They are the sort of people of whom Jesus said, "from him who has not, even what he has will be taken away" (Mark 4:25). Many of these people have at one time made a beginning with the Bible, tried to pray, and attended worship services. But none of it seemed to work with them. They did not keep on.

What accounts for this undeniable difference in response? Since its early centuries, the church has known three accounts. One account is that of Pelagius. To the shiny new believer Pelagius might have said, "Congratulations! You *did* it!" Augustine, however, rejected Pelagius' account. To the recent convert, Augustine might have said, "Thank God! You have been saved by grace!" A third account has always tried to get in between the first two. Certain Catholics, Lutherans, Arminians, and others might say to the born-again Christian, "Thank God—and congratulations! This was a cooperative effort. Praise is due all around."

That is a grossly simplified picture, but it gets the idea across. What we must see is that the Canons follow the second account (Augustine's) and reject the others. All three schemes try to account for the historical, experienced fact that people respond differently to the preaching of the gospel. In this attempt they ask Paul's question: "Why do not all (Jews) believe?" But only the Augustinian-Calvinist tradition gives the Pauline answer. The answer in Romans 9 is divine election and reprobation.

For the sake of convenience, let us divide the material of the First Head of Doctrine into three: first, the historical drama of salvation (Art. 1-4); secondly, the explanation of belief and unbelief according to the decrees of election and reprobation (Art. 5-11,15); thirdly, pastoral advice for the handling of these delicate issues (Art. 12-14, 16-18). Proceeding article by article, we will add appropriate material from the Rejection of Errors and the Conclusion.

Historical Drama of Salvation (Articles 1-4)

The Canons of Dort begin not in eternity with God but in history with man. The Canons begin with the fall. Here we can see something very important. The first question in the whole debate about divine sovereignty and human freedom is the question of the human predicament. How far have we fallen? Are we still free to choose God? Partly free? Or quite enslaved to sin? Are we bright-eyed? Bedimmed? Or blind as moles?

On this the Canons take the sternest view. Chapter III-IV will assert a doctrine of "total depravity." But Chapter I, Article 1 already declares that "all men...lie under the curse, and are deserving of eternal death." Following such texts as Ephesians 2:1 and 5, the Canons assert that fallen humanity is spiritually blind, enslaved, and, in fact, quite dead.

But Article 2 goes on in the drama of salvation. In His fierce determination to recover His creation, God invades with His Son. After the events of Christ's life among us, God calls, equips, and sends out ambassadors with the "joyful tidings" of what Christ has done. These messengers, says Article 3, call sinners to repentance and faith. Some do repent and believe the gospel. They are delivered from God's wrath and graced with eternal life. But others shun the good news. Article 4 says about them what the Bible says: "The wrath of God abides upon those who believe not this gospel."

Explanation of Belief and Unbelief: The Eternal Decrees (Articles 5-11,15)

Why do some believe? God has decreed to give them the gift of faith. Why do others not believe? God has decreed not to give them the gift of faith—without which, because of the fall, they cannot believe. The former decree is the decree of election. The latter is the decree of reprobation. The two sorts of decrees have been worried over by able minds and pious hearts for centuries.

One worrisome problem can be met at once. Article 5 starts out talking about *cause*. That, we recall from chapter 27, is the idea from which Arminius always wanted to flee. Article 5 probes the cause of the unbelief which has just been described in Article 4. Note what it says. It says that God does not cause unbelief; man himself

LES KLYN
11-14-78

does. This is a crucial point, for Arminians have often suspected Calvinists of believing that God causes the reprobate to disbelieve the gospel and then blames and damns them for their disbelief. But the Canons explicitly deny any such horror. In both Chapter I, Article 5 and the Conclusion the Canons assert firmly that such an idea is detestable and blasphemous.

What Article 5 says is what the Belgic Confession says. It says that God elects some from the mass of ruined sinners and gifts them with faith. The rest He passes by. These latter persons have inherited, along with the elect, the original guilt and tendency to sin from Adam's fall. Eventually it produces its dreadful fruit. "In" Adam and by their own sin, the reprobate cause their own unbelief and condemnation.

Article 6 probes deeper. This electing of some and passing by of others is according to God's *decree*. What is meant by "decree"? The article does not say, but likely the notion of purpose or plan or decision is intended. The term *decree*, incidentally, is not found in the New Testament. It does appear several times in the Old Testament, but not in the context of election to salvation. *Purpose* is the New Testament term which appears most often when election is being discussed (Rom. 8:28; 9:11; Eph. 1:9, 11; 3:11; II Tim. 1:9). So perhaps it would be wise to take the Canons' "decree" as "purpose."

138

Here, then, is the clearest statement the Canons make in accounting for the actual, historical belief and unbelief of human beings after the fall: "That some receive the gift of faith from God, and others do not receive it, proceeds from God's eternal decree" (Chap. I, 6). It was from the beginning part of God's plan, His will, His purpose to gift some with faith and not others. These others, because of their original and actual sin, would inevitably perish. It is the same scheme as in the Confession. In neither case is God said to cause unbelief.

But is God said here to cause belief? Article 6 does not itself go that far. It is gentler. God "graciously softens" the hearts of the elect; He "inclines" them to believe. So far, it sounds as if God woos and aids believers, but does not actually cause them to believe. But several articles in Chapter III-IV (11, 12, 14, and 16) use stronger language. God "pervades...opens...circumcises...infuses...quickens...actuates." He "sweetly and powerfully bends" the will (Chap. III-IV, Art. 16). In fact, God Himself "produces...the act of believing." In a celebrated phrase, the Conclusion plainly implies that election is "the fountain and *cause* of faith and good works."

Why do the Canons go so far as to say that God causes belief? We have to go back once again to the fall and its effects. We are hooked on sin and in a spiritual coma. By fallen nature we all resist God's invasion. In order to save, God must break down barriers, move past defenses, disarm rebels, and change hearts. He has to cause belief. Else we would continue to resist—and in that case there would be no hope.

Article 6 closes with the same pairing of election with mercy and of reprobation with righteousness which appears in the Confession. There is likewise the first canonical appearance of a word familiar to us from the Confession—the word "consolation." The Canons will maintain as a recurrent theme that the doctrine of election ought not to be scarifying, but consoling to believers.

Article 7 offers a definition of election and, indirectly, confirms the fact that *purpose* is the main idea behind the use of "decree." The breadth and sweep of this article is remarkable. It is a gracious, evangelical, biblical statement of election. Like the Confession it locates the context of election "in Christ." Christ is the head of the elect community whom God gives to Him. Christ, or His work, is "the foundation of salvation." There is, meanwhile, a forceful reminder that the elect are "by nature neither better nor more deserving

than others," a reminder both of the need for humility in the elect and of the fall as the historical starting point for considering election and reprobation.

If Article 7 offers a glorious description of election, then Article 15 is its opposite number. That article is as close as the Canons come to a definition of reprobation. The reprobate are those sinners whom God leaves, whom He permits to follow their own ways, on whom He does not bestow faith, whom He passes by. The upshot of Articles 6, 7, and 15 is that there is no balanced, symmetrical relation between election and reprobation. They are unequally yoked together. God causes some to believe. But He does not cause the others to disbelieve. He simply leaves them alone.

Articles 8 through 11 turn to some semi-technical points disputed with the Arminians. To understand these articles, we have to know a little about what Arminius said on these issues.

Arminius was deeply afraid of a causal system of predestination according to which God would cause the elect to believe and the reprobate to disbelieve—quite apart from the wishes of the human beings involved. So Arminius made a distinction in predestination. He said there are two kinds of predestination. First, God predestines all believers to be saved and all unbelievers to be damned. He elects a *type* of person (the type which believes) and reprobates another type (the type which disbelieves). This is a "general" predestination which God does without paying any attention to His foreknowledge of what actual persons will do or believe. Then God does a second, or "particular," predestination. He looks into the future at individual persons. He sees His grace and the atoning work of Christ as sufficient for all to believe. He sees His grace freeing the enslaved wills of all persons enough so that those wills can swing either in the direction of belief or of unbelief. God looks to see in each case whether the free will cooperates with His grace or resists it. He then elects all those whom He foresees as finally resisting His grace.

That is approximately what Arminius believed, and that is what his followers believed. Articles 8 through 11 oppose this scheme. Article 8 denies that there are these two decrees of election. Rejection Paragraph 2 is even more detailed and forceful. It denies, first, the distinction between a general election according to type and a particular election of individuals. Then it denies the further distinction between an "election unto faith and another unto salvation." Arminius thought that a believer might be elected "unto faith," but then fall away from his belief and therefore be damned. The Canons cannot find biblical support for either of these Arminian distinctions.

Article 9 is perhaps the heart of Chapter I. There, following Ephesians 1:4, the Calvinist case is strongly made that election is not on account of faith, but rather *for* faith. We are elected not because God foresees that we shall believe, but in order that we might believe. Election is not caused by foreseen faith; rather, faith is caused by election. In one way or another, Rejection Paragraphs 1, 2, 4, 5, and 9 join Article 9 in guarding this essential point. Article 10 is in the same line.

Article 11 previews the doctrine of the perseverance of the saints. Contrary to Arminius, an elect person cannot fall away. In no way can God's election be humanly interfered with.

Pastoral Advice (Articles 12-14, 16-18)

Suddenly the air warms and the atmosphere brightens. We pass from somewhat chilly and technical material into some articles of genuine pastoral concern. How shall believers rightly handle the knowledge of election and reprobation?

Article 12 affirms the Reformed belief that one's salvation is shown by its fruits (cf. Answer 86 of the Catechism). Note that among these fruits the Canons realistically list not righteousness, but "a hungering and thirsting after righteousness." Let a person be sorry for his sin; let him fear God, trust Christ, and yearn for righteousness. If he does these things, he need not doubt his election.

But if a person has assurance of election, will he not loaf and rest from his labors? That is the classic Catholic and Arminian concern—that Calvinists give a person cause for moral stupor and inertia. But Article 13 makes the same point as Part III of the Catechism and Article XXIV of the Confession. The knowledge of election induces humility, ardent love, and moral cleanliness in believers. They are free from anxiety about their salvation and therefore free to serve their Savior. They are moreover heartily motivated by gratitude to do so. But there is a profound distinction made here between those who have a certainty of election and those whose "rash presumption" sinks them into "carnal security." There is to be no idle "chattering" (a better translation than "trifling") about election by people who are not humble and do not act like elect people.

Election may be known, then, provided that it is known with a humble certainty by people with godly fears, sorrows, and hungers. It may also be preached or "published in due time and place" (Art. 14). Indeed, it must be. But here too there is a proviso. Election may be published if it is done "with reverence, in the spirit of discretion and piety." Article 14, together with Articles 12, 18, and others, warns against prying, against "vainly attempting to investigate the secret ways of the Most High." This word of warning, so characteristic of the Reformed reaction to Catholic boldness and speculation, attempts to encourage intellectual as well as moral humility where the doctrine of election is concerned.

Article 16, as we noted in chapter 27, is a fine example of Dort's pastoral interest. The subject is reprobation, but the language is anything but cold and sterile: Spiritually dry believers "ought not to be alarmed." They must "persevere in the use of means," and "humbly . . . wait for a season of richer grace" because of what "a merciful God has promised." What Article 16 really says is that those who are worried about whether they are elect probably have least to worry about. Let them *act* like believers. Let them use the means of grace (the Lord's Supper is most needed by people whose faith is wobbling). Let them seek holiness and be patient. But those who disregard God, who are not at all concerned about faith and election, who "have wholly given themselves up to the cares of the world," have real cause for concern.

Article 17 deals with the Remonstrant fear that the Calvinist doctrine of reprobation might include children of believers who die in infancy. The Remonstrants had insisted that all infants of believers who die before the "use of reason" are saved. Here in Article 17 the Canons graciously agree—albeit in somewhat more muted tones: "godly parents ought not to doubt the election and salvation of their children whom it pleases God to call out of this life in their infancy." While they are immature, the children of believers are protected in the covenant of grace.

The end of Chapter I is typical of all biblical and Reformed discussions of this material. There is an implied acknowledgment in Article 18 of the difficulties in the doctrines of election and reprobation and a confession that even when God's ways are unsearchable they are still just and good.

Conclusion

The Canons, like the Confession, raise all the perennial questions about election and reprobation. We know what they are from our study of the Confession's Article XVI. Yet the intent of these doctrines is clear: They intend to confess God's sovereign grace and freedom. The issue can become very personal and devotional—as we saw in the introduction to this chapter. Whom do you thank for salvation? Whom do you praise? Do you congratulate yourself for being wise enough to see the light? Or do you confess that whatever love for God you find in yourself is "but my answer, Lord, to Thee! For Thou wert long beforehand with my soul . . ."?

Perhaps we might leave this section with a firm grasp of the Canon's teaching about the proper *attitude* for approaching these sensitive doctrines. On the one hand, if we indulge the "rash presumption" that we are elect—while chattering idly about the damned in hell—we may be pretty sure that salvation has not yet come to our house.

Casual assurance and light banter about these matters are canonically forbidden.

On the other hand, we are not to fear God as if He were an enemy whom no humble seeking could find and no ardent desire placate. He is "a merciful God [who] has promised that He will not quench the smoking flax, nor break the bruised reed" (Art. 16). The God of grace seeks not to squelch, or crush, or quench, or break the tender frames and little lights of devout believers who struggle and doubt. He knows our frame; He remembers that we are dust. That is why He has elected to come to us in Christ. Let all who wait for a season of richer grace spend some time following the Christ through passion and suffering and doubt. Let them see to what lengths a loving God will go in the profound work of rescuing His erring children.

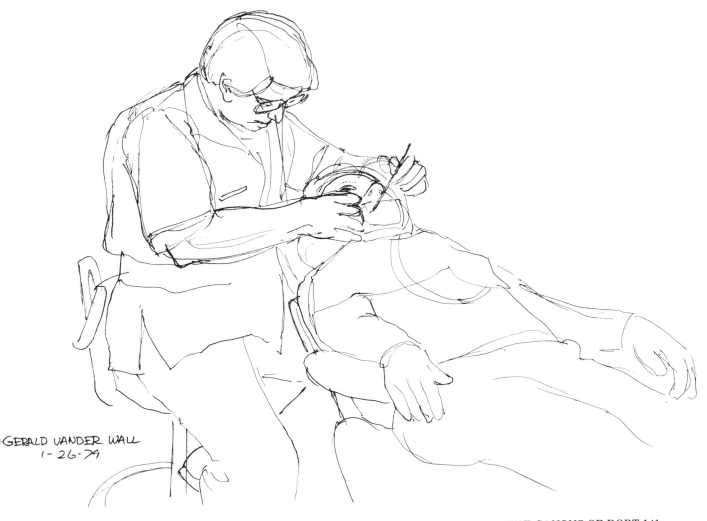

GERALD VANDER WALL
1-26-79

CHAPTER 29
The Death of Christ
and Our Redemption

Canons of Dort, Second Head of Doctrine

Introduction

A certain farmer had five children. Both wealthy and gracious, the farmer provided them with safe lodging, interesting work, plenty of food, and clear direction about the right way to live. They lived that way. The farmer and his sons and daughters were very happy.

But the farmer knew there were other sorts of places in the world beyond his farm. Some were darkened places where people got drunk together and lost their minds. They told each other lies and betrayed their loved ones. Some were soiled places where "adults" could pay to watch diseased and hopeless people pretend to love each other. Many were noisy places where a person with excess money or time could easily dispose of them.

The farmer knew about such places because, although he was a good man, he was not naive. He warned his sons and daughters not to go near any of them. He explained to his children that a person might find the places exciting at first, but that sooner or later he would learn that they were traps. People in them discovered that though they did not always enjoy what they were doing—not really, not in the same way that they enjoyed a good meal after a brisk day's work—they could not give it up. The children said they understood.

In fact, they came to understand the hard way. First the oldest daughter found herself lured to one of the places. Then she persuaded her brother to follow. Soon all the sons and daughters were living in a place which combined all the vices their father had warned them about. There were plenty of things to swallow, inject, or inhale which com-

pletely changed one's mind. There were a number of naked persons with forced smiles and unusual ways. There were scores of opportunities to try one's luck with cunning wheels, cubes, and cards.

The farmer was both angry and heartbroken. He lay awake trying to think of good ways to rescue his children. At last he called in one of his two trusted foremen, a kindly, gentle person nameed Jacob Arminian. Arminian was an Armenian. "Arminian," said the farmer, "use your own method, but get my children back. As you know, all my resources are at your disposal."

Reluctantly, Arminian drove into town. He did not relish this assignment. He brought along clean clothes, methadone, a skilled deprogrammer, nourishing food, and promises of the father's forgiveness. He faced the five children. "Listen," he said kindly. "You have broken your father's heart, but he is willing to forgive and take you back. He has sent me with everything you need to escape this place. But you must come voluntarily. I cannot force you."

Two kids sneaked out the back door. One laughed hysterically. Two others tried to beat up poor old Arminian. Drunk, crazed, hearts sinking, the children deeply resented this reminder of father and home. Arminian finally persuaded two of them to return with him, but they did not stay. The farmer was childless again.

So he turned to his other foreman, a stubborn but honest man by the name of Canon—John Canon. John was the sort of no-nonsense person who would grit his teeth and do what needed to be done. He often disagreed with Arminian about the best way to do a thing. He too was sent with provisions for rescuing all the children. This time the farmer added some secret instructions.

As Canon drove into town he reviewed in his mind Arminian's failure and his own alternative approach. He knew the five kids were too far gone to be persuaded by kindly offers of help. This was a desperate situation and needed emergency measures.

John entered the darkened place. He found the five children variously smirking, slinking, and snarling. "Look," said John plainly. "This is no place for you. You no longer know what's good for you. You are completely out of your minds. Your father wants you all to come home."

Again, one or two attempted escape and the rest tried to attack John. But John was enormously strong and stone sober, while they were neither. He could easily overpower all five. Yet, remarkably, he selected three of the five, dragged them kicking and screaming out of the dark room, wrestled them into the back of his van, and left. At home these three were carefully nursed back to health. From time to time they rebelled again, but each time their father saw to it that they were helped and guided. Eventually, when their minds cleared and their health returned, they freely and joyfully served their father. They could not imagine what had possessed them to seek their comfort in desperate places and among hardened people. But neither could they help wondering now and then about their lost brother and sister. Why had John not rescued them too?

So they approached John. "Your father secretly told me which ones to bring back," said John. "He had his reasons. We are not to ask about them."

The Canons—Chapter II

The second chapter of the Canons of Dort deals with the sort of rescue just described. The Arminians claimed that God intended rescue for all sinners. Christ came for all, died for all, and reconciled all to God, they said. But each sinner has to accept freely the offered grace. And, as Arminius himself freely admitted, many sinners do not accept it. Many sinners whom Christ came to save are hopelessly lost.

The Calvinists disagreed with passion. They said God does not leave so vital a matter as salvation in the hands of sinners who are enthralled and self-deceived. Instead, God fixes it so that every person for whom Christ died is securely saved. God makes sure. He does what is necessary to bring such a person into a state of grace and keep him or her there. Yet He does not save all sinners. He does not even intend to save all of them. And we do not know why.

Chapter II of the Canons makes three claims along these lines: first, that the atoning work of the Savior is of infinite value, sufficient to save all sinners (Art. 1-4); second, that the summons to believe in Christ, issued to all sinners, is (by God's grace) accepted by the elect and is (by their own fault) rejected by all others (Art. 5-7); third, that those who accept are forever guarded and supported by the "golden chain of salvation" so that they cannot be lost again (Art. 8,9).

Christ's Infinite Satisfaction (Articles 1-4)

The material of the first four articles is not new to us. We have read similar descriptions of Christ's atonement in the Catechism (Q & A 12-19) and the Confession (Art. XX, XXI). The prevailing Reformed theory of the atonement is based on the thought of St. Anselm as modified by John Calvin.

Its outline, we remember, is this: Because of our original and actual sins, we deserve punishment. In fact, because God's justice and dignity are supremely great, the punishment for breaking His law and offending His majesty must also be supreme (Art. 1).

Yet God is also supremely merciful. Thus He arranged with His Son to enter our darkness, be cursed as if a miserable sinner, and satisfy God's justice. All this is *vicarious* satisfaction: All this is "for us," "in our stead," "on our behalf" (Art. 2).

Moreover, this satisfaction is of unlimited worth. It is the infinitely valuable work of the divine Son of God—"abundantly sufficient to expiate the sins of the whole world" (Art. 3). Christ's work was no game of charades. It was attended with a real "sense of the wrath and curse of God" (Art. 4).

So far, Calvinists and Arminians might appear to agree. In some measure they do. They agree, for example, that Christ's death was a sacrificial offering to God for human sin. But they also disagree in at least two particulars. First, Calvinists always insist that Christ endured the *full* penalty for the sins of the whole world, and therefore *fully* satisfied God's retributive justice. His work is "abundantly sufficient to satisfy for the sins of the whole world" (see I John 2:2). Arminians deny that Christ's work was a full penalty in complete payment of the staggering debt accumulated by our sin. Rather, they say, His work was an agreed-upon *substitute* for the exact penalty—a substitute which God graciously ordained as a sufficient condition for forgiving all sin. Secondly, Calvinists always seek to present the atonement in such a way that neither the grace nor the justice of God is minimized. Both are fully exercised in the work of redemption. But Armin-

ESTHER AND RICKY VISSER
11-16-78

ians claim that if Christ fully merited our salvation by completely satisfying God's justice, then He *earned* our salvation and there was no grace in it at all. You have to take your pick, say the Arminians. Either Christ fully earned God's forgiveness for us or else God mercifully forgives us out of mere grace. Either of these—but not both.

Calvinists are quick to reply, of course, that grace and justice are not mutually exclusive. Suppose a moneylender demands that a debtor's debt be fully paid. That's justice. But suppose he mercifully arranges for his own son to pay it. That's grace. The two virtues may coexist.

Articles 1-4, then, typically emphasize both God's mercy and His justice. The accumulated penalty for sinners must be fully paid. So says God's justice. For this payment God gave His only begotten Son, "that whoever believes in him should not perish, but have eternal life." So says God's mercy—and so say Articles 5 through 7 of the Second Head of Doctrine.

The Gospel and Response (Articles 5-7)

Article 5 begins with the promise just quoted from John 3:16. It adds the command to repent and believe, a command sewn deep into the fabric of the New Testament. This gospel command and promise, say Article 5, are to be spread to all nations and all persons (Luke 24:47).

The article uses a most interesting word for this action. Command and promise are to be declared "promiscuously." This is a word we usually come upon in other contexts. When we talk of a promiscuous person, we do not ordinarily have a missionary in mind. Yet Article 5 plainly says that missionaries are to be promiscuous in publishing the gospel truth. They are not to make distinctions among people. They are not to judge anybody as too good for the gospel—or too bad. Even with a Reformed understanding that conversion awaits God's powerful work of producing faith in the listener, missionaries are still to preach to all.

Here we have a fascinating feature of the Canons. One might suppose that a doctrine of election would undercut preaching. God has to save a person, after all, by causing him or her to turn in repentance and faith. So why urge the *person* to do this turning? He can't. Like the farmer's children, he may be enslaved to drink, dope, and bed. What help is preaching? Why do it?

It is a good question. And it has an answer. There is, after all, Paul's famous question ("How are they to hear without a preacher?") and Christ's command to preach the gospel (which, as Bavinck says, ought to settle the matter by

144

itself). Moreover, as Paul suggests in Romans (10:14ff.) we know from actual experience how powerfully the word of truth—either "declared" or "published"—can incline us toward God. The proclamation of the Word is a mighty tool, a primary means, in God's work of building His people and making known His will to the world. Election in no way comprises preaching. Indeed, the two are most intimately related. Conversion typically happens *by means of* both Word and Spirit.

Yet, as we saw in chapter 28, not all respond to the preaching of the Word. Articles 6 and 7 repeat what Chapter I of the Canons says about this. The Word does not take hold in some people because of human sin (Art. 6). Without the supernatural work of the Holy Spirit in us, we are stupefied, misled, and immune to the invasion of the gospel. We have no grip on the truth. In many cases, we are not even attracted to it.

But other people do believe and are saved. Why? Not because they are any wiser or more intelligent than those who reject. Not because they are able to see farther or think straighter. Not in any way because they are humbler, abler, or cleaner. Not at all. Rather, they are people who have been dragged, perhaps in spite of themselves, out of the darkness and into the light. There they are kept, guarded, and confirmed in the faith. For their everlasting salvation they are indebted "solely to the grace of God" (Art. 7).

Here we see the Canons aimed most directly at the Arminian error. Poor old Arminian goes to the farmer's sons and daughters with all they need for salvation. He has equipment for cleaning, curing, detoxifying, and transporting. But rescue does not work, in the Arminian scheme, except with those who "appropriate" the help by "their own free will" (Chap. II, Par. 6). God does free their wills to turn to Him, if they want. But they still have to want and do the turning. And many do not. They are still too blind or weak to see and do what is right.

The Golden Chain of Our Salvation (Articles 8 and 9)

We have now to face a sensitive sort of question. Did Christ come to save all? Did He die for all? Was His atoning work intended for all?

Yes, say all Arminians. Christ paid the price of redemption "for all men and for every man, according to the decree, will, and grace of God the Father" (Opinions of the Remonstrants B, 1). Christ "reconciled God the Father to the whole human race" (Opinions B, 2). Thus, "all men have been accepted into the state of reconciliation and unto the grace of the covenant" (Canons II, Par.

5). God intends to save all. He graciously frees the will of all sinners so that they can believe if they will. The only thing that stands in the way of God's realizing His intention is the actual *exercise* of human free will. Human beings are free either to believe (albeit, imperfectly), and thus be saved, or else to disbelieve, and thus frustrate the intention of God.

No, say all Calvinists. That cannot be. God wants all of His sons and daughters back. But He does not intend to bring them all back. The atonement of Christ is limited both in its intention and effectiveness to those who were "from eternity chosen to salvation" (Art. 8).

Let us admit, a final time, that even devout Calvinists swallow this hard teaching with difficulty. It is reluctantly believed because of certain biblical texts (John 10:11,15; John 17:9; Acts 20:28; Eph. 5:25-7; Matt. 1:21; Rom. 8:32-5), but even believers cannot be very enthusiastic about it. For they are obliged to defend a baffling combination of claims: God's plainly revealed will is that no one perish, but all live (Ezek. 33:11; II Peter 3:9). God wants all to be saved. He wants everybody *told* that He wants them saved. Yet they cannot be saved without His powerful work in them. He *can* provide this for all, but He does not. He does not even intend to do so. God wants all saved, but intends to save only some, and nobody knows why.

We are apparently missing some part of this puzzle. We do not understand this doctrine at all. Even St. Paul at least admits his insufficiency: "How unsearchable are his judgments and how inscrutable his ways!" (Rom. 11:33). No one of us can help wondering whether we have got this doctrine of limited atonement right. Perhaps the best we can do is hope that one day there will be some wonderful enlightenment when we no longer see in a glass darkly.

Meanwhile, we *can* see at least one reassuring truth. Those for whom Christ died—every lost one of them—is certainly saved. Here it is not the Calvinists, but the Arminians, who propagate a cruel and unusual doctrine. What Arminians believe (Canons II, Par. 1-6) is that there is no firm connection between Christ's work and a person's salvation. The tie that binds them is very loose. Everything finally depends on a person freely accepting the offered grace. This is *conditional* election. Election happens only on the condition that the person successfully grasp God's hand.

Yet, as we know from our story (and, more importantly, from the Bible) nobody can do that on his or her own. We are too drunk, too dim, too hooked, too scared, too weak. That a person must rise up out of his stupor and embrace a savior who appears alien, embarrassing, and disquieting is a hopeless prospect and a hopeless doctrine. Calvinists have their own difficulties to face with the doctrine of limited atonement. But Calvinists see at least the security, the certainty of salvation in all for whom Christ died. That is one of the glories of Reformed doctrine. And, like other glorious things, it is thoroughly biblical. In the matchless eighth chapter of Romans, St. Paul exclaims:

> For those whom he foreknew he also predestined to be conformed to the image of his Son . . . And those whom he predestined he also called; and those whom he called he also justified; and those whom he justified he also glorified. What then shall we say to this? If God is for us, who is against us? (Rom. 8:29-31)

This is "the golden chain of our salvation." With all of its links God binds the believer to Christ. At no time in the long, mysterious process of salvation is a person left to make his or her personal bond, or to depend on social security. Every link between Christ's work and the everlasting salvation of the elect is unbreakably forged. The grace of God is no mere tissue of polite invitations and genteel announcements of good intentions. It is a stout and thoroughly tested bond which never lets a believer go. In the covenant of grace, says Article 8, choosing, calling, justifying, converting, and cleansing are so linked as to bring the elect "infallibly to salvation." Union with Christ lasts. The golden chain stretches "even to the end," so that Christ, who has faithfully preserved them even to the end, should at last bring them, free from every spot and blemish, to the enjoyment of glory in His own presence forever (Art. 8). Articles 8 and 9 are only saying in other words that nothing "in all creation, will be able to separate us from the love of God in Christ Jesus our Lord" (Rom. 8:39).

Conclusion

People sometimes refer to Chapter II of the Canons as the "limited atonement chapter." Perhaps they do that because of their remorseless attraction to the TULIP acronym—in which the limitation is plainly central.

But the main point of this chapter is rather the security of salvation by grace alone, the theme which Articles 8 and 9 bring to a climax. This theme will be replayed with variations in the rest of the Canons. Start to finish, salvation is planned, worked, supported, and preserved by the grace of God. That grace is powerfully effective. God does whatever is necessary to save His elect.

Thus, to the question "Why are some not elect?" Arminians answer, in effect, that some are too stupid, rebellious, or ornery to believe. Calvinists answer: "We do not know—but we do know it is not because they are too stupid, rebellious, or ornery for God to save them. From their own case, all the elect know that such things cannot stop the God who is determined to save. His grace must prevail."

With that—questions and all—we can live.

PAUL BANDSTRA
11-15-78

CHAPTER 30
Corruption and Conversion

Canons of Dort, Third and Fourth Heads of Doctrine

Introduction

He was an intellectual. He read widely and thought deeply. He studied with excellent teachers and discussed ideas endlessly with learned friends. He relished books—not only their contents, but even the objects themselves. For him, "the set up of the page, the feel and smell of the paper, the differing sounds that different papers make as you turn the leaves became sensuous delights."

He was also a romantic. Knights and chivalry, myths and poetry, faraway places and remarkable people fascinated him. He was not a soft or sentimental person. Yet, the sound of a sea steamer, the taste of salt water, the way certain green hills looked from his childhood home—these filled him with longing. The longing seemed to come, he said, "as from a depth not of years, but of centuries." From time to time it stabbed him when he read, or heard a certain tune, or came suddenly upon a particular landscape when the light was right.

He was an atheist. As a child he had believed in God, but without love or awe. God was to him simply a magician who did not always perform when asked. Later he lost his belief even in the magician-God. He became a materialist. That is, he believed that the material universe—what may be touched, tasted, seen, or heard—is all there is. This belief made him happy. At least it smoothed the sharpest edges off his pain:

> No strictly infinite disaster could overtake you...Death ended all. And if ever finite disasters proved greater than one wished to bear, suicide would always be possible. The horror of the Christian universe was that it had no door marked *Exit.*

Yet materialism began in time to seem less and less plausible to him. He was tormented by the idea that if nothing was real except what was material, then truth, beauty, and right and wrong could not be real in the way he was instinctively sure they were. He gave up materialism.

He became an idealist instead. That is, he believed that what is finally real is not what one touches and sees, but rather what one thinks—or perhaps what one thinks *with*. Mind is ultimate. And there is an ultimate Mind. It is called "The Absolute." Belief in The Absolute offers all the advantages of belief in God with none of the inconveniences. You do not have to "count the cost" if you want to believe in The Absolute since It never bothers you with demands: "It was 'there'; safely and immovably 'there.' It would never come 'here'; never (to be blunt) make a nuisance of Itself."

But soon he was on his way even beyond idealism. He happened to come upon a number of people he admired. Strangely, to a person these new friends believed not merely in an Absolute, but in God. These people had depth. These people cared about telling the truth, restraining lust, and dealing fairly with others. Moreover all these people seemed to be Christians and thoroughgoing supernaturalists. They influenced him profoundly.

As he looked back, years later, he could see that his intellectual movement was being guided, that his longing had an object of whom he was not aware, that it was not by chance that he met and became acquainted with Christians. The "great Angler" had set the hook and was bringing him in; the great Adversary of all atheists was making his move. "The Absolute" turned out to be *alive!*

What must he do? He felt he had a choice to "open the door." Yet the choice did not appear to be his own: "It did not really seem possible to do the opposite." Not that he *wanted* to meet God. He was not searching for God (you might as well talk about "the mouse's search for the cat"). In fact, more than anything he wanted to believe that his only comfort in life and in death was that he was his own. But the Angler, the Adversary, could not be denied his prey. The final capture is described in a passage already classic in Christian literature:

> You must picture me alone in that room...night after night, feeling, whenever my mind lifted even for a second from my work, the steady, unrelenting approach of Him whom I so earnestly desired not to meet. That which I greatly feared had at last come upon me. In the Trinity term of 1929 I gave in, and admitted that God was God, and knelt and prayed: perhaps, that night, the most dejected and reluctant convert in all England...The Prodigal Son at least walked home on his own feet. But who can duly adore that Love which will open the high gates to a prodigal who is brought in kicking, struggling, resentful, and darting his eyes in every direction for a chance of escape?...The hardness of God is kinder than the softness of men, and His compulsion is our liberation.

The joy for which this human being longed was found, by surprise, to lead beyond itself to the personal source of all good. In fact, even when he did not know it this man had always been longing for God.

The man is, of course, C. S. Lewis, and the story of his early life is *Surprised by Joy.* The Lewis story is an apt introduction to Chapter III-IV because both give account of the movement from corruption to conversion. In its own way, Chapter III-IV also observes that "the hardness of God is kinder than the softness of man, and His compulsion is our liberation."

In this chapter we will find little that is completely new. Dort says things more than once. That is mainly because the several issues which it disputes with the Arminians are all related. What we find here is a kind of enlargement, or blowup, of details from the broad picture already drawn in Chapters I and II. Let us examine first those articles which deal with human corruption (1-5) and then those which describe human conversion (6-17).

Corruption (Articles 1-5)

Articles 1-5 enlarge what is said in Chapter I, Article 1. In greater detail, they describe the corruption from which we need conversion. This corruption came to a humanity originally created with built-in virtues and delights. Article 1 catalogs the choice gifts which Adam and Eve possessed, and then tragically forfeited. They had wholesome knowledge of God, a hearty willingness to do the right, pure "affections," or relations, with God and each other, and general holiness. But, inexplicably, they revolted. They did it, "by...free will," even if at "the instigation of the devil."

The result is dismally well known. Everything was reversed. All was turned upside down. The gifts were spoiled. The clarity and light in which God had been apparent were turned to blindness and darkness; straight wills were now perversely bent, pure relations adulterated. They who had been holy became wicked, rebellious, and stubborn. "The world" and "worldliness" crept over creation.

This world has since hosted the birth of every child. All children, beginning with Cain and Abel, are born into this zoo of lusts and bent creatures. It is not long before children get the hang of doing wrong. Do they get it, as the Pelagians taught, by aping their parents? No, says Article 2. The corruption is deeper than that. Children do wrong not merely by imitation, but by second nature. It is almost as if the tendency to selfishness were passed along genetically. It is almost as if the inclination to stubbornness were given along with two-leggedness. A bad strain has gotten into the stock.

Now "all men are conceived in sin," says Article 3. This does not mean, of course, that the sexual act which conceived each of us was contrary to the will of God and should never have been performed. That is absurd. Many such acts faithfully reflected married love, however imperfect. Rather, this first clause of Article 3 says we are all involved in common human fallenness from conception on. We are not innocents who are later corrupted. We are rather by *nature* "children of wrath." We have a depravity not of nurture so much as of nature.

Is it a *total* depravity? It is. But let us understand what we mean. The phrase "total depravity" (which the Canons do not employ) has often led people to think Calvinists were radical pessimists or even misanthropes. That is a mistake. The Canons nowhere say that unregenerate people always do what is utterly wrong. There is no suggestion that if an atheist has a choice between hugging his children and throttling them he will throttle them every time. Nothing of the sort. Article 4 plainly acknowledges "glimmerings" of

2ND GRADE
ORANGE CITY CHRISTIAN
11·16·78

the knowledge of God in natural man. Unregenerate people often know the difference between good and evil and show "some regard for virtue." Atheists may be no more in favor of cruelty to children than some self-professed Christians.

"Total" depravity refers, then, not to every feature of every act a person does, but rather to the broad scope or sweep of sin. Sin has gotten into every department of our lives. No area is exempt. We are contaminated specimens, and the contamination is thorough. It is not that every act is rotten through and through. It is rather that even our best acts are spoiled or marred. Even when we display what Article 5 calls "good outward behavior," there is likely to be an unholy motive attached to it. Natural depravity means that every facet of our lives, however shining and attractive, is still flawed and impure.

Article 4 goes a bit further. If by His common grace God allows unconverted persons some "glimmerings" of the truth about Him and His will, it is not as if such glimmerings were powerful enough to light the way home. They are not. In fact, though by common grace we are capable of some relative good, we are "incapable of *saving* good." If we are preserved from always doing what is utterly evil, while unconverted, we are still "*prone* to evil." We are inclined to do it, attracted by it, bent toward it. Evil is our natural habitat. That is why the glimmerings are finally not sufficient for salvation. If we were to open our eyes and hearts to the light that is given us, perhaps we should see our sin and be cleansed. But, in fact, because of our natural inclinations, we tend to suppress the truth (Rom. 1:18). We introduce so many impurities into our moral atmosphere—we throw up such a smoke screen between God and ourselves—that we render the light "wholly polluted." Thus, except for conversion, we make ourselves "inexcusable before God." We get ourselves into a position where we are "neither able nor willing to return to God" (Art. 3).

This last phrase is, of course, pointed at the Arminians. In chapter 28 we said Calvinists and Arminians already disagree about the seriousness of the fall, about whether our depravity is total or limited. That is roughly true. But now we are in a position to draw the distinction a bit more sharply.

The Arminians before Dort actually sounded quite Calvinistic on the seriousness of the fall. True, they did say that all human beings after the fall have it within their power to turn to God and be saved. But no reputable Arminian was willing to say that people can do that on their own. They need the grace of God to remove the slavery to sin and the spiritual death which resulted from the fall. Then they can believe.

So, strictly speaking, Arminians agree with Calvinists that natural man after the fall is impotent, dead in sin, and blind to spiritual things. Apart from the grace of God he cannot repent. Thus, when the Calvinists at Dort looked at the third Opinion of the Remonstrants, the one on human corruption, they could not tell that it was unscriptural. What seemed unscriptural to them was what followed—namely, the Arminian idea of conversion. Hence the treatment of opinions three and four together in Chapter III-IV.

The Arminian idea of conversion has an important preface. According to it, God's *common* grace—the grace with which He visits everybody—is sufficient to render a person able to repent and believe. That is really the nub of the Arminian-Calvinist dispute in the Third and Fourth Heads of Doctrine. Practically all the Rejections of Errors have to do with it in one way or another. Both parties see humanity naturally sunk in depravity after the fall. But Arminians claim that God so graces all fallen creatures (every one of which God intends to save) that they can believe. All they have to do is rise up and do it. Calvinists, on the other hand, deny that God's common grace has this effect. Only God's special grace does—and it, while limited to the elect, goes on to *assure* that the elect person is saved.

Think of it this way: Arminians say that after the fall God's common grace in effect returns everybody to the place Adam had—free to believe or not. In every human life, God efficiently removes the slavery introduced by the fall so as to let a person repent—if only (s)he *will.* The Adam-test is run over and over again. Some fail the test. They are lost. Some pass. God foresees that they will, and graciously allows their faith to take the place of a perfect life. They are the elect. They are elected on the basis of God's foreseeing that they will pass the Adam-test.

No, says Dort. Both Scripture and "the experience of all ages" (Chap. III-IV, Par. 5) deny the Arminian scheme. We know by *experience,* as well as by Scripture, that not everybody has the necessary and sufficient means for conversion. For example, not everybody hears the gospel.

Not even the Ten Commandments—part of which practically everybody knows from state criminal codes or from his own conscience—are sufficient. Here Article 5 follows Paul in Romans 7. The most the law can do is to show us our guilt. By itself, the law offers us neither strength to do right nor a Savior from the wrong we cannot help doing. We need outside help for conversion.

Conversion (Articles 6-17)

The rest of the articles in Chapter III-IV describe in detail what we know of such outside help. God arranges for His will and Word to be revealed to many. Some He regenerates. These are powerfully and thoroughly converted. Of these C. S. Lewis spoke truly: "The hardness of God is kinder than the softness of men, and His compulsion is our liberation."

Because this section says a number of things we have heard before, we can review it briefly. Article 6 is the transition to the new section. The light of nature is insufficient, so God has provided the ministry of the Holy Spirit; the law is bad news to sinners, but God has sent His good news "concerning the Messiah."

Who gets exposed to the gospel? Who hears the good news? That is up to God. Some unconverted persons "happen" to come upon strong Christians, as Lewis did. Others do not. But it is never a matter of the pious ones getting an advantage. None of us are naturally pious. Even God's chosen people could claim no advantage in natural goodness ("How odd of God/to choose the Jews"). Article 7 says that it is odd of God to choose any of us.

Article 8 stresses the well-meant offer of the gospel, a matter we considered in chapter 29. Articles 9 and 10 repeat the familiar ideas that disbelief in the well-offered gospel is to be attributed to human sin while belief is to be attributed to God's grace. Article 10 adds an important note: Election is not merely to salvation, but also to a task. Those who are translated "into the kingdom" are called to do the work of the kingdom. They are not to bask, sit, congratulate themselves, discuss the reprobate, or rest. They are "to show forth the praises of Him who has called them out of darkness into His marvelous light" (see I Pet. 2:10).

Articles 11-14 are the heart of this section. Here we find some vivid, almost passionate, descriptions of the manner of conversion. How does it *work?* It works, says this cluster of articles, irresistibly and incomprehensibly. The regeneration by which old things in us are made new is both powerful and mysterious.

Article 11 speaks of irresistible grace. Here we see the great Adversary of atheists making His move. It is all action language—a march of verbs. God "illuminates...pervades...opens...softens." He "circumcises...infuses...quickens...renders...actuates...strengthens." Article 14 will say frankly that God *produces* the act of believing. The point is that nothing is left to chance. Every elected sinner is at last brought to his knees by this terrible love, this severe mercy, this "hardness of God which is kinder than the softness of men." Nobody can finally hold out against God's grace. Nobody can outlast Him. Every elect person comes, as C. S. Lewis did, to "give in and admit that God is God." The article concludes with an utterly Reformed reminder about the purpose of all this. It is parallel to the reminder at the end of Article 10. The elect are not to sit around feeling warm and saved. They are to "bring forth the fruit of good actions."

Article 12 is the highlight of the chapter. At its center lies a beautiful description of regeneration.

RON LUBBERS
1-26-79

The work of regenerating a spirtually dead soul

> is evidently a supernatural work, most powerful, and at the same time most delightful, astonishing, mysterious, and ineffable; not inferior in efficacy to creation or the resurrection from the dead.

So empty of commitment to God is unregenerate man that the birth of such commitment is akin to creation, akin to making something out of nothing! So dead is fallen spiritual life that successful attempts to revive it can only be called resurrection!

So the hardness of God is kinder than the softness of men. Both Articles 11 and 12 add the rest: His compulsion is our liberation. At the end of both articles is an acknowledgment of human free will *after* regeneration. We have been forcefully unhooked from our dependence on sin. Now we can freely serve God. God "quickens" the will and makes it "pliable" (Art. 11). The will now "becomes itself active." In Article 16 the point is made even more sharply. Regeneration works not only powerfully, but also gracefully and mysteriously. It "does not treat men as senseless stocks and blocks." Rather, those bent by the fall are bent back upright "sweetly and powerfully." Once again there is "freedom of our will."

Two final issues raised by this section may be briefly considered. The first is the matter of attitude. Again and again the Canons warn those who think they are elect that election produces gratitude and humility—not "haughtiness, as if we had made ourselves to differ" (Art. 15). Moreover, people who know themselves saved by grace are to pray for such as "have not yet been called." Going beyond the Canons, we would today say that we must ourselves send and be ambassadors to them. Meanwhile, no Christian is to pretend to discern who is elect and who is not. We are not privy to the secrets of God. If someone makes a profession of faith, says Article 15, and amends his life, then we are to assume his sincerity. We are to judge and even *speak* of him " in the most favorable manner." That goes even for those, such as politicians and celebrities, for whom a profession of faith might conceivably be professionally advantageous.

The last issue raised by Articles 6-17 is another we have met before. In all the Canons' talk about election, there is never a minimizing of the need to use ordinary gospel *means* of salvation. No fatalism is allowed. Nobody is permitted to say:

"Either God will save me or else He won't, so it doesn't matter what I do." Article 17 insists on this. We are to preach and listen to the gospel. We must reverently partake of the sacraments. With a mixture of firmness and humility, we are to exercise church discipline. These are *means* of grace. This is the ordinary way of salvation and nurture.

Conclusion

The end of Article 17 mentions something mature Christians have come to know through experience: God's grace does not work in a vacuum. It works in and through ordinary lives and commonplace events. And it works especially when we do not merely wait for it to spark or restore our faith, but also steadfastly "perform our duty." Here is a primary method of escape from spiritual dryness and depression. We are summoned to act like Christians—going to church, attending to sacraments, living as Christians should. We are summoned to do our duty even when we do not feel like it. That is not popular advice in a day in which bumper stickers advise us to do what feels good—and only that. But it is sound advice nonetheless. Nobody is promised that in the Christian life (s)he will always *feel* joy. The sort of faith which tries constantly to rub some feeling back to its original shine is a desperate and lonesome faith. There may be times, by God's grace, when we get shivers down the spine, and a racing of the pulse. But that is not what we are after. We are to "perform our duty" so that "His work is advanced" and His glory manifested. *That* is what we are after.

Even joy itself, as Lewis says at the conclusion of his autobiography, was never meant by God to be our final object. "It was valuable only as a pointer to something other and outer:

> When we are lost in the woods the sight of a sign-post is a great matter...But when we have found the road and are passing signposts every few miles we shall not stop and stare... not on this road, though their pillars are of silver and their lettering of gold. "We would be at Jerusalem."   *(Surprised by Joy)*

CHAPTER 31
The Perseverance of the Saints

Canons of Dort, Fifth Head of Doctrine

Introduction

Everyone grows older. After age thirty, it is said, the "sense of transience" is awakened. It occurs to you in some reflective moment that you may already have lived almost half your life. You find yourself astonished, every time anew, at how certain children have *grown*! Your group at church is no longer called the "*Young* Couples." Gradually you notice that nobody your age is still called a "promising young woman," or "a man with a big future." If you are athletic, you have to admit the effects of aging. You are not as fast, not as agile, not as quick as before. It hurts you to watch aging professional athletes. These are people past their prime at thirty-three. They have "lost a step."

Some people age gracefully. If they are Christians, they do it with a sense of the grace of God which preserves them. The know that their "outer nature is wasting away." But they are also firmly aware that their "inner nature is being renewed every day" (II Cor. 4:16). Here are people with age spots, crow's feet, and gray in whatever hair is still firmly rooted. Yet, some part of the beauty of God has come upon them in the midst of their years, and they have become heartier, keener, and more assured in the things of the faith. They have used their years to practice the Christian virtues, and in everything important—wisdom, patience, peace, love for God and neighbor—these people have not declined, but advanced. They are on their way, with a pilgrim's progress, to a "city set on a hill." The closer to it they come, the stronger they get.

Other people do not age gracefully. They make expensive, and sometimes pitiable, attempts to seem younger than they are. They watch a lot of television and take the advice of its sponsors.

Thus they acquire (Grecian) formulas, iron tonics, and skin smoothers. Some acquire young lovers. A few pay high-priced surgeons to lift certain bodily parts. There is so much of one's fading youth to be preserved and so little time to do it! The effects of aging must be put off or held back. If not lifted up, they can at least be covered up. In any event, one must *act* young! A mother can try to dress like her twenty-year-old daughter. A father, soft and out of shape, can test his heart and tear his cartilage over weekend sports. Both can affect teenage jargon and amuse all those whom they are trying to impress. The movement toward old age is a sad decline, as all good secularists know, and a person has to fight back with all the money, ingenuity, and drugstore foolishness at his or her disposal. You are over the hill, you are getting weaker, and you thoroughly resent it.

Christian and secular views of aging are directly opposed. One sees advance; the other, decline. One sees the flower of human life continually growing. The other sees it withering. One claims the climax of human life occurs at death! The other sees it lost somewhere in the beauty and ignorance of youth (Why is youth wasted on the *young?*).

It is not that Christians are blind to change and decay. They know something of the poignance of aging. Old friends die. Youthful dreams must at last be abandoned. A snapshot falls out of a book, or you discover an old letter, and memories come back. Your own body has succumbed, here and there, to the encroachment of old age. Here it has stiffened; there it has begun to sag. And all of this has gone so fast! Why are the years so short? Christians have their share of human wonder and wistfulness about aging.

But Christians have something else too. They have a sense of permanence in the midst of change.

It gives them poise. They dare to believe that they are going to live forever. They know as well as anybody else that the days of man are as the grass of the field. But Christians go on from there. They also know that the lovingkindness of the Lord is from everlasting to everlasting. In other words, Christians believe with all their heart that the one, stable, permanent fact about human life is that a gracious God loves and preserves His children. Those whom He rescues He also preserves—both for this life and for the life which is to come.

Chapter V of the Canons of Dort is about such preservation. It is entitled "The Perseverance of the Saints." But it is actually less about the saints and their perseverance than about God and His preservation. Let us take it in two sections: first, God's preservation of His people (Art. 1-8); then, believers' assurance of their preservation (Art. 9-15).

God's Preservation of His People (Articles 1-8)

The first eight articles say this: God's people still sin daily. Some sin so seriously as to "highly offend God" and "incur a deadly guilt" (Art. 5). But in His great mercy, God permits none of them to be *finally* lost. Meanwhile, even when they sin "enormously," God's people do not *totally* lose their faith or His grace, not even temporarily. All along God inspires in His people such repentance and faith, such longing for His favor, that at last they "reign with the lamb of God in heaven" (Art. 2). God's purpose for His elect cannot be blocked. So Article 8, which summarizes this whole section concludes:

> ...His counsel cannot be changed nor His promise fail; neither can the call according to his purpose be revoked, nor the merit, intercession, and preservation of Christ be rendered ineffectual, nor the sealing of the Holy Spirit be frustrated....

In this profoundly Calvinistic confession, appeal is made to the grace which sustains redemption firmly and lastingly. In a way which reminds us of "the golden chain of our salvation" (chap. 29), this confession points to the bedrock of Christian security—God's faithfulness.

In so many ways the Bible speaks of God's faithfulness. In the Old Testament we hear the voices of those who cry out of the depths, who wait for the Lord "more than watchmen for the morning," who urge on the whole people of God:

> O Israel, hope in the Lord!
> For with the Lord there is steadfast love, and with him is plenteous redemption.
>
> (Ps. 130:7)

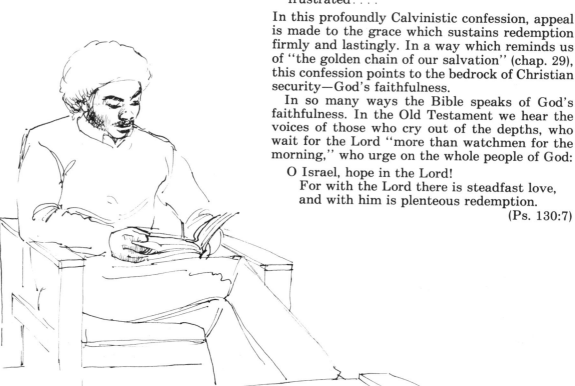

VERNON PROCTOR
12-14-78

And we hear the ageless, searching wisdom of him who says:

> As for man, his days are like grass...
> But the steadfast love of the Lord is from everlasting to everlasting upon those who fear him....
>
> (Ps. 103:15,17)

In the new age, the testimony continues:

> [Nothing] in all creation, will be able to separate us from the love of God in Christ Jesus our Lord. (Rom. 8:39)
>
> ...I am sure that he who began a good work in you will bring it to completion at the day of Jesus Christ. (Phil.1:6)

On the lips of our Lord Himself is a haunting reassurance to which Calvin pointed again and again:

> My sheep hear my voice, and I know them, and they follow me; and I give them eternal life, and they shall never perish, and no one shall snatch them out of my hand. (John 10:27,28)

To these texts Reformed people have always turned for their sense of security and permanence in a shifting and dangerous world. Elaborating on the splendid Answer 54 of the Catechism ("Of this community I am *and always will be* a living member"), Article 8 refers to that divine mercy which keeps, and which keeps for good. In fact, says Article 8, the whole Trinity is at work in promising, calling, preserving, interceding, and sealing. This work is irrevocable, unbreakable, irreversible, utterly final.

Why do the Canons need to say this? Because Arminians (and other Christians) deny it. The Arminian position is that believers *can* persevere, but it is up to them to do it. Believers are helped toward final salvation by the preserving grace of God, but nothing about the process is completely sure. A true believer can totally fall from grace (Chap. V, Par. 7,8). He may then be born again repeatedly, but if he wants to be finally saved he must see to it that he perseveres. Successful perseverance is a *condition* of his election and salvation. Many true believers fail the test of perseverance and are lost forever (Par. 3, 4).

In support of this teaching, Arminians (and like-minded Christians) point to biblical texts which warn believers against apostasy, and to texts which suggest that believers have in fact fallen away. Moreover, they insist that God does not intrude upon that human freedom which wants to lock Him out.

But Dort and all Calvinists read the matter differently. They find the Arminian position quite depressing and hopeless. Taking the preservation texts (quoted above) as their anchor, Calvinists understand the biblical warnings against apostasy simply as divine means for inducing repentance and godliness (Art. 13). They moreover deny that any genuine believer in the Bible is said to fall away. And they repudiate the notion that God allows the freedom of fallen human beings to stop Him from completing His appointed rounds of gathering, protecting, and preserving His people.

So Articles 1 through 8 state the Calvinist doctrine of God's gracious preservation. True, even converts still sin (Art. 1). Pilgrims on their way up to the new Jerusalem sometimes slide back part way. There are daily lapses and weaknesses. There are defects which mar even "the best works of the saints" (Art. 2). Worse than that, there are sometimes "great and heinous sins" performed by great and heroic saints (Art. 4).

This last observation reminds us of a fascinating feature of the Christian life—a feature at once disturbing and reassuring. The disturbing part is that believers may be deeply divided persons. Genuine piety and genuine wickedness may cohabit in the greatest saints. For centuries before Dort, David and Peter had been cited as examples. Dort mentions them too. Take David. Here is a lickerish peeping tom, an ingenious killer, a crafty master of cover-up. Yet, according to tradition, it is this same man who wrote the greatest psalm of confession ever to appear among God's people:

> Have mercy on me, O God, according to thy steadfast love; according to thy abundant mercy blot out my transgressions.... (Ps. 51:1)

In this heartbroken prayer we see misery and mercy "flowing mingled down." Here is a reassurance for all God's people. What the Canons say in Articles 1-8 is that no matter how deeply God's people sin, their sin is never deeper than His grace. No matter how lasting their suspension of "the exercise of faith," their persistence cannot outlast God's mercy.

Hence, the pressure to confess and come clean turns out to be a pressure built by God (Art. 7). Shame after sin is a means by which God draws His children out of the shadows and into His fatherly light (Art. 5). It is not that the hazards and lapses of the Christian life are trivial or unreal. Article 5 is unflinching in its description of the grieving, wounding, and alienating effects of sins by believers. Sin always leaves its mark on the sinner—and usually on many others as well. David, we recall, came to penitence only after

DICK SONDERFAN
1-25-74

wrecking the home and removing the life of Uriah the Hittite. None of this is denied by Dort. Yet, mysteriously and powerfully, God uses even tragic sin as an occasion for progressing in the godly life. A believer in the new age who flees from things which are dingy or cruel or cheap or depressing—a believer who "flees for refuge to Christ crucified"—finds that he is strengthened in his pursuit of "the goal of perfection" (Art. 2). In the great rhythm of the godly life, those who see their sin, and honestly confess it, are both forgiven and fortified for the way ahead. Once again they "experience the favor of a reconciled God." What is more, they "henceforward more diligently work out their own salvation with fear and trembling" (Art. 7).

Yet all along it is God who is at work in them. In the combining of these last two statements, Dort simply reproduces the paradoxical language of Philippians 2:12 and 13. We are called to persevere. We have to repent. We must exercise godliness. Yet, as it turns out, "God is at work...both to will and to work for His good pleasure." In these articles and in the corresponding paragraphs, Dort is intent upon refuting any notion that we stand on our own. We do not. If we were not shored up by God's grace, we would cave in to the "temptations of the world and of Satan" (Art. 3). Any persevering we do, any standing upright, all progress toward perfection is to be charged to God's mercy which "confirms" and "powerfully preserves" His people "even to the end" (Art. 3).

Assurance of Preservation (Articles 9-15)

But now comes the inevitable question: How can a person be sure of all this? In particular, how do *I* know that these great truths about preservation apply to *me*?

Article 9 begins simply by claiming that believers *can* have assurance of preservation. In Chapter I, Dort affirmed election and the assurance of election. Chapter V just draws out the implications. Every elect person must persevere. And every person who knows that he is elect will also know that he will persevere.

That is the general conceptual frame of the two chapters. But, of course, this frame or skeleton needs to be fleshed out with reference both to the struggle and joy of the Christian life as believers live it. The background is always the Arminian denial of assurance. Arminians think such assurance removes all the risk and freedom of faith. They think a person cannot know he will persevere till he does it. There are no advance guarantees. In this Arminians represent the position of practically all Christians but Calvinists. Only the Roman Catholic Council of Trent offers much of an exception. There are special cases, said Trent, in which God grants private revelations by which certain saints are assured.

Dort denies that assurance springs from private revelations—or at least from revelations "contrary to or independent of the Word of God." And Dort emphatically affirms the possibility of assurance. Article 10 offers three grounds of assurance: first, "from faith in God's promises"; second, "from the testimony of the Holy Spirit"; and third, "from a serious and holy desire...to perform good works." These have been often discussed and argued about. The discussion centers around the fact that the first of these grounds is "objective" and external to the believer while the second and third grounds are "subjective," or dependent on the believer's own perceiving. Which of these is final?

Dort says we need all three. None is enough by itself. The first ground of assurance, the objective one, is that God has made certain "promises... abundantly revealed in His Word." God has promised to be faithful to His people. That, as we have already suggested above, is the bedrock of a believer's security and the heart of the covenant of grace. It is an objective fact: God is faithful.

But, of course, the question arises: How do I know He will be faithful to *me*? How do I know *I* am in the covenant of grace? Suppose it is true that God is gracious; how is this true for me?

Just as in Chapter I, Dort answers this sort of question by pointing in the end to "fruits of election." I gain assurance, says Dort, subjectively. I gain it by noting in *myself* a "holy desire to preserve a good conscience and to perform good works." This notoriously Reformed idea (cf. Heid. Cat. Answer 86) has always been controversial. Historians have often found in it the explanation for the whole Reformed "ethos" or life-style. A few important scholars have even argued that the rise of Western capitalism is owed to this idea. Did the Puritans not strive to prove to themselves that they were elect? Did they not therefore diligently do their duty, work hard, save thriftily, invest prudently, and make much money? Is that not a prime way of telling that the Lord loves you and wants to keep you? You tell by referring to your bank balance!

Actually, this "good works" ground has nothing particularly to do with making money. It means instead to reassure a believer that if his conscience bothers him, that is a good sign. God is using the believer's conscience as a moral warning system to preserve him. Any good works the believer actually does may be regarded as genuine fruits of faith. But then they must *be* fruits of faith—and not merely attempts at self-aggrandizement. Believers are obliged to face the fact that this third ground all by itself is very dangerous indeed. If it does not tempt a person to despair over his lack of progress, it may tempt him to pride. He is likely either to give up or to puff up. Neither reaction is any good.

Perhaps the key to assurance lies in the middle ground—"the testimony of the Holy Spirit, witnessing with our spirit that we are children and heirs of God." This special work of the Spirit both *applies* the gospel promises to believers and also *stimulates* them to do works of gratitude.

Thus this second ground links the first with the third.

But what is this elusive "testimony of the Holy Spirit" like? Will I get a warm feeling in the middle of my chest? Will I cultivate a permanent Christian smile? Will I tell everyone that I am thrilled to pieces? Not necessarily. The mysterious testimony of the Holy Spirit gives a person a quiet sense of conviction. Perhaps that is as near as we can come to describing its effect. A person is *convinced* by the Holy Spirit that scriptural promises are true. What is more, he is convinced that they apply to *him*. The same Spirit who guides us "into all the truth" (John 16:13) also bears "witness with our spirit that we are children of God" (Rom. 8:16).

The "we" is important. We must see assurance, as well as the rest of the Christian life, broadly enough. Assurance is not merely a private treasure, a secret possession of prayer closets and bedrooms. The context of assurance is always the community of God's people. Article 1 begins with a call to "the communion" of Christ. Article 9 echoes the Catechism's great Answer 54 by affirming our perseverance as "true and living members of the Church." Article 14 insists that assurance is fostered by the work of the church—by preaching and sacraments. Article 15 sums up this whole line of thought by emphasizing that the teaching of perseverance is an "inestimable treasure" of "the bride of Christ"—that is, the church.

It is crucial to see this. We have already taken account in chapter 22 of church discipline as one of the church's "marks." We are to keep "one another on the right road" (Rom. 15:14, Phillips). At some times in our lives we need nothing so much as a strong warning to get back on track. But there are other times when reassurance is needed.

We see this in the case of David. David had sinned grievously. Likely an examination of his own life would not have revealed much of "a holy desire . . . to do good works." Indeed, to the family of Uriah, David was a holy terror. If we may judge from Psalm 51, David felt joyless and abandoned. To a godly man that is one of the wages which sin pays. Now, interestingly, the same man who came to David with rebuke from God also comes with reassurance. Nathan the prophet had told David a soft little lamb story—with a point like a lance. But David does not get the point till Nathan sticks him with it: "*You* are the man" (II Sam. 12:7). David is penitent: " 'I have sinned against the Lord.' And Nathan said to David, 'The Lord also has put away your sin . . . .' "

So it goes in the fellowship of God's people. There is a time for warning and a time for reassurance. There is a time for saying "You must not do that!" or, "You have to do that at once!" But there is also a time for saying, "The Lord has put away your sin. He still loves you. Now let's see what can be done."

We need to be preserved. We also need *assurance* that God preserves and still loves us. So often God works both preservation and assurance through other saints, through flesh and blood, by way of the church, through the very body of Christ. Most of us are too proud to submit ourselves to others for such help. But we need it. We need to walk with each other, lean on each other, take both warning and assurance from each other. It is one of the ways by which God Himself preserves and assures.

Conclusion

Articles 12 and 13 repeat the familiar canonical warning against pride, laziness, and a general tendency among the "assured" to throttle back the old plant and take one's ease. Real believers, say the Canons, would not do that. True faith *inevitably* produces good works. True children of God could not live with themselves or with their own conscience if they became careless or scornful of piety. The point is that anyone who wants to take his ease has probably not yet got the salvation he is so sure of. Real believers are sure of their election—but not *too* sure. They are secure—but not "carnally secure."

But if carnal security is to be shunned, so is "carnal doubt." Article 11 admits some of the continuing struggle of the Christian life, and assures those tempted to despair that with temptation God also provides the way of escape (I Cor. 10:13). There are times for most believers when all the zest has gone out of the Christian faith. It does not mean much to us at the moment, and we know it. Prayer is a bore. We are weary in well-doing. Preaching is powerless to move us. We wonder if the whole Christian enterprise has not been a sadly human mistake.

Yet we cannot quite let go. There are too many ties which bind. A sociologist might mention community pressures, family ties, old memories and the like. But, as we discover, the matter seems deeper and more mysterious than that. Among the threads which still tie us to the faith may be honest fear, a conscience which will not die, and, for many, an intolerable sense of the emptiness and meaninglessness of a godless life.

So we plug along for a time. We keep on. We do our duty. We make ourselves pray a little. We ask for more life, more depth, more enthusiasm. We confess sin; we admit our lackluster faith and the weakness of our grip on God.

And one day the darkness lifts. Strangely, "from a depth not of years, but of centuries," the assurance returns. Veteran Christians know the return is not easy. It has come through pain and perseverance. And there are still questions we want to ask. There are still places where we are tender and weak. There is no adequacy of our own. Yet we seem to behold God's gracious countenance again. And we discover that God has never left us. It is we ourselves who have taken a journey into some far country.

The Holy Spirit has been at work, says Article 11. He has brought us back. It is this person, this Comforter, who both assures us of God's favor and also stimulates good works of gratitude.

So we must never give up. We must *look* up, aware that the same Lord who has embraced us all along will let nothing snatch us from His hand. This is a truth which the church has always

tenderly loved and constantly defended...as an inestimable treasure; and God, against whom neither counsel nor strength can prevail, will dispose her so to continue to the end. Now to this one God, Father, Son, and Holy Spirit, be honor and glory forever. Amen.

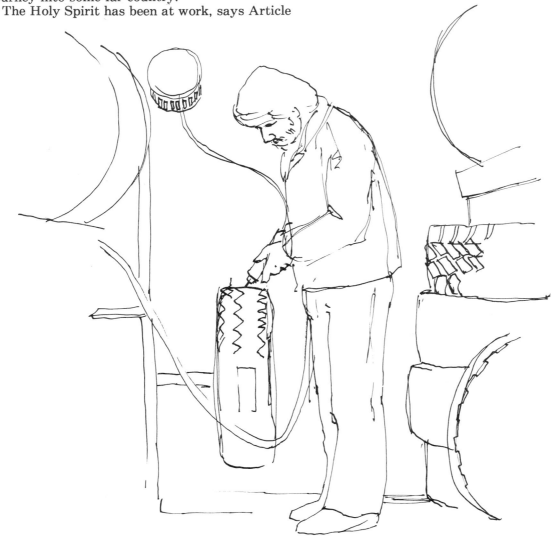

LESTER KLYN
STUDDING TIRES
11.14.78

BIBLIOGRAPHY

Acts of Synod, 1973. Grand Rapids: Board of Pub. of the Chr. Ref. Church, 1973.

Armstrong, Brian. *Calvinism and the Amyraut Heresy.* Madison: University of Wisconsin Press, 1969.

Aulen, Gustaf. *Christus Victor.* New York: Macmillan Co., 1969.

Baillie, Donald. *God Was in Christ.* London: Faber and Faber, 1948.

Baillie, John. *Our Knowledge of God.* New York: Charles Scribner's Sons, 1959.

Bainton, Roland. *The Reformation of the Sixteenth Century.* Boston: Beacon Press, 1952.

Baird, Henry Martin. *Theodore Beza.* Heroes of the Reformation, vol. 4. New York and London: G. P. Putnam's Sons, 1899.

Bangs, Carl. *Arminius.* Nashville: Abingdon Press, 1971.

Barnow, A. J. *The Making of Modern Holland.* New York: W. W. Norton & Co., 1944.

Barth, Karl. *Church Dogmatics,* vol. IV/1. Edinburg: T & T Clark, 1955.

Berkhof, Hendrikus. *Well-Founded Hope.* Richmond: John Knox Press, 1969.

Berkhof, Louis. *The History of Christian Doctrines.* Grand Rapids: Baker Book House, 1973.

———. *Systematic Theology.* Grand Rapids: Wm. B. Eerdmans Pub. Co., 1949.

Berkouwer, G. C. *The Church.* Grand Rapids: Wm. B. Eerdmans Pub. Co., 1976.

———. *Divine Election.* Grand Rapids: Wm. B. Eerdmans Pub. Co., 1960.

———. *Faith and Perseverance.* Grand Rapids: Wm. B. Eerdmans Pub. Co., 1958.

———. *The Person of Christ.* Grand Rapids: Wm. B. Eerdmans Pub. Co., 1954.

———. *The Work of Christ.* Grand Rapids: Wm. B. Eerdmans Pub. Co., 1965.

Bettenson, Henry. *Documents of the Christian Church.* New York: Oxford University Press, 1950.

Bratt, John, ed. *The Heritage of John Calvin.* Grand Rapids: Wm. B. Eerdmans Pub. Co., 1973

———. *The Rise and Development of Calvinism.* Grand Rapids: Wm. B. Eerdmans Pub. Co., 1959.

Brunner, Emil. *Our Faith.* London: SCM Press, 1949.

Calvin, John. "Preface to Olivetan's New Testament," *Calvin: Commentaries.* Library of Christian Classics, vol. 23. Edited by Joseph Haroutunian. Philadelphia: Westminster Press, 1958.

Calvin, John. *Institutes of the Christian Religion.* Translated by F. L. Battles. Philadelphia: Westminster Press, 1960.

Calvin, John. *The Sermons of M. Iohn Caluin upon the Fifth Booke of Moses Called Deuteronomie.* Translated by Arthur Golding. London: H. Middleton for G. Bishop, 1583.

Carnell, Corbin Scott. *Bright Shadow of Reality.* Grand Rapids: Wm. B. Eerdmans Pub. Co., 1974.

Centennial Discourses of the Reformed (Dutch) Church in America (1876). New York: Reformed Church in America, 1877.

Daane, James. *The Freedom of God.* Grand Rapids: Wm. B. Eerdmans Pub. Co., 1973.

Davidman, Joy. *Smoke on the Mountain.* London: Hodder and Stoughton, 1955.

De Jong, Peter Y. *The Church's Witness to the World.* Pella, Iowa: Pella Pub., 1960.

———, ed. *Crisis in the Reformed Churches; Essays in Commemoration of the Great Synod of Dort, 1618-19.* Grand Rapids: Reformed Fellowship, 1968.

De Vries, Peter. *The Mackerel Plaza.* Boston: Little, Brown, 1958.

Dickens, A. G. *Reformation and Society in Sixteenth-Century Europe.* London: Thames and Hudson, 1966.

Dobson, James. *Hide or Seek.* Old Tappan, N. J.: F. H. Revell Co., 1974.

Dowey, Edward A. *A Commentary on the Confessions of 1967 and an Introduction to the Book of Confessions.* Philadelphia: Westminster Press, 1968.

———. *The Knowledge of God in Calvin's Theology.* New York: Columbia University Press, 1952.

Dulles, Avery. *Models of the Church*. Garden City, NY: Doubleday, 1974.

Flannery, Austin P., ed. *Documents of Vatican II*. Grand Rapids: Wm. B. Eerdmans Pub. Co., 1975.

Fuhrmann, Paul T. *An Introduction to the Great Creeds of the Church*. Philadelphia: Westminster Press, 1960.

Graham, Billy. *Angels: God's Secret Messengers*. Garden City, NY: Doubleday, 1975.

Greeley, Andrew. "When Religion Cast Off Wonder, Hollywood Seized It." *New York Times*, Nov. 27, 1977.

Hageman, Howard G. "Does the Reformed Tradition, in 1975, Have Anything to Offer to American Life?" *The Reformed Journal*, March, 1975.

————. "The Gift of Office." *The Banner*, Oct. 14, 21, 1977.

Harrison, R. K. *Introduction to the Old Testament*. Grand Rapids: Wm. B. Eerdmans Pub. Co., 1969.

Hendry, George. *The Westminster Confession for Today*. Richmond: John Knox Press, 1960.

Herberg, Will. *Protestant, Catholic, Jew*. New York: Harper & Row, 1960.

Hick, John, ed. *The Myth of God Incarnate*. Philadelphia: Westminster Press, 1977.

Hoekema, Anthony. "The Heritage of Dort," *The Acts of Synod 1968*. Grand Rapids: Board of Pub. of the Chr. Ref. Church, 1968.

————. "The New Great Planet Earth." *The Banner*, Feb. 24, 1978.

Huxley, Julian. *Religion Without Revelation*. London: Watts & Co., 1941.

Kahl, Joachim. *The Misery of Christianity*. Translated by N. D. Smith. Harmondsworth, Middlesex, England: Penguin Books Ltd., 1971.

Kelley, Dean. *Why Conservative Churches Are Growing*. San Francisco: Harper & Row, 1977.

Kelly, J. N. D. *Early Christian Creeds*. 3rd ed. New York: David McKay Co., 1972.

Kittel, G., ed. *Theological Dictionary of the New Testament*. Grand Rapids: Wm. B. Eerdmans Pub. Co., 1964.

Kromminga, D. H. *The Christian Reformed Tradition*. Grand Rapids: Wm. B. Eerdmans Pub. Co., 1943.

Kromminga, John. "Church Discipline as a Pastoral Exercise." *The Reformed Journal*, Nov. 1977.

Kuyper, Abraham. *Calvinism*. Grand Rapids: Wm. B. Eerdmans Pub. Co., 1961.

Leith, John H. *Creeds of the Churches*. Chicago: Aldine Pub. Co., 1963.

————. *An Introduction to the Reformed Tradition*. Atlanta: John Knox Press, 1977.

Lewis, Clive Staples. *The Four Loves*. London: Geoffrey Bles, 1960.

————. *The Great Divorce*. London: Geoffrey Bles, 1946.

————. *Mere Christianity*. London: Geoffrey Bles, 1952.

————. *Reflections on the Psalms*. New York: Harcourt, Brace & Co., 1958.

————. *The Screwtape Letters*. New York: Macmillan Co., 1947.

————. *Surprised by Joy*. London: Geoffrey Bles, 1955.

————. *The Weight of Glory*. New York: Macmillan Co., 1949.

"Living: Pushbutton Power." *Time*. Feb. 20, 1978.

Luther, Martin. *Three Treatises*. Philadelphia: Muhlenberg Press, 1943.

MacDonald, John D. *Condominium*. Philadelphia: Lippencott, 1977.

Machen, J. Gresham. *Christianity and Liberalism*. Grand Rapids: Wm. B. Eerdmans Pub. Co., 1946.

Mackintosh, H. R. *Types of Modern Theology*. New York: Scribner, 1937.

Marin, Peter. "The New Narcissism." *Harper's Magazine*, Oct. 1975.

Masselink, Edward. *The Heidelberg Story*. Grand Rapids: Baker Book House, 1964.

McKinley, O. Glenn. *Where Two Creeds Meet: A Biblical Evaluation of Calvinism and Arminianism*. Kansas City, Mo.: Beacon Hill Press, 1959.

McNeill, John T. *The History and Character of Calvinism*. New York: Oxford University Press, 1967.

Menninger, Karl. *Whatever Became of Sin?* New York: Hawthorn Books, 1973.

Metzger, Bruce. *An Introduction to the Apocrypha*. New York: Oxford University Press, 1957.

Miller, H. B. "Millenium Now." *The Trentonian*, Feb. 26, 1978.

Minear, Paul. *Images of the Church in the New Testament*. Philadelphia: Westminster Press, 1960.

Molinari, P. "Intercession of Saints," *Catholic Encyclopedia*, vol. 12.

Mouw, Richard J. "Bad Sermons." *The Reformed Journal*, Nov. 1976.

————. "Baptismal Politics." *The Reformed Journal*, July, 1978.

————. *Politics and the Biblical Drama*. Grand Rapids: Wm. B. Eerdmans Pub. Co., 1976.

The Nature and Extent of Biblical Authority. Grand Rapids: Board of Pub. of the Chr. Ref. Church, 1972.

Niebuhr, H. Richard. *Christ and Culture*. New York: Harper and Bros., 1951.

Nygren, Anders. *Agape and Eros*. London: Society for Promoting Christian Knowledge, 1932.

O'Collins, G. *What Are They Saying About Jesus?* New York: Paulist Press, 1977.

Orlebeke, C. and Smedes L., eds. *God and the Good*. Grand Rapids: Wm. B. Eerdmans Pub. Co., 1975.

Osterhaven, Eugene. *Our Confession of Faith*. Grand Rapids: Baker Book House, 1964.

Pannenberg, Wolfhart. *Jesus—God and Man.* 2nd ed. Philadelphia: Westminster Press, 1968.

————, ed. *Revelation as History.* New York: Macmillan Co., 1968.

Pelikan, Jaroslav. *Historical Theology.* New York: Corpus, 1971.

Phillips, J. B. *Your God Is Too Small.* New York: Macmillan Co., 1955.

Pieters, Albertus. *The Facts and Mysteries of the Christian Faith.* Grand Rapids: Wm. B. Eerdmans Pub. Co., 1926.

Piper, John. "Is Self-Love Biblical?" *Christianity Today,* Aug. 12, 1977.

Plantinga, Alvin. *God, Freedom, and Evil.* New York: Harper & Row, 1974.

————. "On Being Honest to God." *The Reformed Journal,* April, 1964.

Psalter Hymnal Supplement. Grand Rapids: Board of Pub. of the Chr. Ref. Church, 1974.

Rauschenbusch, Walter. *Theology for the Social Gospel.* New York: Macmillan Co., 1917.

Roberts, R. C. *Rudolf Bultmann's Theology.* Grand Rapids: Wm. B. Eerdmans Pub. Co., 1976.

Russell, Bertrand. "A Free Man's Worship," *Why I Am Not a Christian.* New York: Simon and Schuster, 1957.

Ryle, Gilbert. *Concept of Mind.* New York: Barnes and Noble, 1949.

Schaff, Philip. *The Creeds of Christendom,* 3 vol. 6th ed. New York: Harper and Bros., 1931.

Schleiermacher, Friedrich. *The Christian Faith.* Edinburgh: T & T Clark, 1928.

Smedes, Lewis. *All Things Made New.* Grand Rapids: Wm. B. Eerdmans Pub. Co., 1970.

Spykman, Gordon. *Never On Your Own.* Grand Rapids: Board of Pub. of the Chr. Ref. Church, 1969.

Stewart, James. *A Man in Christ.* New York: Harper.

Stilma, Lize. *Dordrecht in Pocket-Size.* Baarn: Hollandia D. NV., 1966.

Stob, Henry. "Civil Disobedience." *The Reformed Journal,* April, 1972.

Stroup, G. "Chalcedon Revisited." *Theology Today,* April, 1978.

Tawney, R. H. *Religion and the Rise of Capitalism.* London: John Murray, 1960.

Thompson, E. T. *Through the Ages, A History of the Christian Church.* Richmond: CLC Press, 1965.

Tillich, Paul. *The Shaking of the Foundations.* New York: Charles Scribner's Sons, 1950.

Tolstoy, Leo. *The Kingdom of God Is Within You.* Edited and translated by Leo Wiener. Boston: L. C. Page and Co., 1932.

The Truth that Leads to Eternal Life. Pennsylvania: Watchtower Bible and Tract Society, 1968.

Ursinus, Zacharius. *Commentary on the Heidelberg Catechism.* Grand Rapids: Eerdmans Pub. Co., 1956.

Van Halsema, Thea. *Glorious Heretic.* Grand Rapids: Wm. B. Eerdmans Pub. Co., 1961.

————. *Three Men Came to Heidelberg.* Grand Rapids: Christian Reformed Publishing House, 1963.

Verduin, Leonard. "Around the Pulpit as a Conversation Piece." *The Banner,* Sept. 3, 10, 17, 1976.

————. *The Reformers and Their Stepchildren.* Grand Rapids: Wm. B. Eerdmans Pub. Co., 1964.

Walker, Williston. *A History of the Christian Church.* New York: Charles Scribner's Sons, 1959.

Weber, Max. *The Protestant Ethic and the Spirit of Capitalism.* New York: Charles Scribner's Sons, 1958.

Westerhoff, John H. III. *A Colloquy on Christian Education.* Philadelphia: United Church Press, 1972.

Will, George F. "Moderns in Marin County." *The Washington Post,* July 31, 1977.

Wittgenstein, Ludwig. *On Certainty.* Edited by G. E. M. Anscombe and G. H. Van Wright. Translated by Denis Paul and G. E. M. Anscombe. Oxford: Blackwell, 1969.

Wolterstorff, Nicholas, and Mouw, Richard. "Are 'Bad Sermons' Possible? An Exchange on Preaching." *The Reformed Journal,* Nov. 1977.

Wolterstorff, Nicholas. "Letter to a Young Theologian." *The Reformed Journal,* Sept. 1976.

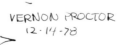

VERNON PROCTOR
12·14·78

POSTSCRIPT

Since the textbook *A Place to Stand* is part of a complete adult curriculum, each chapter has a companion *POSTSCRIPT* which serves as an aid to group study. Neal Plantinga is the author of the textbook; the Education Department staff added *POSTSCRIPT*. The Teacher's Manual for this course (available separately) explains how the *POSTSCRIPT* study guide can be used in each class session.

As you read the chapters of *A Place to Stand*, you are invited to use section *A* (under each *POSTSCRIPT*) for writing your personal comments and/or questions. The remainder of each *POSTSCRIPT* can be completed during the class session.

POSTSCRIPT
Introductory Session

Agenda

A. Introduction of class members

You may be surprised how little others know about you! Take a minute to tell something about yourself, your family, your work, or whatever else you'd like others in the class to know about you.

B. Our study of the textbook, *A Place to Stand*
1. Table of Contents
2. POSTSCRIPT
3. Adult Curriculum Plan
4. Class procedures
   a) Schedule
   b) Attendance
   c) Refreshments
   d) Visitors
   e) Variety of methods (lecture, group work, discussion, devotionals, etc.)

C. Goals of our study

Although none of us (including the teacher!) really know much about the new course we're about to begin, it's still a good idea to think about what we hope to learn. Following are goals for which this course was written. Please check those goal statements which seem *most* important to you.

After completing this course, I'd like to be able to

_____ 1. identify the key features of the creeds confessed by our church—be familiar with their basic structure and content.

_____ 2. explain how the creeds came into existence and were developed.

_____ 3. intelligently discuss some important theological issues the church faced and is facing.

_____ 4. show how the Scriptures are expressed in the creeds.

_____ 5. apply the creeds to my own daily life.

_____ 6. do *something* positive in church or community as a result of our study of the creeds, something such as . . . _____

_____

POSTSCRIPT 1
The Nature and Shape of the Ecumenical Creeds

A. Reflections on chapter 1

B. The case against the creeds

With others in your group, outline a response to *one* of the following arguments against the creeds. (If you can find texts to support the response, excellent; you're also invited to use *A Place to Stand* for reference, if you wish.)

1. Against using the creeds for identity

The identity of the church and its members must be based on the person and presence of Jesus Christ alone. Creeds and confessions are man-made devices which can tempt us to look away from Christ, away from God's Word, to hear only our own wisdom. "For no other foundation can any one lay than that which is laid, which is Jesus Christ" (I Cor. 3:11).

To confirm our beliefs
Give us a basis to follow (rules)

2. Against using the creeds for education/evangelism

New believers welcomed into the church, and new infants born into the church, must learn to make their *own* confessions. The *credo* (the "I believe") which is demanded, however, is not a set of words written by men but a testimony given by the Spirit. " Now we have received not the spirit of the world, but the Spirit which is from God, that we might understand the gifts bestowed on us by God. And we impart this in words not taught by human wisdom but taught by the Spirit, interpreting spiritual truths to those who possess the Spirit" (I Cor. 2:12,13). What Christians need to know and learn is not creeds but the Bible; the education program of the church should be Bible-centered, not creed-centered.

3. Against using the creeds to unify worship

The unity we experience in worship must come not from adherence to some human formulation of words, but from the profound unity secured through Christ's Spirit. What makes us one is not *our* words, but *the* Word, Jesus. We are one because we know nothing "except Jesus Christ and him crucified" (I Cor. 2:2). To use creeds in worship detracts from the unity we have in Christ.

Phillipeans 2:11
Mat. 28:20

4. Against using the creeds to defend the faith (polemics)

When faith is under attack and heresies threaten to divide Christ's body, how is the true faith to be defended? Certainly not by quoting the words men have written in creeds! No, the only way to defeat heresy is by that Word, the Scriptures, which comes from God. "For the wisdom of this world is folly with God. . . . So let no one boast of men" (I Cor. 3:19,21).

Can be helpful in defending your faith.

POSTSCRIPT 2
The Apostles' Creed

A. Reflections on chapter 2

① How the early church used the Apostle's creed.

② How the creed can be divided.

B. Survey of the articles of the Apostles' Creed, with guide questions.

1. *I believe in God the Father, Almighty, Maker of heaven and earth.*
   - Of what is God the Father? Why is God's omnipotence highlighted?

   The creator.

2. *And in Jesus Christ, His only begotten Son, our Lord;*
   - How can Jesus be the *only* begotten Son when Christians are also the children of God?

   Jesus was the first. Christians are the adopted children of God.

3. *Who was conceived by the Holy Spirit, born of the virgin Mary;*
   - Why is it so difficult for some people to believe the virgin birth?
   - Why is there such heavy emphasis on the events of Christ's life in articles 3-7?

   unnatural & illogical.
   The Nostics taught that Jesus really wasn't human.

4. *Suffered under Pontius Pilate; was crucified, dead, and buried; He descended into hell;*
   - Why is Pontius Pilate mentioned in the Creed?
   - Is it important to include the burial?
   - What does it mean that Jesus descended into hell?

   important time during history
   the burial proves he is dead.
   when he was on the cross without suffering it was like a living Hell.

5. *The third day He arose again from the dead;*
   - Is the resurrection the single most important item of our faith?

     yes
   - Is Jesus still human—does He still have a body?

     Has a glorified body.

---

6. *He ascended into heaven and sitteth at the right hand of God the Father Almighty;*
   - What is heaven? Where is it? What does it mean to sit at God's right hand?

     Heaven is where God and Christ are. — Heaven is everywhere. The right hand is a place of honor.

---

7. *From thence He shall come to judge the living and the dead.*
   - Why the distinction between "living" and "dead"?

     They were afraid if they died before Christ's coming they wouldn't be judged.
   - Should Christians fear the final judgment?

     NO.

---

8. *I believe in the Holy Spirit.*
   - What's the connection between Jesus and the Holy Spirit?

     The Holy Spirit is our connection with Christ.

---

9. *I believe a holy catholic Church, the communion of saints;*
   - What does it mean to call the church "holy"?

     Holy in Christ.
   - Can all Christians be called saints?

     A saint is, not an exceptionally good person.
   - What is the connection between the two phrases of this article?

     It is defining what the church is.

---

10. *The forgiveness of sins;*
    - Can you see a connection between articles 9 and 10?

      we can be called saints because of the forgiveness of sins.
    - If a person does not believe in the forgiveness of sins, what alternative is there with respect to what is done about sin?

      None

---

11. *The resurrection of the body;*
    - Upon what is this belief based?

      *Phillipians 3:21
      I corinthians 15:35-41*
    - What alternative is there for persons who do not believe in the resurrection of the body?

---

12. *And the life everlasting. Amen.*
    - What is the difference between eternal life and everlasting life?

      everlasting further defines eternal.

POSTSCRIPT 3
The Nicene Creed

A. Reflections on chapter 3

B. What are some key differences you have
observed between the Nicene Creed and the
Apostles' Creed?

C. The Letter of Arius to Eusebius, Bishop of Nicomedia, c.321

To his dearest lord, the man of God, the faithful and orthodox Eusebius, Arius, unjustly persecuted by Pope Alexander on account of that all-conquering truth which you also champion, sends greeting in the Lord.

Since my father Ammonius is going into Nicomedia, I thought it my duty to salute you by him, and at the same time to advise that naturally charitable disposition of yours, which you display toward the brethren for the sake of God and his Christ, how grievously the bishop attacks and persecutes us, and comes full tilt against us, so that he drives us from the city as atheists because we do not concur with him when he publicly preaches, "God always, the Son always; at the same time the Father, at the same time the Son; the Son co-exists with God, unbegotten; he is ever-begotten, he is not born-by-begetting; neither by thought nor by any moment of time does God precede the Son; God always, Son always, the Son exists from God himself."

Eusebius, your brother, Bishop of Caesarea, Theodotus, Paulinus, Athanasius, Gregory, Aetius, and all the other bishops of the East, have been condemned for saying that God existed, without beginning, before the Son; except Philogonius, Hellanicus and Macarius, men who are heretics and unlearned in the faith; some of whom say that the Son is an effluence, others a projection, others that he is co-unbegotten.

To these impieties we cannot even listen, even though the heretics threaten us with a thousand deaths. But what we say and think we both have taught and continue to teach; that the Son is not unbegotten, nor part of the unbegotten in any way, nor is he derived from any substance; but that by his own will and counsel he existed before times and ages fully God, only-begotten, unchangeable.

And before he was begotten or created or appointed or established, he did not exist; for he was not unbegotten. We are persecuted because we say that the Son has a beginning, but God is without beginning. For that reason we are persecuted, and because we say that he is from what is not. And this we say because he is neither part of God nor derived from any substance. For this we are persecuted; the rest you know.

POSTSCRIPT 4
The Athanasian Creed

A. Reflections on chapter 4   *Colossians 1: 15 - 20*

B. The Athanasian Creed defends the doctrine of the Trinity (3-28) and the doctrine of the incarnation (29-43) against various heresies and misinterpretations, some of which are described below. The first three statements relate to the Trinity; the remainder to the incarnation.

Please use the Athanasian Creed to develop a brief response to the statements. In your response, try to refer to specific verse(s) of the Creed. Chapter 4 of *A Place to Stand* may also be consulted.

1. The New Testament clearly talks about the Father as being God, about Christ as being God, and about the Holy Spirit as being God. In several places, it puts all three together, as in Matthew 28:19: "Baptizing them in the name of the Father and of the Son and of the Holy Spirit." Since the New Testament does not hesitate to say there are three Gods, neither should we.

2. The Bible insists there is only one God, but describes Him in three roles: First we read about God creating the world, then about God redeeming the world in Christ, and finally about God as Spirit. History is like a three-act play in which God first acts as Creator, next as Redeemer, and finally as Sanctifier.

3. In John 14:28 Jesus says, "The Father is greater than I." This shows the Son is inferior to the Father. And in John 16:13 Jesus says the Holy Spirit will not speak on His own authority. This shows the Spirit is less than both the Father and the Son. So there are three levels of deity; the highest is the Father, next is the Son, and the lowest is the Holy Spirit. They aren't all equal.

Verse 25

---

4. Jesus sometimes got tired and hungry, but God never gets tired and hungry. Jesus changed water into wine, but human beings can't do that, only God can. So it's clear that Jesus is both God and man—sometimes He acted as God, and sometimes He acted as a human being.

Verse 30
34
37

---

5. God changed into a human being when Jesus was born. John 1:1 says that the Word became flesh.

Verse 35

---

6. Since God is omniscient, Jesus, being God, must have known everything when He walked the earth.

Verses 35 & 36

---

7. Jesus is made up of both God and man. But it's obvious that when two different qualities are mixed, a hybrid results. So Jesus is a hybrid, a third kind of being, halfway between God and man.

Verse 37

---

8. To be human is to be sinful. The more human we are, the more sinful we become. Jesus was not sinful; therefore, it's obvious that He couldn't have been as truly human as we are.

Verse 32

TEST ON PART I
The Ecumenical Creeds

Which Creed(s) . . .

_____ 1. is the longest?

_____ 2. is the shortest?

_____ 3. is of uncertain authorship (in its present form)?

_____ 4. was intended to educate beginners in the faith?

_____ 5. has twelve articles?

_____ 6. includes a full discussion of the Trinity and the incarnation?

_____ 7. refutes the heresies of tritheism and modalism?

_____ 8. was *not* written primarily to refute heresy?

_____ 9. warns that its statements must be believed for salvation?

_____ 10. mentions Pontius Pilate?

_____ 11. has the most material on the Holy Spirit?

_____ 12. has a *filioque* phrase which caused the church to split into Western (Latin) and Eastern (Greek) branches?

_____ 13. was used to identify early Christians?

_____ 14. speaks of Jesus as "begotten, not made, being of one substance with the Father"?

_____ 15. has been called "the Creed of creeds"?

_____ 16. refutes the beliefs of Arius?

_____ 17. contains the phrase "descended into hell"?

_____ 18. grew out of the trinitarian baptismal formula?

_____ 19. has a trinitarian structure?

_____ 20. was not completed by the council after which it was named?

Answers

1. Athanasian	11. Nicene
2. Apostles'	12. Nicene
3. All three creeds	13. Apostles'
4. Apostles'	14. Nicene
5. Apostles'	15. Apostles'
6. Athanasian	16. Nicene
7. Athanasian	17. Apostles'
8. Apostles'	18. Apostles'
9. Athanasian	19. Apostles' and Nicene
10. Apostles' and Nicene	20. Nicene

POSTSCRIPT 5
Introduction to the Heidelberg Catechism

A. Reflections on chapter 5

General characteristics
1. Biblical
2. Ecumenical
3. Christ Centered
4. Devotional
5. autobiographical
6. addressed to the whole person.

B. Discussion notes

POSTSCRIPT 6
Misery

A. Reflections on chapter 6

B. Reviewing the Misery section of the Catechism

1. *Knowledge* of our misery (Q & A 3, 4, 5)

   a) Rephrase Question 3 without using the word *misery*.

   b) How does the English word *misery* differ ~~exile~~ from the German word *Elend*? Is it possible for a person to be miserable without feeling miserable?

   c) What is remarkable about the form of the law quoted by the Catechism? In what respect does this form of the law make us especially conscious of our misery?

   It quoted Christ rather than the 10 commandments.

   It exposes our sin more clearly than the 10 Commandments

   d) How does Q & A 5 relate to our knowledge of misery?

2. *Source* of our misery (Q & A 6, 7, 8)

   a) Identify the different relationships of man to God described in Q & A 6, 7, 8.

created in his own image

---

   b) Is human nature good or <u>evil</u>? What happened to human nature when Adam and Eve sinned?

human nature was poisoned.

---

   c) What happens to us when we are born again?

sins are forgiven

---

3. *Consequences* of our misery

   a) How do you react to this statement about the nature of sin: Sin is a type of sickness.

---

   b) What word does the Catechism use for sin in Q & A 7 and 9? What other terms might also adequately describe the nature of sin?

disobedience
corruption
rebellion

---

   c) How can God be angry about the sins we are born with? Is this fair?

---

   d) What does it mean that God punishes our sins in eternity? If God is merciful, how can He punish sin eternally?

He is totally just.

POSTSCRIPT 7
Deliverance

A. Reflections on chapter 7

B. Choose the Catechism question and answer
which you think captures the essence of each of
the following headings from chapter 7 in *A
Place to Stand*. Jot down a reason or two for
each of your choices.

1. Faith in Our Deliverer (Q & A 12-28)

   Representative question and answer:

   Reason for choice:

2. The Events of Christ (Q & A 29-52)

Representative question and answer:

Reason for choice:

3. The Benefits of Christ (Q & A 53-64)

Representative question and answer:

Reason for choice:

4. Sacraments and Discipline (Q & A 65-85)

Representative question and answer:

Reason for choice:

POSTSCRIPT 8
Gratitude

A. Reflections on chapter 8

B. Structure of the third section of the Catechism
   1. How does the Catechism think of the life of
      gratitude? (Of what does that life consist?)

   Law and prayer.
   good works and the law go hand in hand.
   Devout words

   2. What happens when one of these aspects of
      gratitude is emphasized at the expense of
      the other?

   gratitude will suffer.

C. The Law

1. What are the three uses of the law? Which use does the Catechism stress? Can you illustrate (which use is stressed) by referring to Q & A 86 and 91?

   1) civil Protection
   2) Theological or religious.
   3) guide for redeemed life.

2. Which use of the law is stressed in your worship services? Would the commandments be better read after the confession of sin (as guidelines for a departing congregation) than before the confession of sin (as a call to repentance)?

D. Prayer

1. Take a few minutes to page back through Q & A 122-129. What are your impressions of the Catechism's treatment of the Lord's Prayer?

   Deepens the meaning of the prayer. Practical.

2. What does the "Amen" (Q & A 129) say to you personally about your prayers?

TEST ON PART II
Survey of the Heidelberg Catechism

A. Identify...

1. the two authors of the Heidelberg Catechism.

2. the prince who wanted them to write a Catechism.

3. within five years, the year the Catechism was written.

4. the language it was first printed in.

5. the two basic reasons why it was written.

6. the first country outside of Germany to use the Catechism.

7. the three main parts of the Catechism.

8. the longest and shortest of those parts.

9. the part in which the sacraments are found.

10. the part in which the Ten Commandments are found.

11. the third use of the law.

12. what the Catechism means by "misery."

13. the two characteristics of the Catechism's treatment of the Lord's Prayer.

14. the part of the Catechism which illustrates that good deeds must be accompanied by good words.

Answers

1. Ursinus and Olevianus
2. Prince Frederick
3. 1563
4. German
5. To unify the people and instruct them in the truths of the Scripture
6. Netherlands
7. Misery, Deliverance, Gratitude or Sin, Salvation, Service
8. Longest: Deliverance; shortest: Misery
9. Deliverance
10. Gratitude
11. As a guide to redeemed living or living a life of gratitude
12. The condition (not necessarily the feeling) of being alienated from God by our sins
13. Devotional, prayer-like; demanding action of us; practical; all requests, rather than praise or thanks; humble; confident
14. Gratitude

184

B. Match the Catechism question on the left
   with its answer on the right:

Questions

_____ WHAT IS YOUR ONLY COMFORT
IN LIFE AND IN DEATH?

_____ BUT ARE WE SO CORRUPT
THAT WE ARE TOTALLY UNABLE TO DO ANY GOOD
AND INCLINED TOWARD ALL EVIL?

_____ WHAT IS TRUE FAITH?

_____ BUT WHY ARE YOU CALLED A CHRISTIAN?

_____ WHAT GOOD DOES IT DO YOU, HOWEVER,
TO BELIEVE ALL THIS?

_____ YOU CONFESS THAT BY FAITH ALONE
YOU SHARE IN CHRIST AND ALL HIS BLESSINGS:
WHERE DOES THAT FAITH COME FROM?

_____ WHAT DO WE DO THAT IS GOOD?

_____ WHAT IS GOD'S WILL FOR US
IN THE SIXTH COMMANDMENT?

_____ HOW DOES GOD WANT US TO PRAY
SO THAT HE WILL LISTEN TO US?

_____ WHAT DOES THAT LITTLE WORD "AMEN" EXPRESS?

Answers

1. I am not to belittle, insult, hate, or kill my neighbor—
   not by my thoughts, my words, my look or gesture,
   and certainly not by actual deeds—
   and I am not to be party to this in others;
   rather, I am to put away all desire for revenge.

   I am not to harm or recklessly endanger myself either.

   Prevention of murder is also why
   government is armed with the sword.

2. Because by faith I am a member of Christ
   and so I share in his anointing.
   I am anointed
   to confess his name,
   to present myself to him as a living sacrifice of thanks,
   to strive with a good conscience against sin and the devil
   in this life,
   and afterward to reign with Christ
   over all creation
   for all eternity.

3. This is sure to be!

   It is even more sure
   that God listens to my prayer,
   than that I really desire
   what I pray for.

4. Only that which
   arises out of true faith.

5. First, we must pray from the heart
   to no other than the one true God,
   who has revealed himself in his Word,
   asking for everything he has commanded us to ask for.

   Second, we must acknowledge our need and misery,
   hiding nothing,
   and humble ourselves in his majestic presence.

   Third, we must rest on this unshakable foundation:
   even though we do not deserve it,
   God will surely listen to our prayer
   because of Christ our Lord.
   That is what he promised us in his Word.

6. That I am not my own,
   but belong—
   body and soul,
   in life and in death—
   to my faithful Savior Jesus Christ.

7. In Christ I am right with God
   and heir to life everlasting.

8. Yes, unless we are born again,
   by the Spirit of God.

9. The Holy Spirit produces it in our hearts
   by the preaching of the holy gospel,
   and confirms it
   through our use of the holy sacraments.

10. not only a knowledge and conviction
    that everything God reveals in his Word is true;
    it is also a deep-rooted assurance,
    created in me by the Holy Spirit through the gospel
    that, out of sheer grace earned for us by Christ,
    not only others, but I too,
    have had my sins forgiven,
    have been made forever right with God,
    and have been granted salvation.

Answers

Matching: 6, 8, 10, 2, 7, 9, 4, 1, 5, 3

POSTSCRIPT 9
Introduction to the Belgic Confession

A. Reflections on chapter 9

B. Notes on the life and times of de Bres

C. Comparing the Confession to the Catechism

    1. Purpose:

_____

    2. Style (the way the documents are organized and written):

_____

    3. Content:

POSTSCRIPT 10
There Is One Only God

A. Reflections on chapter 10

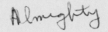
Almighty

B. Bible study

For each attribute listed, please answer these questions:
1. What does the first passage say about God?
2. According to the second passage, how does Christ show the attribute?
3. What does the third passage say about Christians reflecting the attribute?

SAMPLE   Attribute: spiritual
   a)   John 4:24 teaches that God is spirit.
   b)   John 1:32 teaches that Jesus was baptized with the Spirit.
   c)   I Corinthians 3:16 teaches that God's Spirit dwells in Christians (the church) as in a temple.

ATTRIBUTE	GOD	CHRIST	CHRISTIANS
spiritual	John 4:24	John 1:32	I Corinthians 3:16
eternal	Psalm 90:2	John 1:1-3	John 3:16

incomprehensible	Job 11:7 (or Romans 11:33 or Isaiah 40:28)	Ephesians 1:9,10	Ephesians 3:8,9 (or I Corinthians 13:12)
invisible	I Timothy 6:16	John 1:18 (or Colossians 1:15)	I John 3:2

1) has immortality and dwells in unapproachable light. Whom no man has ever seen or can see.
2) No one has ever seen God
3) When he appears we will be like him. We shall see him as he is.

immutable	Ezekiel 24:14	Hebrews 7:28	Hebrews 10:14

1) unchangeable
2) being made perfect forever
3) we will be made perfect because christ died for our sins

infinite	I Kings 8:27	Colossians 2:9	Colossians 2:10

1) not contained

almighty	Psalm 115:3 (or Jeremiah 32:27)	Matthew 28:18	Acts 1:8

1) Power to do anything
2) Given power from God
3) Filled with the power

perfectly wise	Romans 16:27	I Corinthians 1:30	I Corinthians 4:10

1)

just	Psalm 145:17	Revelation 19:11	Amos 5:24

good	Psalm 100:5	John 10:11 (or Mark 10:18)	Hebrews 13:20,21

fountain of all good	James 1:17	Luke 4:18	Romans 15:2

POSTSCRIPT 11
How God Is Known

A. Reflections on chapter 11

B. Book I

Our Confession (Art. II) calls the universe "a most elegant book...leading us to see clearly the invisible things of God." The following passages show why we can make that confession. Read them and state the main point of each:

1. Psalm 33:6

2. Psalm 119:89

3. Psalm 19:1-4

4. Romans 1:20

C. Book II

Article II goes on to speak about God's second book, "His holy and divine Word," by which God "makes Himself more clearly and fully known to us." Scan the last half of "Knowledge of God by Means of the Universe," chapter 11 of *A Place to Stand*, and state two reasons why this second book has become necessary:

1.

2.

Read and react to the following quote from John Calvin:

Just as old or bleary-eyed men and those with weak vision, if you thrust before them a most beautiful volume, even if they recognize it to be some sort of writing, yet can scarcely construe two words, but with the aid of spectacles will begin to read distinctly; so Scripture, gathering up the otherwise confused knowledge of God in our minds, having dispersed our dullness, clearly shows us the true God.

(*Institutes* I, vi, 1)

D. Discussion notes

POSTSCRIPT 12
The Bible

A. Reflections on chapter 12

B. The Heidelberg Catechism says nothing specific about the Scriptures; the Belgic Confession has five articles on that subject. Most of us could probably write or say quite a few things about the Bible...but suppose we limited ourselves to a single, brief sentence stating what we believe to be the most important things about the Scriptures. What would you write?

We believe that the Bible....

C. As we study what the Belgic Confession says about the Bible, look for a parallel to your own statement. Also be prepared to raise any questions you might have on the articles and to summarize each article in your own words.

Article III

Questions:

Summary:

Article IV

Questions:

Summary:

Article V

Questions:

Summary:

Article VI

Questions:

Summary:

Article VII

Questions:

Summary:

POSTSCRIPT 13
The Trinity

A. Reflections on chapter 13

B. Study of John 17, Jesus' prayer for the church

1. Jesus begins His prayer with the words, "Father, the hour has come; glorify thy Son...." What, specifically, has Jesus been doing and saying to prepare His disciples for His final hour? (Skim chapters 13-16.) How does chapter 17 fit in with the pre-crucifixion events?

2. Write descriptive headings for each section of Christ's prayer as recorded in John 17.

   a) Verses 1-5:

   b) Verses 6-19:

   c) Verses 20-26:

3. Find evidence for the idea of *unity* or *oneness* in each section of the prayer.

4. What is the purpose of this unity between God and believers?

_____

5. What are the results of union for believers? What must happen if this unity is to be achieved?

_____

6. Does it seem strange to you that Christ does not directly mention the role of the Spirit in bringing this oneness about? Why or why not?

_____

7. What, if anything, has this study of John 17 added to what the Belgic Confession has to say about the Trinity in Articles VIII-XI?

_____

8. At what times in your life do you feel most strongly the oneness in Christ you have with other believers?

POSTSCRIPT 14
Creation and Providence

A. Reflections on chapter 14

B. Article XII

1. The service idea is prominent in Article XII.
   From that perspective, what is the purpose
   of creation? Of providence?

   To serve your creator

2. "There are two equal and opposite errors into which our race can fall about the devils.
   One is to disbelieve in their existence. The
   other is to believe, and to feel an excessive
   and unhealthy interest in them. They themselves are equally pleased by both errors,
   and hail a materialist and magician with the
   same delight."

   (from Lewis' *The Screwtape Letters*)

   Which error is more common today? Why?

3. Is belief in angels and demons as important as the Confession, by the space devoted to it, suggests?

_____

4. Read these three important New Testament "creation passages": John 1:1-3; Hebrews 1:1,2; Colossians 1:15,16. What is the common element in these passages?

   creation by God

_____

C. Article XIII

1. A little boy dashes into a street and is struck dead by a car. Grieving Christian relatives say, "The Lord took him." Comment.

_____

2. A young wife is dying of leukemia. What would you not want to say to her and to her husband in an attempt to comfort them? What, in the context of the Confession's view of providence, might you say that would be of genuine Christian comfort?

_____

3. What can we learn from the Confession's steadfast refusal to address certain difficult questions about the cause of evil in our world?

_____

D. Discussion notes

a brief
atements.
f disagree-
rticles XIV
and

1. "A few days   proud father
(first time!) of the   iful child God
ever made! Holding litt   ily in my arms
now, I marvel at this miracle of life and
goodness. Somehow, I can't accept the notion (taught by my church) that Emily is
already sinful. What has she *done* that could
be called sinful? If she should die tonight,
would God send her to hell for her sins? I
really think, down deep, that the only way
Emily will become sinful is by imitating us
(her parents) and others. If we can just *love*
Emily enough and be good models of Christian behavior, I know she'll be able to hang
on to most of the goodness and purity I see
in her right now. I think that kind of love
and that kind of parenting will raise a
generation that will start turning our sinful
old world upside down and make it what
God intended it to be—a good place to live."

2. "Take a realistic look at our sick world and
you'll see crime, war, famine, terrorism,
child abuse...and a hundred other evils.
Frankly, I don't want to bring a child into a
place like this, a world that could blow itself
to nuclear hell in a matter of minutes. A
good many people who insist on bringing
children into this hopeless world are selfish
beyond words; they think only of themselves, not of their children and their
children's children. I'm not saying everyone
should think the way I do, but I know
what's best for me. I'll get along and maybe
find some happiness in my own way. But
real joy will come only when this world ends
and my new life in heaven begins."

3. "When I see the permissive way some parents raise their kids, I want to scream at them to wake up and recognize that kids, like everyone else, will be bad if given the chance. It isn't hard to see, right from the start, that kids are born sinners. Don't think for a minute little ones are perfect! They know just how to get their way! Seems to me what parents have to do is to control the naturally sinful nature of their young. Strict discipline will work wonders. And the kids can never get too much religious training from the church and school. With that kind of upbringing, the young would come to repentance in Christ. Poverty and crime would diminish. The whole problem is we're afraid to discipline our kids, and so we live in a world of spoiled rotten brats."

4. "Most Christians go around with a frown instead of a smile...and that's all wrong. Sure, we are all born sinners and we sin until the moment we die. The Bible teaches that and our church preaches that (too much, I think). But when we are born again, everything changes for the better! After all, we're on our way to heaven! If a Christian can't smile his way through life, he's not worthy of being called a Christian. If we raise our children to think in terms of what we Christians are *in Christ,* to know His joy and love, the world becomes paradise. Our Christian smiles—through thick and thin—can make it all happen."

C. Try writing what you consider to be a Christian view of our humanity, including especially the role of parents, as did the statements in section *B*.

POSTSCRIPT 16
Election

A. Reflections on chapter 16

B. For today's session, we suggest an "open-book survey" of chapter 16, skimming through each section of this chapter and discussing whatever concerns you the most. We've included a few questions (below) on each section that you may also want to discuss.

1. Introduction

a) Do you think distinguishing between "task-election" and "salvation-election" is helpful? Can you find evidence for "task-election" in Ephesians 1:4-10?

b) This section makes the point that it is usually "salvation-election" that causes us discomfort, that raises problems. Do you agree? If so, what kinds of questions/concerns/problems does the idea of salvation-election cause us?

2. Election as Mercy for Sinners

c) Please skim this section. Are there any thoughts here (or perhaps biblical references) which best capture for you the *mercy* aspect of election, the comfort it can bring?

3. Election in Christ

   d) React to this statement from the text: "Practically speaking, it (being elect in Christ) means at least that our election...comes when we are joined to Christ's body, the church."

---

4. Justice and Our Difficulty with Election

   e) Do we sometimes feel as if we are not elect? If so, why? How can we be comforted?

---

   f) On the other hand, are we sometimes too smug about our own election? If so, why? How can we be made less complacent?

---

   g) Read Luke 13:22-30. What does this passage tell us about our election questions? Why is Jesus so reluctant to answer the question, "Will those who are saved be few?" What is the significance of His injunction, turned back upon the questioner, to "strive to enter by the narrow door"?

C. Discussion notes

POSTSCRIPT 17
Incarnation

A. Reflections on chapter 17

B. Do you think Jesus might have...
   — yawned during a long service in the synagogue?
   — laughed heartily at one of Peter's jokes?
   — been tempted by lust or pride or laziness?
   — complained about the heat before beginning one of His sermons?
   — mistaken James for John until He got a closer look?

Reflect on the two main errors in Christological thought. Think especially about which error Christians *tend* to lean toward.

C. Which phrases from the Belgic Confession (Articles XVIII and XIX) best indicate to you the heart of our belief about the natures of Jesus Christ?

D. Study of Philippians 2:5-11

   1. What phrases (vss. 6,7) indicate that Christ existed first as God, then as God-man? Can you think of any other biblical passage to support this?

2. Note that the phrase "emptied himself" connects "form of God" and "form of a servant [man]." Of what did Christ "empty himself"?

3. What's the meaning of "did not count equality with God a thing to be grasped"? (vs. 6)

4. What are the two stages in Christ's humiliation? (vss. 7,8)

5. What events in history mark the beginning of Christ's exaltation? How can we avoid explaining Christ's exaltation (vss. 9 and 10) as a regaining of His divine nature which was set aside during His stay on earth?

6. Paul clearly means the passage for our instruction (vs. 5). We are to "have this mind among yourselves . . . ." What practical applications can we draw from the verses which follow?

POSTSCRIPT 18
Atonement

A. Reflections on chapter 18

B. The *Christus Victor* Theory

Heart of the theory: A universal battle between God and the devil, won by Christ at the resurrection.

Man had been created by God that he might have life. If now, having lost life, and having been harmed by the serpent, he were not to return to life, but were to be wholly abandoned to death, then God would have been defeated, and the malice of the serpent would have overcome God's will. But since God is both invincible and magnanimous, He showed His magnanimity in correcting man, and in proving all men, as we have said; but through the Second Man He bound the strong one, and spoiled his goods, and annihilated death, bringing life to man who had become subject to death. For Adam had become the devil's possession, and the devil held him under his power, by having wrongfully practised deceit upon him, and by the offer of immortality made him subject to death. For by promising that they should be as gods, which did not lie in his power, he worked death in them. Wherefore he who had taken man captive was himself taken captive by God, and man who had been taken captive was set free from the bondage of condemnation.

(Irenaeus,
A.D. 130-200)

1) Captivity to Evil Powers

2) Sends Christ as liberator. Conqueror of Evil.

3) Conquers Evil through resurrection.

4) In christ we share victory over Evil.

204

C. The Example Theory

Heart of the theory: A demonstration of the way to full human life by Christ's sinless life.

God had forgiven sins before Christ came. Forgiveness is an act of grace and must be free and without demand for compensation for sin. God is love and has voluntarily assumed the burden of suffering brought on by man's sin. This act of God's grace, taken freely and without the necessity of making satisfaction for sin, awakens in men gratitude and love for God. In Jesus Christ, who is both man and God, men see what men should be, are brought to recognize their sin, and by God's love seen in Christ are won to a response which releases new springs of love which issue in right conduct. In this fashion, the sinner becomes a new creation, a different self.

(Views of Abelard,
A.D. 1079-1142)

1) Moral Weakness.
2) Sends christ as a model.
3) Lives perfect life..
4) Turn from sin and imitates christ.

D. The Satisfaction Theory

Heart of the theory: An expiation of human guilt by Christ's death as a substitute for sinners.

What greater mercy can be conceived than that God the Father should say to the sinner—condemned to eternal torment, and unable to redeem himself—'Receive my only Son, and offer Him for thyself,' while the Son Himself said—'Take me, and redeem thyself'?
And what greater justice than that One who receives a payment far exceeding the amount due, should, if it be paid with a right intention, remit all that is due?
(Anselm, *Cur Deus Homo?*
A.D. 1033-1109)

We believe that God, who is perfectly merciful and just, sent His Son to assume that nature in which the disobedience was omitted, to make satisfaction in the same, and to bear the punishment of sin by His most bitter passion and death.
(de Bres, Belgic Confession
A.D. 1561)

1) Disobedience
2) Sent his Son to make satisfaction for punishment the only sacrifice.
3) Poured out His precious blood to purge away our sins.
4) Remission of sins.

POSTSCRIPT 19
Justification and Faith

A. Reflections on chapter 19

Faith
Grace
Bible
Christ

B. Article XXII

1. Against *what* is most of paragraph one aimed?

   that we need anything but Christ

2. Stated positively, what is the main point of the first paragraph? (What does de Bres seem to stress?)

   Christ is sufficient for our salvation —

3. *Sola fide* (faith alone) was one battle cry of the Reformation (see Rom. 3:28). Yet in paragraph two, Article XXII finds it necessary to "speak more clearly" than this. Why? What do you see as a key word the article uses to describe faith?

   instrument.

4. Read again those parts of Article XXII which talk of our union with Christ as a result or end of our faith. Do you agree with chapter 19's assertion that "union with Christ is...that vast communion with Christ in which all that we are and do is part of His new Creation?"

C. Article XXIII

1. Sentence one of Article XXIII contains a capsule definition of salvation or justification. But it's not in the language we would use to explain the term to, say, a new Christian or our inquiring twelve year old. How *would* you explain justification in a way that appeals more to basic human needs? How would you explain the connection between faith and justification?

acceptance (forgive and accept.)

Faith is the way in which we accept this.

2. How is true "self-acceptance" possible? (See paragraph two of Article XXIII.)

3. Underline the benefits, listed in Article XXIII, of Christ's obedience (which we appropriate through faith). Reflect with others in the class on the extent to which we actually experience these blessings. Is the warning (with which Article XXIII closes) appropriate for us?

POSTSCRIPT 20
Sanctification

A. Reflections on chapter 20

B. How is a smoker's battle like salvation?
Think of as many comparisons as you can,
listing them under the headings below. Then
evaluate the analogy: Is it helpful? At what
points does it break down?

Old Life (smoker before quitting; person
before justification)

New Life (smoker after quitting; Christian
during sanctification)

C. Below are statements related to the process of sanctification. Please react by circling one of the five responses which follow each statement. Consider Articles XXIV and XXV, as well as chapter 20, when making your response. Also be ready to explain your choice.

1. It's impossible to have faith and *not* do good works. If there are no fruits of faith in my life, it's clear that I haven't been justified. I'm fooling myself into thinking I'm a Christian.

   (strongly agree)
   agree
   not sure
   disagree
   strongly disagree

2. God's acceptance of us is at least *somewhat* conditional on our doing good works. Lack of good works indicates a lack of faith. And if we have no faith, we cannot be justified (accepted) by God, in spite of what Christ has done for us. God won't accept us without at least an attempt on our part to bear fruit.

   strongly agree
   agree
   not sure
   (disagree)
   strongly disagree

   Phil. 3:9
   Gal. 2:16

3. Sanctification (being made holy) means that, as a Christian, I should be getting rid of those personality flaws (temper, pessimism, shyness, irritability, nervousness, etc.) which belong to my old, unrenewed life.

   strongly agree
   agree
   not sure
   disagree
   strongly disagree

4. My non-churched neighbor donates $100 toward the building of a new medical clinic for treatment of the poor. I do the same. God recognizes my gift and rewards it, but not my neighbor's.

   strongly agree
   agree
   (not sure)
   disagree
   strongly disagree

5. Sanctification is only a personal, private matter between each individual and God. The church should bring persons to justification, and then aid in their sanctification. The church should never meddle in such areas as politics or labor or abortion or racial discrimination. Those things will be taken care of when individuals correct their personal vices and faults.

   strongly agree
   agree
   not sure
   (disagree)
   strongly disagree

POSTSCRIPT 21
Intercession

A. Reflections on chapter 21

B. Our approach to God—a Litany

Leader: The Lord reigns; let the peoples tremble...The Lord is great in Zion; he is exalted over all the peoples. Let them praise thy great and terrible name! Holy is he! (Ps. 99:1-3)

Group: Jesus said... "I am the way, and the truth, and the life; no one comes to the Father, but by me." (John 14:6)

Leader: Extol the Lord our God; worship at his footstool! Holy is he! (Ps. 99:5)

Group: And the Word became flesh and dwelt among us, full of grace and truth... And from his fullness have we all received, grace upon grace....(John 1:14,16)

Leader: Extol the Lord our God, and worship at his holy mountain; for the Lord our God is holy! (Ps. 99:9)

Group: He was despised and rejected by men; a man of sorrows, and acquainted with grief...yet he bore the sin of many, and made intercession for the transgressors. (Isa. 53:3,12)

Leader: Be still, and know that I am God. I am exalted among the nations, I am exalted in the earth! (Ps. 46:10)

Group: And being found in human form he humbled himself and became obedient unto death, even death on a cross. (Phil. 2:8)

Leader: ...men cannot look on the light when it is bright in the skies, when the wind has passed and cleared them. Out of the north comes golden splendor; God is clothed with terrible majesty. The Almighty—we cannot find him. (Job 37:21-23)

Group: No one has ever seen God; the only Son, who is in the bosom of the Father, he has made him known. (John 1:18)

Leader: ...he is great in power and justice, and abundant righteousness he will not violate. Therefore men fear him. (Job 37:23,24)

Group: Christ is able for all time to save those who draw near to God through him, since he always lives to make intercession for them. (Heb. 7:25)

Leader: ...stop and consider the wondrous works of God...Do you know the balancings of the clouds, the wonderous works of him who is perfect in knowledge? ...Can you, like him, spread out of the skies, hard as a molten mirror? Teach us what we shall say to him.... (Job 37:14-19)

Group: Since then we have a great high priest who has passed through the heavens, Jesus, the Son of God...who in every respect has been tempted as we are, yet without sinning. Let us with confidence draw near to the throne of grace, that we may receive mercy and find grace to help in time of need. (Heb. 4:4-16)

Leader: And I heard every creature in heaven and on earth and under the earth and in the sea, and all therein, saying.... (Rev. 5:13)

Group: "To him who sits upon the throne and to the Lamb be blessing and honor and glory and might for ever and ever!" (Rev. 5:13)

Leader: And the four living creatures said, "Amen!" And the elders fell down and worshiped. (Rev. 5:14)

POSTSCRIPT 22
Church

A. Reflections on chapter 22

B. Imagine that an artist was commissioned to paint a picture that would somehow communicate the nature of the church. Being an accommodating type with plenty of time, our artist painted six pictures, which are now presented for your choice. The picture you select will be captioned *The Church* and will be displayed for public observation.

1. Against the background of a dark and sinister planet earth, a cluster of human beings of all ages and races and times, clothed in white and arms linked, are kneeling before the cross of Christ.

2. Under the shadow of a cross, a large group of people of all ages and races and times are working together, apparently helping each other in various ways—some are raising crops, some are serving food, some are healing, some are comforting, some are teaching, etc.

3. A runner is straining toward the finish line, face contorted with effort, every muscle straining forward, every part of mind and body working together to achieve victory.

4. A large Bible lies open on a high pulpit. A preacher is about to read the Bible to an attentive congregation.

5. A group of adults, with children sitting among them and watching, are being served the bread and the wine of the Lord's Supper. The adults' faces show the intensity of the moment, as they commune with their Lord and each other.

6. A church, shining white in the sun, is surrounded by shadowy figures in semi-darkness; the figures depict the attraction of various sins. Near the door of the church several of its members are struggling to rescue a fellow member from the grip of one of the shadowy figures.

-Which picture, if any, would you select to best represent *The Church*? Can you find support for your choice in Articles XXVII-XXIX of the Belgic Confession? In the Bible?

-Are there any pictures which you think are not biblically and confessionally accurate? Explain.

-Would you want to add any pictures that would more effectively and completely communicate the nature of the church in our world?

C. What "picture" of your congregation do you think your unchurched neighbors have? Suppose such persons tell you they want to be Christians in their own way, without joining the organized church. What would you say to convince them of the importance of becoming an active part of the body of Christ?

POSTSCRIPT 23
Church Order

A. Reflections on chapter 23

B. Article XXX

1. Chapter 23 notes that it is a Reformed conviction that all office is service. "All officers serve in their ruling and rule in their serving."

   What do John 13:12-15 and Ephesians 4:11 and 12 say about the servant aspect of officebearing? What do I Timothy 5:17 and I Peter 5:1-3 say about the ruling aspect of officebearing? Which aspect, if any, should dominate?

   Examine the duties of pastor and council, as listed in Article XXX, for evidence that these officers "serve in their ruling and rule in their serving."

2. "When I was a little kid sitting in church, I would see those elders march in, so sober and stern-looking. When I went to catechism class, I met another of those sober types, this time quizzing me relentlessly on sin, salvation, and service. And there was house visitation where the pastor and an elder pressed me on my commitment to Christ and actually had me convinced they knew all about my secret sins! I never really got over those impressions of elders."

   Do our children see pastors, elders, and deacons in this way? If so, how can we teach them that officebearers are servants of Christ and of all believers? Or is the problem today a lack of respect for the officebearer? If so, how can we teach our children to honor those through whom God governs His church?

3. The last sentence of Article XXX speaks of "faithful men" to be chosen for church office. Does this mean "faithful women" may

not be chosen? How does chapter 23 of *A Place to Stand* explain de Bres' terminology?

___

C. Article XXXI

1. Do the procedures for electing elders and deacons in your congregation give the prospective officebearer adequate time and assistance in determining whether he/she is actually being called by God? Are people ever mistaken about having a call to office? How can you tell (they are mistaken)?

___

2. What does this article say to the gifted but unordained person who works up his own ministry in some storefront church, even calling himself "Reverend"? Does this article have anything to say to the itinerant evangelist who holds a tent revival? And what about para-church ministries such as Campus Crusade, Young Life, World Vision, Salvation Army, etc?

___

3. George and Edna find it difficult to listen to some of their pastor's sermons—and with good reason, for their pastor too often uses the Bible as a basis for moral examples and spiritual pep talks. George and Edna admit there's nothing really heretical about these sermons, but point out that they limit the message of the Scriptures and are superficial and inept.

    Considering the last paragraph of Article XXXI, as well as the Reformed view of preaching, what should George and Edna do? May they select from the pastor's sermons only those which, in their judgment, are indeed the Word of God? Or are they bound to regard all of what the pastor says as "God's Word" to them?

___

D. Article XXXII

Suppose you're serving on the council of your congregation. A group of younger church members requests the council to recommend dropping the evening sermon for a series of religious films. According to Article XXXII, what standards should you apply when making such a judgment? If time permits, try applying and reaching a tentative decision.

POSTSCRIPT 24
Sacraments

A. Reflections on chapter 24

B. Here is how one man—John H. Westerhoff III, a nationally prominent figure in the field of religious education—once celebrated the sacraments of the Lord's Supper and baptism. In our session today, we'll be evaluating his experience in the light of Articles XXXIII-XXXV of the Belgic Confession.

Celebrations*

One night not long ago, I was in the living room of a suburban home near a small West Coast college campus. A young priest in sports clothes had invited me to join him and his congregation for a celebration. These adults, teenagers, and children met regularly to celebrate their common faith and life. A long dining room table was set with loaves of bread and bottles of wine, fruit, and cheese.

The whole house had a festive atmosphere, with colorful paper flowers and birds hanging from the ceiling. I was greeted with a bag decorated on the outside with dayglow letters reading, "We care." Inside was a large red and yellow sheet of tissue paper with a hole in the middle and a variety of other things. We each picked a partner to dress in the paper costume. We read them part of an anonymous poem we had found somewhere: "I love you. You're more valuable than anything in the earth and I like you better than anything in the world."

We fed each other Hershey Kisses. We stuffed a balloon with confetti, blew it up, tossed it in the air, punctured it with a pin. As the confetti fell over us, we blew party horns. The daily news programs blaring from the two television sets in the room were turned down as someone began to strum a guitar. Everyone joined in the folk song "Turn, Turn, Turn" as we made our way to the table.

There, we each greeted our neighbors with the ancient kiss of peace. Everyone had a part in the reading of Scripture and in original, brief, simple prayers. We prayed the Lord's Prayer, but following "thy will be done on earth as it is in heaven," reports from the day's newspaper were read. We each made our confession of apathy in the face of need; this was followed by a hug of forgiving affection from a neighbor. An offering of money and fair housing pledge cards was made that evening. Each person made personal affirmations of what he believed. Some were moving. "I believe in God, which is to trust that someone, somewhere, is not stupid." Together we affirmed our understanding of the Christian faith: Where there is life there is death, but where there is death there is hope. We acknowledged that with such a perception of life we could affirm the negative aspects of our times as the birth pangs of a new age.

Our priest broke the bread and blessed it. He poured the wine and blessed it, each person serving his neighbor. We joined hands and sang joyfully, concluding with Jesus' words to Simon Peter, "Simon, son of John, do you love me more than these?" And we answered with Peter's words, "Yes, Lord, you know that I love you." And our host responded as did Jesus, "Feed my lambs."

As we sat at the table to share the bread, cheese, wine, and fruit, we struggled to decide what we must do during the next week in order to make good our celebration in action in the world. Two hours later, as a community, we formulated some definite resolves for action, sang "We Know They Are Christians by Their Love," and with a kiss of peace departed into the night.

• • •

I remember another significant adventure in celebration, a baptism that went something like this. The couple whose baby was to be baptized carefully chose from among their friends those who had the same faith, values, life styles as themselves. They invited them to their home and told them to bring party decorations. We entered the living room where the baby was resting in a bassinet. All joined in decorating the room. When we were finished, we sat on the floor in the new, festive environment and sang. The baby seemed to love it. Then we began to talk about the world in which we lived and the world we hoped would someday be. Champagne was passed about and everyone toasted the baby, stating what he was personally going to do on behalf of the baby to help make that vision of a new world a reality. The parents said what they intended to do for their child. Together we knelt around the baby. Water was poured from his baby bottle into a dish, and the parents and I placed our hands in the water and onto the child's head, baptizing him into the faith community. We all joined hands and sang, and the party went on.

*Reprinted from a *A Colloquy on Christian Education*, ed. John H. Westerhoff III. Copyright © 1972 United Church Press. Used by permission of The Pilgrim Press.

C. Use the following questions to compare Westerhoff's celebrations with the celebration of the sacraments described in Articles XXXIII-XXXV

1. Where is it held, and who are present?

2. What preparation is made for the sacrament?

3. How is the sacrament itself conducted?

4. How is Christ acknowledged in the sacrament?

5. What follow-up is there?

D. Opinions

Why (do you suppose) people feel the need to celebrate the sacraments as Westerhoff describes them? Is there anything positive to be learned from "Celebrations"? What implications, if any, are there for our own celebration of the sacraments?

POSTSCRIPT 25
Civil Government

A. Reflections on chapter 25

B. Article XXXVI introduces a number of interesting state/church questions. To focus our discussion, first take inventory of where you (individually) stand on the issues described below. Circle the one (1) if you totally disagree with the stand taken on the issue; circle the ten (10) if you agree entirely with the stand. Take into consideration the danger of sacralism as well as the positive guidelines found in Article XXXVI and in such passages as Romans 13:1-7 and Acts 5:29.

1. If the president were to order all citizens to turn down their thermostats to save money . . . while he jets around the country in style, I feel no obligation to do as he says. Calvin and de Bres have too high a view of those who govern. Their calling is no higher than that of, say, mothers, or pastors, or journalists who criticize rulers. Nobody in power gets my respect (and sometimes even my obedience) unless (s)he deserves it.

   disagree 1 2 3 4 5 6 7 8 9 10 agree

2. In any given community, Christians ought to work together to force closings of stores open on Sunday. Boycotts and other public pressure should be used. If possible, local ordinances should be drawn up to enforce such closings. The Sunday is the Lord's Day and should be respected as such.

   disagree 1 2 3 4 5 6 7 8 9 10 agree

3. A little blue porno barn opens a few blocks down the street from the local Reformed church. The church should do all

it can to get the city to close down the theater on the grounds that such places have demonstrably harmful social effects.

disagree 1 2 3 4 5 6 7 8 9 10 agree

---

4. Prayer and Bible reading ought to be allowed in our public schools, especially when a majority of those attending any given school are Christian. This is still a Christian nation; our public institutions ought to reflect that.

disagree 1 2 3 4 5 6 7 8 9 10 agree

---

5. Our country continues to build more and more nuclear weapons. In the sixties we had about one hundred missiles aimed at key locations in Russia. Today, as part of a policy which the government calls Mutually Assured Destruction (MAD), we have over ten thousand bombs ready to go, and another twenty thousand in stockpiles, enough to destroy any enemy dozens of times. The church ought to preach and teach and support nuclear disarmament. Building more bombs is a clear violation of the sixth commandment.

disagree 1 2 3 4 5 6 7 8 9 10 agree

---

6. It's impossible for the state to be "impartial" while unnecessarily requiring some of its citizens to pay extra for their children's education in Christian schools. For this reason, churches should support plans which require the state to financially support (but not control) *all* legitimate forms of education.

disagree 1 2 3 4 5 6 7 8 9 10 agree

C. *Summarize* the principles of state/church relations which have emerged from our study today. You might list your statements under the headings of *STATE* and *CHURCH*.

POSTSCRIPT 26
The Last Judgment

A. Reflections on chapter 26

B. Bible study
   Working in small groups, outline a brief
   answer to *one* of the following questions. Base
   your answer on group study of the Scripture
   passages and Article XXXVII. Also, please jot
   down any additional, related questions raised
   by the group.

   1. What will life be like just before Christ's
      return? (Matt. 24:3-28)

2. What will the appearance of Christ be like?
(Matt. 24:29-31, 36; Acts 1:11; I Thess. 4:16)

_____

3. By whom and on what basis will we be
judged? (Matt. 25:31-46; Rom. 2:6-8; Rev.
20:12, 22:12; II Cor. 5:10; Jas. 2:18-26)

_____

4. When Christ comes, what will happen to
believers? To unbelievers? (Matt. 25:34, 41;
I Cor. 15:42-44, 51-53; Phil. 3:20, 21)

_____

5. When Christ comes, what will happen to the
devil? To the world? (II Thess. 2:8; Rev.
20:10; Isa. 65:17, 66:22; Rom. 8:19-23; II
Pet. 3:12, 13

TEST ON PART III
The Belgic Confession

Match:

_____ "one only simple and spiritual Being" (Art. I)

_____ "a most elegant book" (Art. II)

_____ "He makes Himself more clearly and fully known" (Art. II)

_____ "Tobit, Judith...Maccabees" (Art. VI)

_____ "For They are all three co-eternal and co-essential" (Art. VIII)

_____ "proceeds from the Father and the Son" (Art. XI)

_____ God's "messengers...to serve His elect" (Art. XII)

_____ "This doctrine affords us unspeakable consolation" (Art. XIII)

_____ "capable in all things to will agreeably to the will of God" (Art. XIV)

_____ "a corruption of the whole nature and a hereditary disease" (Art. XV)

_____ "really assuming the true human nature with all its infirmities, sin excepted" (Art. XVIII)

_____ "the remission of our sins for Jesus Christ's sake" (Art. XXIII)

_____ "are of no account towards our justification" (Art. XXIV)

_____ "outside of it there is no salvation" (Art. XXVIII)

_____ "ascribes more power and authority to itself...than to the Word of God" (Art. XXIX)

_____ "the council of the Church" (Art. XXX)

_____ "visible signs and seals of an inward and invisible thing" (Art. XXXIII)

_____ "of 'that' which Christ has done for them" (Art. XXXIV)

_____ "their office is ...also to protect the sacred ministry" (Art. XXXVI)

_____ "according to what they have done in this world, whether it be good or evil" (Art. XXXVII)

1. providence
2. the true church
3. the false church
4. infant baptism
5. God
6. original sin
7. the Bible
8. ministers, elders
9. Apocryphal books
10. angels
11. the universe
12. the last judgment
13. the Holy Spirit
14. the image of God
15. justification
16. magistrates
17. incarnation
18. the Trinity
19. sacraments
20. good works

Answers

5, 11, 7, 9, 18, 13, 10, 1, 14, 6, 17, 15, 20, 2, 3, 8, 19, 4, 16, 12

POSTSCRIPT 27
Introduction to the Canons

A. Reflections on chapter 27

B. Notes on the writing of the Canons of Dort

C. Structure of the Canons

1. The Canons of Dort are divided into four sections (the third and fourth "Heads of Doctrine" are combined). What are the two parts of each section? Which of the two is longer?

_____

2. Give evidence that the structure and language of the Canons are polemical.

_____

3. How are the Scriptures used in the Canons? Where are they cited the most?

POSTSCRIPT 28
Divine Election and Reprobation

A. Reflections on chapter 28

B. According to the first two paragraphs of the
Conclusion of the Canons of Dort, what are
some of the Arminian misunderstandings of
the Calvinist teachings on election and reprobation? Feel free to put the statements from
the Conclusion in your own words.

C. Preparation for Calvinist/Arminian role-play
   1. Position I'm taking: Calvinist or Arminian.

   _____

   2. Item from section *B* (above) to be discussed.

   _____

   3. Notes for my attack (Arminian) or defense
      (Calvinist). Refer to Articles 1-11, First
      Head of Doctrine (Chapter I), for ideas.

POSTSCRIPT 29
The Death of Christ and Our Redemption

A. Reflections on chapter 29

B. Review, if necessary, the parable at the beginning of chapter 29. Then, for each statement below:

- discuss how the parable teaches it.
- decide what the Arminian version of the statement would be.
- find direct support for the statement in Articles 1-9, and Paragraphs 1-6, of the Second Head of Doctrine.

1. We are too blind, too rebellious, to come to Christ on our own by simply exercising our free will.

2. God does what is necessary—by His Word and Spirit—to bring us into gracious fellowship with Himself.

3. God does not save us all, or even intend to (limited atonement).

4. All the elect are assuredly saved through the death of Christ.

_____

5. The message of salvation must be preached to all people, and must include the gospel command and promise.

_____

6. We confess we do not know why some are elect and others are not.

_____

C. (Optional) Parables, even good ones, are not perfect; they tend to "break down" when pressed on every detail. What weaknesses do you find in the parable from chapter 29? Do you think the parable is worth remembering as illustrative of a key teaching of the Canons of Dort?

_____

D. Does it really matter all that much whether we have Arminian or Calvinist views of redemption? What possible difference does it make to us as Christians?

POSTSCRIPT 30
Corruption and Conversion

A. Reflections on chapter 30

B. Articles 1-5 "Total Depravity"

Which of the following statements are supported by Articles 1-5?

__T__ 1. Depravity is inherited, not learned.

__F__ 2. Total depravity means people everywhere are about as bad as they can be.

__T__ 3. Total depravity means that our total lives are affected by sin; nothing we do is pure righteousness.

__F__ 4. Total depravity is a term which applies only to the unregenerate; once we are converted, we are no longer "totally depraved."

__T__ 5. God's common grace prevents unregenerate people from doing what is totally evil.

__F__ 6. This common grace is sufficient to lead unregenerate people to a saving knowledge of the Lord Jesus Christ.

__F__ 7. After the fall, God's common grace in effect returns everybody to the place Adam had—free to believe or not to believe.

__F__ 8. The law of God, in itself, points unregenerate people toward the cross.

C. Articles 6-17 "Irresistible Grace"

1. From Article 11, define "irresistible grace." What does chapter 30 mean when it says of Article 11, "Here we see the great Adversary making His move"? How would the Arminian describe God's work in the human heart?

_____

2. Read Article 12, then reflect on regeneration as "a new creation" (see II Cor. 5:17) and as a "resurrection" (see Rom. 6:4-11; Eph. 2:1,5). What do these descriptions say to you?

_____

3. Cite and discuss one vivid biblical example showing God's irresistible grace and regenerating power in bringing sinners home.

_____

4. If you're willing, share with the class the means that God has used to work in your life, bringing you not only to conversion but also to growth and Christian maturity. Put another way, is there evidence from your own life that God's compulsion was (is) your liberation?

_____

5. What antidote does Article 17 suggest for spiritual dryness? What cure does it suggest for slavery to the need for religious "highs" and ecstasy?

POSTSCRIPT 31
The Perseverance of the Saints

A. Reflections on chapter 31

B. God's preservation of His people (Chapter V, Articles 1-8)

1. How did God "preserve" Peter, despite his "lamentable fall"? Discuss the seriousness and the effect of Peter's sin (see Article 5) and how God immediately began working to move Peter to "a sincere and godly sorrow" (Art. 7 and Luke 22:54-62).

2. How might an Arminian account for Peter's repentance and subsequent life of service for the Lord?

3. In a sentence or two sum up what God's preservation means to us, as believers who may, at times, be "deeply divided between genuine piety and genuine wickedness" (chap. 31).

C. Assurance of preservation (Chapter V, Articles 9-15)

1. How did God assure Peter that He would never let him go? (See Mark 16:7 and John 21.) Which, if any, of the three grounds of assurance listed in Article 10 were probably at work in Peter's life?

2. To what extent was Peter's assurance given in the context of the community of God's people?

3. Share with two other persons in your class:
   a) One text (or experience) which has assured you that God will let nothing snatch you from His hand.
   b) Your own degree of assurance—at this point in your spiritual journey—that you will always be God's child.

TEST ON PART IV
Canons of Dort

Each of the following five pairs includes a Calvinistic statement and an Arminian statement. Indicate by a *C* or an *A* which is which:

1. ____ "The election of particular persons is decisive, out of consideration of faith in Jesus Christ and of perseverance . . . as a condition prerequisite for electing."

   ____ "This election was not founded upon foreseen faith and the obedience of faith . . . ; but men are chosen to faith and to the obedience of faith. . . ."

2. ____ ". . . it was the will of God that Christ by the blood of the cross, . . . should effectually redeem . . . all those, and those only, who were from eternity chosen to salvation and given to Him by the Father."

   ____ ". . . Christ has merited reconciliation with God and remission of sins for all men and for every man. . . ."

3. ____ "We do not believe that all zeal, care, and diligence applied to the obtaining of salvation before faith itself and the Spirit of renewal are vain and ineffectual. . . ."

   ____ ". . . without the regenerating grace of the Holy Spirit, they are neither able nor willing to return to God, to reform the depravity of their nature, or to dispose themselves to reformation."

4. ____ "Faith is therefore to be considered as the gift of God, not on account of its being offered by God to man, to be accepted or rejected at his pleasure, but because it is in reality conferred upon him, breathed and infused into him. . . ."

   ____ ". . . sufficient grace for faith and conversion falls to the lot not only of those whom God is said to will to save according to the decree of absolute election, but also of those who are not actually converted."

5. ____ ". . . we do not see how (a true believer) can be certain that he will never afterwards be remiss in his duty but will persevere in faith . . . ; neither do we deem it necessary that . . . a believer should be certain."

   ____ "Of this preservation of the elect to salvation and of their perseverance in the faith, true believers may and do obtain assurance according to the measure of their faith. . . ."

Answers

1. A Opinions of the Remonstrants A, 7
   C Canons of Dort I, Art. 9
2. C Canons II, Art. 8
   A Remonstrants B, 3
3. A Remonstrants C, 3
   C Canons III-IV, Art. 3
4. C Canons III-IV, Art. 14
   A Remonstrants C, 6
5. A Remonstrants D, 8
   C Canons V, Art. 9

234

ADULT EDUCATION CURRICULUM PLAN

DIVISION I: STUDIES IN SACRED SCRIPTURE

A. *Revelation Series*

An ongoing series of studies of individual Bible books. (Some available 1979)

B. Survey Series

A one-year survey of the major groupings of Bible books.

DIVISION II: GOD'S WORK IN HISTORY

A. Church History

A one-year course covering Biblical periods, major periods of church history, and patterns of development in North American church history. Text written by Frank Roberts. (1980)

B. Christian Reformed Church History

A course covering the origins and development of the Christian Reformed Church.

DIVISION III: TRUTH FOR LIFE

A. *A Place to Stand*

A one-year course covering the Apostles', Nicene, and Athanasian creeds; and the Heidelberg Catechism, the Belgic Confession, and the Canons of Dort. Includes a text written by Cornelius Plantinga, Jr., Teacher's Manual, Teacher's Kit, and a copy of the creeds and confessions. (1979)

B. *Beyond Doubt*

A one-year course explaining the Reformed faith as answers to questions life raises. A practical, life-related, devotional study based on a text by Cornelius Plantinga, Jr. (1980)

DIVISION IV: LIVING IN THE PRESENCE OF GOD

A. Family Living

A one-year course treating the concerns of Christian families, beginning with marriage and continuing to death.

B. Christian Living

A one-year course examining various life situations requiring Christian moral response.

DIVSION V: THE BODY OF CHRIST IN MINISTRY

A one-year course centering on the practical concerns of the church's corporate ministry.